THE GATEWAY OF
UNDERSTANDING

THE GATEWAY
OF UNDERSTANDING

By CARL A. WICKLAND, M.D.

Author of
"THIRTY YEARS AMONG THE DEAD"

Member of
CHICAGO MEDICAL SOCIETY
ILLINOIS STATE MEDICAL SOCIETY
AMERICAN ASSOCIATION FOR THE
ADVANCEMENT OF SCIENCE

In Collaboration with
NELLE M. WATTS
CELIA L. GOERZ

Published by
NATIONAL PSYCHOLOGICAL INSTITUTE
Incorporated
2208 W. 11th ST., LOS ANGELES 6,
CALIFORNIA

PRINTED IN THE UNITED STATES OF AMERICA

DEDICATED TO

MY WIFE

ANNA W. WICKLAND

WHOSE HUMANITARIAN IMPULSES
AND UNSELFISH DEVOTION TO AN IDEAL
HAVE MADE THIS RESEARCH POSSIBLE
AND TO THE INVISIBLE CO-WORKERS
WHO HAVE SO FAITHFULLY
INSPIRED AND GUIDED OUR EFFORTS

The Author
CARL A. WICKLAND, M.D.
Pioneer Psychiatrist

Carl A. Wickland was born February 14th 1861 at Liden, Norland Province, Sweden. In his youth Carl Wickland learned, from his father, the trade of cabinet maker, and later that of watchmaker.

In 1880 he left Sweden and arrived in St. Paul, Minn. in 1881. He married Anna W. Anderson in 1896 and shortly thereafter they moved to Chicago where Carl Wickland entered Durham Medical College from which he graduated in 1900. He followed the general practice of medicine while specializing in research in mental illnesses.

Dr. Wickland became chief psychiatrist at the National Psychopathic Institute of Chicago in 1909, where he remained until 1918. Later the Wicklands moved to Los Angeles, California, where the doctor founded the National Psychological Institute, a non-profit corporation for research in psychology. At the sanitarium, operated by the National Psychological Institute, from six to ten patients at a time were cared for and brought back to sanity and health.

In 1924 Dr. Wickland, in collaboration with Nelle Watts, Celia and Orlando Goerz, his assistants, wrote and published THIRTY YEARS AMONG THE DEAD, a book that has become a classic in abnormal psychology. This book had five editions in the U.S.A. and three printings in England. This book was translated and published in the Netherlands under the title DERTIG JAREN ONDER DE DOODEN. Title of the Spanish translation was 30 ANOS ENTRE LOS MUERTOS.

The first edition of GATEWAY OF UNDERSTANDING was published in 1934. Shortly after the death of Dr. Wickland, Wing Anderson, a pioneer in sleep suggestion therapy for the correction of psychosomatic ills, purchased copyrights and plates of the Wickland books. Public demand led to the publication of this sixth edition of GATEWAY OF UNDERSTANDING. The American Edition of THIRTY YEARS AMONG THE DEAD is temporarily out of print but the English Edition can be obtained from the National Psychological Institute.

A decade after the death of Dr. Wickland in 1945 orthodox psychiatry lags a half century behind Dr. Wickland in knowledge and efficiency in the cure of insanity.

"Read not to condemn,
but to weigh and consider."

CONTENTS

		Page
INTRODUCTION—THE WHY OF EXISTENCE		xvii
CHAP. I.	THE SCIENCE OF LIFE	1
CHAP. II.	PSYCHIC RESEARCH	19
CHAP. III.	VERIFICATION OF SPIRIT IDENTITY	40
CHAP. IV.	DEATH AND THE FUTURE LIFE	64
CHAP. V.	OBSESSION	93
CHAP. VI.	MULTIPLE PERSONALITIES AND PSYCHIC INVALIDISM	114
CHAP. VII.	DOGMA SPIRITUALIZED	142
CHAP. VIII.	PICTORIAL RELIGION	168
CHAP. IX.	IS THERE A GOD?	176
CHAP. X.	CHRISTIAN SCIENCE	190
CHAP. XI.	REINCARNATION AND THEOSOPHY	207
CHAP. XII.	DANGERS OF OCCULT PRACTICES	228
CHAP. XIII.	THE GREAT DESIGNER	250
CHAP. XIV.	ORIGIN OF RELIGIONS	261
CHAP. XV.	THE GOLDEN THREAD OF TRUTH	279
CHAP. XVI.	THE SOUL'S JOURNEY	298

ILLUSTRATIONS

PORTRAIT . . . . , Frontispiece

FACING PAGE

THE WILD ROSE 168

NIGHT'S SWIFT DRAGONS CUT THE CLOUDS
FULL FAST 170

DAWN OF THE CHRISTIAN ERA 172

FLIGHT INTO EGYPT 174

A LITTLE CHILD SHALL LEAD THEM 175

FOREWORD

"Truth wears no mask,
Bows at no human shrine,
Seeks neither place nor applause,
She only asks a hearing."

Truth must imply a thorough knowledge of any subject to which the term is applied. Too often mere belief or disbelief are accepted as evidence of truth; this attitude has prevailed all through the ages and largely predominates today in dogmatic creeds, cults and isms.

But there is an ever-increasing number of individuals who are unable to accept mere beliefs as facts but desire reasonable evidence pertaining to the seeming enigma of life. To these, and to the liberal-minded scientist, man-of-law, churchman, physician, educator, reformer, humanitarian and philanthropist, this volume is cordially inscribed.

Carl A. Wickland, M.D.

INTRODUCTION

The Why of Existence

THE world stands today between two domains of thought: Science, which presents a knowledge of the Laws of Nature and Matter; Religion, which teaches Morality and Spirituality. These two activities are not irreconcilable, but yet a gap exists between them which must be bridged by a Spiritual Science based on actual knowledge of the inter-relationship of the two worlds, the visible and invisible.

What is the purpose of Life? In this age of unrest and disturbance many earnest minds are seeking the fundamentals underlying life itself. Humanity is still kept in subjection by fear and superstition, by repressive laws, by dogmas, creeds and false doctrines, and has not yet attained liberation through a fuller understanding.

Happiness is unquestionably the goal of all human endeavor; all activities have this one aim in view. There are various conceptions of happiness, some confined entirely to physical, others to mental pleasures, while still others reach for spiritual happiness. What is this happiness, sought for through the ages?

Happiness is not a thing; it is a condition of mind. This universal search, whether fulfilled or not, must indicate the existence of one Universal Principle, drawing all mankind to one ultimate, common attainment. It is evident that this Universal Principle has projected a visible universe for the purpose of individualizing humanity, and the goal of individualization is the acquirement of wisdom, which can only be attained through experience and reason.

Man has four stages of Consciousness: first, the Unconscious State of Infancy; second, the Consciousness of External Things; third, the Self-Conscious Stage; fourth, God-Consciousness.

xvii

From the Unconscious State of Infancy man gradually develops into a Consciousness of External Things, or the phenomenal world, the prevailing state of humanity at large; this is followed by the Self-Conscious Stage, when the individual begins to question why he exists. Then, when through experience, suffering and service he gradually comprehends the necessity of these previous stages whereby wisdom is slowly acquired, an intelligent realization ultimates of the One-ness of the soul with the Origin of its Being, and man attains that happiness for which he has so blindly been striving, the God-Consciousness.

Mankind is the highest order of manifestation in this objective world and possesses faculties wherewith to ascertain the purpose of existence. The Creator can give us the faculties for the attainment of Wisdom but he does not give us Wisdom itself. We could not appreciate it, nor would it be of any value to us unless acquired through individual experience.

Love and Wisdom are the ultimates of knowledge gained through experience in life; the physical plane is an elementary school wherein humanity must learn its fundamental lessons. God is Love; God is Wisdom; God is Life. "God is Spirit" (John 4:24), "in Him we live, and move and have our being." (Acts 17:28.) A spark of the Divine Principle is innate in every soul and is waiting to find expression through understanding.

Ignorance and selfishness, individual and racial, are the root of much seeming injustice. If humanity were primarily interested in the problems of Life itself, selfishness would be obliterated.

God has provided natural resources requisite for life's expression, and therefore, natural and material resources were originally intended for the use of all, and not for the exclusive few. "He that loveth not his brother whom he hath seen, cannot love God whom he hath not seen." (I John 4:20.)

When humanity has advanced, through experience and reasoning, to a realization of these fundamental laws, and has learned to practice the Golden Rule, then injustice will cease, and the longed-for Millennial Dawn will have arrived.

"Understanding is a wellspring" of happiness. It is necessary that man's thinking faculties be evolved before he can progress into a higher condition of understanding and happiness. Man will not think unless he is obliged to, but pain and suffering cause thinking and "Thought is the solver of Nature's problems."

Therefore, experience of various kinds is absolutely necessary until the soul has arrived at the stage where it can reason on these problems. "Nature keeps a dear school, but fools will not learn in any other." "Fools" in a sense, that as infants we are unconscious even of our very existence, but enter this life to learn.

Difficult conditions cause us to think; adversity is a school wherein strength is developed by resistance. Life is a process of removing one shell of ignorance after the other. Our destiny is the ultimate attainment of happiness, but "The garment of our destiny is woven by ourselves." God has given us elementary principles, but they must come to fruition through experience.

Life's seeming injustice plays a definite part in the evolutionary plan, for when he who has seen the shadows of life finally attains the enlightenment of higher understanding, sympathy will have been developed for the suffering of others and thereby he will become a greater factor for service.

To understand justice we must comprehend the purpose of life and the inter-relationship of the two worlds, physical and spiritual, visible and invisible. Earth life is only temporary and justice must be considered from the two planes. As Paul says: "First . . . that which is natural then that which is spiritual." (I Corinthians 15:46.)

Psychic Research so easily demonstrates through genuine mediums, especially trance mediums, that transition, or so-called death, is only a sleep and an awakening.

This process is so natural that many fail to realize the change for a longer or shorter time, hence the importance of the human mind clearly understanding this simple fact while yet in the body, so when transition occurs and the individual recognizes that something unusual has happened he will be open-minded and spirits of friends and others who have gone before can then manifest themselves to him and welcome him to the new life.

There is no need to fear the passing from the visible to the invisible world; living an honest, upright life according to the dictates of conscience and maintaining an open-minded attitude constitutes all the religion that is necessary.

If those who have lived mis-spent lives will be honest with themselves and recognize the mistakes made and wrongs committed while in the physical, they need not fear death, for the pathway of reformation in the new world is always open to all who are willing to reform their thoughts and actions and seek earnestly for enlightenment.

The selfish-minded and the skeptic, as well as the wilful evil-doers, who have had no aspiration to understand life's meaning, and who lack the spiritual oil of understanding and the light obtained through reason and faith, will find themselves in darkness after transition.

The absence of such light of necessity leaves the soul in obscurity which can only be outgrown by replacing the mental attitude of ignorance and obstinacy with the spirit of a child, in other words, by developing a newness of spirit through seeking to understand the meaning of existence.

The Intelligences of the Spirit world are urging humanity to realize that most of the wrongs and misery in the world are directly due to human indifference to knowledge of the continued existence of those departing from the visible to the invisible sphere. Only through such knowledge will a higher state of civilization be established and redemption be obtained from the prevailing mental darkness concerning the true purpose of life.

Psychic Research is sweeping away the fear of death, proving that so-called death is merely a transition to a broader life where, through progressive stages of ever-broadening understanding, the soul is led from the death of ignorance into life more abundant.

Present-day psychical revelations are opening wide the portals between the two worlds, showing the folly of blind faith as well as blind, unreasoning skepticism and verifying the biblical injunction, "Know the truth and the truth shall make you free." (John 8:32.)

Humanity becomes free from the bondage of ignorance and unhappiness when, having paid the toll of Experience and acquired Knowledge, through Reason—the Gateway of Understanding—it ultimately attains Liberation and Happiness.

CHAPTER I

The Science of Life

AS ALL great discoveries have grown out of crude beginnings which at first met with intense opposition from skeptics and non-progressives, so also does that greatest science of all, The Science of Life, too often meet with ridicule and unbelief when facts discerned through careful research in this mooted problem are presented by the investigator.

Pertaining to the inner meaning of life, the world is mentally yet largely in the situation of the African natives who for years gathered curious stones and, unaware of their value, used them as playthings or for barter until educated man discovered the true nature of the stones and revealed the beautiful diamond.

When potatoes were introduced into Scotland in 1728 the clergy indignantly denounced them as unfit for consumption by Christians because they were not mentioned in the Bible; France scoffed at all early efforts to introduce potatoes into the national diet and in England the British labor leader publicly shouted that potatoes were fit only for hogs and cattle and not for men.

As late as 1840 an Eastern city passed an ordinance against the use of bathtubs, and umbrellas were at one time denounced by the clergy as being contrary to the biblical statement that "The Father which is in Heaven . . . sendeth rain on the just and on the unjust." (Matthew 5:45.)

When Benjamin Franklin made his kite and key experiments in an endeavor to prove that lightning was electricity, he was ridiculed as a dreamer and he himself little realized what his experiments would lead to. For he, like Prometheus, stole fire from heaven and gave man that marvelous electric force which with its effulgent light replaced the candle, revolutionized industries and aided in the development of innumerable avenues of research, resulting in vast progress in mechanics and chemistry and making possible the telegraph, telephone, automobile, airplane, radio and countless other inventions which greatly advanced knowledge and civilization.

When Morse petitioned Congress for an appropriation to construct a telegraph line from Baltimore to Washington, a skeptical congressman sarcastically offered as an amendment to the bill the suggestion that Mr. Morse at the same time establish a telegraph line to the moon. We need not here refer to what telegraphy has done for human achievement.

Andrew D. White relates in "A History of the Warfare of Science with Theology in Christendom": "When the Copernican doctrine that the earth and planets revolve about the sun—perhaps the greatest and most ennobling of scientific truths—was upheld by Galileo as a truth and proved to be a truth by his telescope, the church forbade all books which affirmed the motion of the earth."

The theological opponents disproved Galileo's theory of the revolution of the earth on its axis by placing a crowbar in a hole in the ground, with the idea that if Galileo was right the crowbar would fall out. As it did not do so, Galileo was deemed a heretic and condemned to imprisonment and saved his life only by retracting during his trial. But as he left his accusers he declared under his breath, "And yet it moves!"

White states further: "Copernicus escaped persecution only by death; Giordano Bruno was burned alive as a monster of impiety; Newton was bitterly attacked for dethroning Providence."

"When quinine was introduced in Europe in 1638 it was stigmatized as an invention of the devil and the opposition was so strong that it was not introduced in England until 1653."

"As late as 1770 religious scruples were still felt regarding the lightning-rod of Benjamin Franklin, the theological theory being that the storm is the voice of God."

"In 1847 when the Scotch physician advocated the use of anaesthetics in obstetrical cases he was met by a storm of opposition. From pulpit to pulpit Simpson's use of chloroform was denounced as impious and contrary to Holy Writ; texts were cited abundantly, the ordinary declaration being that to use chloroform was 'to avoid one part of the primeval curse on woman.' "

Dogmatic theologians have constantly endeavored to frustrate scientific research in Nature's Arcana and even today are strenuously opposing the important fact and reality of the communication of Intelligent Spirits from the Invisible World.

If one probes into the physics of the universe with mathematics or the telescope, the plaudits of the multitude are freely given, even when the endeavor is made to convince the novice in these matters that a straight line is not straight at all.

When a physicist delves into the infinitesimal Arcana of Nature, searching for the laws underlying various manifestations, such as the causes of diseases, he receives the laudation which these efforts deserve.

But let the investigator carry his research into the apparent mystery of existence, the meaning of life and the inter-relationship of the two worlds, foremost of all sciences, and he is either at once lampooned, anathematized and consigned to the limbo of superstition or relegated to the ranks of mountebanks and charlatans which infest this field of investigation.

A recent newspaper editorial, which questioned the possibility of spirit return, concluded with the statement: "Even if spiritualism were true there would be no great loss to the world if it should vanish."

The term "Spiritualism" is often misconstrued and limited to spirit phenomena. Spiritualism, in a higher sense, concerns the study of man's nature and discernment of the relationship of the human ego with the Source of its being, or Spirit per se.

The search for the Source of being is an innate prompting within the individual which urges him onward toward an indefinable goal. All phases of existence, all manifestations, all experiences are a revelation of natural laws which are indices of a Divine Source. Nothing is recognized as supernatural; all is natural. The universe acts under natural and

3

intelligent laws; however, many laws of nature are still unknown to man.

The dissatisfied urge of the ego in the transient, everyday life is clearly indicative of an ultimate objective in existence higher than mere material mortal. What is this urge but an emanation from the Source of Life, prompting the soul to rise higher, an urge which finally guides the soul in its journey to a full realization of its One-ness with the All in All. "To live with God—to know God with perfect knowledge, is the highest point of human development and happiness," states Spinoza.

The two terms, Spiritualism and Spiritism, are often used synonymously, yet, in a broader sense, they are quite distinct when each is defined according to its particular sphere.

Spiritism pertains especially to phenomenal existence and manifestations; it also is of great importance as it gives evidence of the survival of the ego after the shadow-form of the physical is discarded, and it establishes communication between the visible and invisible world.

Thus, Spiritism is an important link, proving to those yet in the mortal form that there is no death, merely a simple transition from the grosser manifest to the next School of Experience. It is like a beacon light of encouragement to the weary traveler, showing, as it does, that there is no need of fear or doubt concerning what lies on the other side of the grave.

Porter Evans, research specialist, formerly of the University of Michigan Engineering School, after certain experiments in his laboratory with a medium, announced that psychic revelations merited scientific inquiry. "No explanation possible could be found in electro-magnetic phenomena . . . Are there other media in or beyond the ether, to which certain persons are responsive? . . . It has seemed to me that time is a measure of distance in the infinite, and that, as Spinoza sought the sub specie aeternitatis, Einstein also seeks 'the viewpoint of eternity,' and that science may yet explore a new world in which the old rigid time sequence will be upset."

Unthinking skeptics little realize the important mission which intelligent spirits are carrying on in the world for the

4

good of mankind. From the standpoint of reason alone it is self-evident that those on the Invisible Side not only retain interest and affection for friends and kindred remaining in the physical, but, having entered into a broader and happier sphere of life and the realization that there is no death, only a beautiful progression, their concern for those left behind becomes stronger and keener than formerly.

Following twelve years of tireless effort made by Sir Arthur Conan Doyle and his loyal companion, Lady Doyle, to impart to others a knowledge of survival and the possibility of the communication of discarnate minds with those still in the body, Sir Arthur left a spoken message to the world, one of the H. M. V. records, made some weeks before his passing, wherein he says in part:

"There is nothing in this new knowledge to destroy the foundations of your present belief, but on the contrary it adds a knowledge and a feeling of security such as no other system of philosophy has been able to give. The basis of all religions is that we live after death, and the proving of the truth of this basis is to my mind the most essential work in this age of perplexity and materialism, when good and earnest men honestly doubt whether death is not the end."

"People ask, What do you get from Spiritualism? The first thing you get is that it absolutely removes all fear of death. Secondly, it bridges death for those dear ones whom we may love. We need have no fear that we are calling them back for all that we do is to make such conditions as experience has taught us will enable them to come if they wish, and the initiative lies always with them. They have many times told us that they could not come back if it were not God's will, and that it makes them intensely happy to be able to help and comfort us, to tell us about their happy life in that world to which we are in our turn destined to come."

"We bring important facts, new facts which will revolutionize the whole thought of the human race both in religion and in science. It is the great question of the future, and it will end by making religion a real living thing, so that all doubt of God's goodness or of the destiny of mankind will be forever banished, since we will each be in actual touch with what is higher than ourselves and the communion of saints will at last be an established fact."

Since from the broader vantage ground intelligent spirits are more fully aware than before of the heart-aches, struggles, disappointments and grief of those in the physical, is it not natural that their hearts should go out to those who need their sympathy and an assurance that the departed are not "dead"?

Human life is constantly destroyed by disease, accidents, floods and all manner of catastrophes; the mother loses her beloved child, the husband is separated from his wife, families are broken up. Loved ones are left in keenest distress and, facing a blank wall of silence, cry out: "What has happened to our dear ones? Are they actually dead? Shall we ever see them again?"

What satisfaction or comfort is given these grief-stricken souls at this cruel separation? The churches have "hope," they have "faith" that there is "something beyond," since the Bible intimates that there is a life hereafter, but they offer merely a belief in an irrational, dogmatic theory concocted during the dark ages of ignorance and mental darkness.

"If a man die, shall he live again?" (Job 14:14.) Those weeping for ones who have passed from the physical life may ask their spiritual advisers concerning the enigma of transition and whether existence actually continues, but these advisers are usually unaware of the beautiful fact of spirit communication and cannot give the mourners any definite assurance. They offer only vague advice to "trust in the Lord and all will be well," failing to carry out the admonition: "Add to your faith ... knowledge." (II Peter 1:5.)

Had church leaders the actual knowledge of a life hereafter they could give to the grief-stricken ones absolute assurance that there is no death, only a mere transition into a broader realm of life, and that their loved ones are ever near. An advanced spirit stated: "Rivers and mountains, hills and villages do not express to me what I call the spirit land; I am in the hearts and souls of my friends."

Confucius said: "Bemoan not the departed with excessive grief! The dead are devoted and faithful friends!"

6

In "There Is No Death," Bulwer Lytton wrote:

"Ever near us, though unseen,
The dear immortal spirits tread;
For all the boundless universe
Is life—there are no dead."

The churches stand today, as they did in the Dark Ages, in their own light and persistently substitute dogma for the Science of Life. The church teaches a life after this but when proof is offered that spirits communicate from the invisible side, which demonstrates that there is no death, the churchman promptly denies the facts. "Neither will they be persuaded, if one rise from the dead." (Luke 16:31.) "Ye entered not in yourselves, and them that were entering in, ye hindered." (Luke 11:52.)

It is indeed unfortunate that instead of cooperating in such research the church assumes that communicating intelligences are not of human origin but devils to be shunned. This is a false attitude, for, while it is true, as experience has amply revealed, that many spirits are by no means angels as yet, neither are they devils; their condition is but the end-product of human ignorance and selfishness.

All spirits are redeemable through education; experience has proven that a vast number are not even aware of being so-called dead and, instead of progressing, remain in the earth sphere, a situation for which the church is much to blame, since it is itself ignorant of the actual condition after transition.

Intelligent Spirit Forces urge humanity to obtain a true understanding of life while here and a realization of the true relationship between the two worlds, then we will not produce such vast numbers of earthbound spirits as at present.

The church maintains three tenets: that the dead go either to the grave, to heaven, or to hell. Psychic science has shown that these three premises are false, since the "dead" go to no such places. "The mind is its own place, and in itself can make a Heaven of Hell, a Hell of Heaven." (Milton.) "For as he thinketh in his heart, so is he." (Proverbs 23:7.)

Death, so-called, is only a sleep and an awakening, which process is so simple that a great majority, after leaving the

7

physical and finding themselves possessing a body, visible to them but invisible to mortals, do not at first realize their changed situation. "There is a natural body, and there is a spiritual body ... first ... that which is natural then that which is spiritual." (I Cor. 15:44, 46.)

Nor does this process change the mental attitude which the individual maintained when in the body; skeptical then, skeptical now. His ideas, habits and notions of all kinds are still the same.

The Christian has the same experience for similar lack of understanding of the transition process; in fact, orthodox spirits are the most difficult to enlighten and convince regarding their true situation since in life they disbelieved in spirits and expected at death to "go to God" directly.

This is a belief taught by the churches and yet it is false even according to the teachings of the Bible. "God is love; and he that dwelleth in love dwelleth in God." (I John 4:16.) "He that followeth me shall not walk in the darkness, but shall have the light of life." (John 8:12.) "God is Spirit" (not *a* spirit; *we* are spirits) "and they that worship him must worship him in spirit and in truth." (John 4:24.) "God is light." (I John 1:5.)

Too frequently church membership and activities incident to the same, as well as ethical observances, are maintained with the hope of "being saved from hell" (a procedure which might be termed, obtaining a celestial fire insurance policy), or to "serve the Lord" with the hope of receiving a reward in the future life—a "crown of glory."

This attitude is a form of selfishness as it is not founded upon the great innate law which underlies life, that we are in a broader sense our brothers' keepers. "Bear ye one another's burdens." (Galatians 6:2.) "For none of us liveth to himself." (Romans 14:7.) This implies improved economics and betterment of our fellowman's conditions for mental advancement. Self-interest of the few and disregard for the welfare of the many indicate that selfishness "is the root of all evil"—selfishness plus ignorance, we would say.

Humanity should be bound together in one social fabric, in other words we should be our brothers' keepers not merely in theory but in fact. Failure to recognize this law is indeed one of the great stumbling blocks in the progress of civilization.

"It is not in intelligence that we lack for overcoming of evil, but we lack the unselfish responsible devotion of men in the service of the common weal." (Prof. Albert Einstein.)

Untold misery exists on both planes of existence as a consequence of ignoring this law which is a scientific truism that must be recognized ere humanity ever may advance to a higher plane of civilization. Service is essential. "When the power of imparting joy is equal to the will, the human soul requires no other heaven." (Shelley.)

The more we serve the more we lay up treasures for ourselves, not expected rewards but the thoughts of happiness and good-will of those to whom kindness has been extended, and the satisfaction of knowing that we have been the means of helping others a little along the road of life, which we cannot travel alone. "Love is the fulfilment of the law." (Romans 13:10.)

It should be apparent to the thoughtful that we are all travelers in this mundane sphere journeying onward to the next school and we must strive to help others by giving them opportunities physically and mentally to attain a better understanding of life's higher possibilities. Practice of the Golden Rule will help make this earth a real paradise. "No soul can attain to spiritual wisdom that neglects the foundation principle of humility of spirit." ("Illuminated Brahminism.")

The greatest service we can render the Lord is to use the minds with which he has provided us for the purpose of learning to understand his wondrous handiwork in manifest creation. "Good understanding giveth favour." (Proverbs 13:15.) "How much better is it to get wisdom than gold! Yea, to get understanding is rather to be chosen than silver." (Proverbs 16:16.) "Happy is the man that findeth wisdom, and the man that getteth understanding." (Proverbs 3:13.)

In proportion as we understand and appreciate the revealed nature of the Creator, in that proportion will our minds go out in adoration, not worship. An art connoisseur adores a masterpiece, but he does not worship it; worship would be idolatry. We adore music, the language of the

9

spheres, in proportion as our minds are quickened to it, but we do not worship it.

The churches generally limit themselves to morals and idealism, which are only half the issue. They do not follow up adequate research pertaining to the meaning of existence here and hereafter. Faith is only the key, or urge, to which should be added understanding obtained by the application of thought and research which will culminate in a realization that "passeth all understanding."

"Christian prelates, who so violently oppose the possible admission of the spiritual world to a recognition as a sentient reality forget that their whole system had its foundation in similar phenomena, and in their blind zeal to exclude the light from the world are deliberately closing the avenues of the mind from receiving the only knowledge of a spiritual kind that is worth obtaining, and thereby hold the mental powers upon the old plane of fabulous tradition or crafty fabrication." ("Illuminated Brahminism.")

It is a recorded fact that psychic phenomena occurred at Epworth during 1716 and 1717 in the house of Samuel Wesley, father of John Wesley, the founder of Methodism; noises and disturbances of various kinds continued for many months, causing great annoyance to the members of the family. The influence, which was named "Jeffry," made particularly loud noises if any one attributed these sounds to rats or other natural causes.

In "News from the Invisible World," John Wesley wrote: "I am asked over and over, 'Did you ever see an apparition yourself?' No, nor did I ever see a murder, yet I believe there is such a thing. Yea, and murder in one place or another is committed every day. Therefore, I cannot, as a reasonable being, deny the fact. The testimony of unexceptionable witnesses fully convinces me of both one and the other."

"The sentiment for which we are pleading has," he reiterates, "the sanction of the highest antiquity. Philo (Jewish philosopher, B. C. 20-A. D. 40) speaks of it as a received notion of the Jews that the souls of good men officiate as ministering spirits. The Pagans, in the earliest ages, held that the spirits of their deceased friends continued near them, and were frequently engaged in performing acts of kindness, hence the deification of their kings and heroes and the custom of invoking the names of those who were dear to them."

"The soul receives not its perfections or activity from the body," he continues, "but can live and act out of the body; yea, much better, having then its perfect liberty, divested of that heavy incumbrance which only clogged and fettered it."

"Perhaps glorified spirits of just men made perfect may," . . . he says, "be employed in carrying on the purposes of God in the world; . . . as ministering spirits, they may minister, and watch over the interests of those who on earth were dear to them, either by the ties of nature or religion."

Merle Crowell wrote: "Keep open the windows of your mind. There is no adequate reason why the average man should ever close his mind to fresh 'slants' on life. He does, just the same. Nothing is more tragic, or more common, than mental inertia. For every ten men who are physically lazy, there are 10,000 with stagnant minds. And stagnant minds are the breeding places of fear."

Life is a mind school. In observing the throngs of people passing to and fro in congested avenues of daily traffic, an attempt to read physiognomies and analyze the various individuals brings the realization that the minds of most are principally engaged with matters pertaining to every-day physical existence. Few faces express that radiance which usually indicates a thinking or analytical mind.

The great majority of persons are so engrossed with physical cares which cannot be neglected that the problems pertaining to existence receive very little attention. Should one interrogate throngs of people, as they pass along, regarding their interest in and understanding of the problems of life and what becomes of the dead, the majority would laugh at the interrogator and consider him a freak.

Those who give some thought to the matter are usually satisfied to associate themselves with creeds which suit their fancies but which too often are only opiates to the soul, since most creeds and doctrines are confined to the acceptance of legendary beliefs of revelations presumed to have emanated from an anthropomorphic (man-shaped) God.

11

Aside from creeds or superstitious practices, all religions have their foundation in the recognition of spirit manifestations of one kind or another. The Christian religion particularly emphasizes a spirit background. "Jesus . . . went up into the mountain to pray . . . there talked with him two men which were Moses and Elijah, who appeared in glory." (Luke 9:28-31.) Jesus himself definitely proved the survival of spirit by his appearance to the apostles after his death.

This "discerning of spirits" is one of the psychic gifts enumerated by Paul. (I Cor. 12:10.) In Hebrews 1:14 we find: "Are they not all ministering spirits, sent forth to do service?" In I John 4:1 is stated: "Beloved, believe not every spirit but try the spirits whether they are of God: because many false prophets are gone out into the world." The incident of the spirit of Samuel speaking to Saul in the presence of the Woman of Endor is too well known to require repetition. (I Samuel 28:7-20.)

The Bible alludes clearly to the existence of spirits both good and bad, as for instance, "For our wrestling is not against flesh and blood . . . but . . . against the spiritual hosts of wickedness in the heavenly places." (Ephesians 6:12.) It also contains the admonitions: "Add to your faith . . . knowledge." (II Peter 1:5.) "Prove all things; hold fast that which is good." (I Thessalonians 5:21.)

What more important attitude could the churches adopt in order to obtain knowledge than replace their present aloofness with diligent efforts to ascertain for themselves the reality and truth of the continued existence of the spirit after death, knowledge which is so easily obtained through unprejudiced Psychic Research?

The devotees of the churches may be likened to the prisoners whom Plato describes. "Let me show in a figure how far our nature is enlightened or unenlightened: Behold! human beings living in an underground cave which has a mouth open towards the light and reaching all along the cave; here they have been from their childhood and have their legs and necks chained so that they cannot move, and can only see before them, being prevented by the chains from turning round their heads. Above and behind them a fire is blazing at a distance and between the fire and the prisoners there is a raised way, like the screen which marionette players have in front of them, over which they show the puppets . . ."

"Men pass along the wall carrying all sorts of vessels, statues and figures of animals . . . which appear over the wall . . . Strange prisoners—like ourselves . . . They see only their own shadows, or the shadows which the fire throws on the opposite wall of the cave . . . To them . . . the truth would be literally nothing but the shadows of the images."

But many minds will not be satisfied with mere shadows. Old outworn creeds and dogmas no longer satisfy the intelligent thinkers of the present day and the teaching of the same has at the present time a tendency to drive many from both church and religion. Religion, to the churchman, is chiefly a belief in an anthropomorphic God, whose Son was crucified as a mediator for the supposed sins of mankind, and that any one believing this story shall be saved.

Discerning minds recognize this story as illogical and unreasonable and reject it, but unfortunately often reject with it the true spiritual Science of Life and become atheists, denying the possibility of a future life or the existence of an Architect of the Universe. Progressive evolution is evident on every hand and so must also the understanding of the meaning of life become progressive and rationalized.

Even the alert minds of the children of today demand truth and reason instead of meaningless traditions and beliefs. A little girl inquired of her Sunday School teacher, "If Eve was the only woman how could Cain get a wife in another country?" but was told, "We must not ask questions about God's wonderful mysteries."

Another small girl, having been informed at Sunday School that the Communion Service was a partaking of the flesh and blood of Jesus, came home weeping and said, "I love Jesus, but I don't want to eat and drink him!"

After the story of the crucifixion had been narrated in Sunday School, a boy returned home to be asked by his mother what the lesson had been. "Oh, mother!" he answered, "you wouldn't be interested. It was all about pounding nails in Jesus."

And when a child is asked what the Sunday School text was and, remembering he has been told "The Father shall give you another Comforter," announces that "God is going to send us a new quilt," the need for a clear and reasonable presentation of the Science of Life should become readily apparent.

"The greatest task of the next hundred years will be the fulfillment of man's intellectual and moral needs," declared Dr. Robert A. Millikan, world famous physicist.

Marvelous inventions and educational facilities, with their wonderful revelations of Nature's Arcana, have quickened thought activity to a high degree. Hence the church cannot stand still but must supply the necessary pabulum, or spiritual food, to satisfy the unrequited demand of the hungry soul for a broader and an evidential conception of life's meaning.

The problem of the seeming enigma of existence has been an outstanding one since the dawn of human existence and is still a riddle to countless at the present time, especially to analytical minds that reject the theological doctrines of Christianity as illogical and unreasonable. For Christian orthodoxy implies that the Creator made many mistakes in the creation of mankind and that this lack of forethought required the sacrifice of a "Savior" as a vicarious atonement to rectify these presumed blunders.

From childhood, dissatisfaction with such teachings made it impossible for the writer to reconcile a God of Love with the tyrannical and cruel Lord of the Bible. My parents were adherents of the Baptist faith and I had imbibed this doctrine from earliest infancy but an inner sense always rebelled against its acceptance. This led me later to study various cults and religions until my attention was drawn to psychic phenomena which gave an entirely different interpretation of life and proved definitely that there is no death.

Incidentally it also made clear that many of the Bible stories are allegorical, not historical, and that "salvation" is an individual process, one of realizing that all experiences of the mortal are only transitory. Death is only a sleep and an awakening, an entry into the next school of broader opportunities wherein advancement depends upon rational living while in the physical, upon the use made of the reasoning faculties and upon the understanding acquired of the inter-relationship of the two worlds.

After investigations of various psychic media which resulted in convincing, as well as not-so-convincing evidence, I found that Mrs. Wickland, my wife, was an unusually sensitive intermediary through whom spirit Intelligences could directly communicate with the greatest ease.

These Intelligences stated that there is in reality no death, but a natural transition from the visible to the invisible world and that advanced spirits are ever striving to communicate with mortals to enlighten them concerning the higher possibilities which await the progressive spirit. But death—the freeing of the spirit from the body—is so simple and natural that a great majority do not, for a longer or shorter period, realize the change, and owing to a lack of education concerning the spiritual side of their natures, they continue to remain in their earthly haunts.

They maintained that many such spirits were attracted to the magnetic aura of mortals, although the spirit, as well as the mortal might be unconscious of the intrusion, and thus, by obsessing or possessing their victims, they ignorantly or maliciously became the cause of untold mischief and misery, often producing invalidism, immorality, suicide, crime and seeming insanity.

The risk of interference from this source, constituted, they said, the gravest danger to the unwary novice in Psychic Research, but to be in ignorance of these facts was an even greater risk, especially in the case of the susceptible neurotic.

These Intelligences also stated that by a system of transfer, that is, by attracting such obsessing entities from the victim to a psychic intermediary, the correctness of the hypothesis could be demonstrated and conditions could be shown as they actually exist. After this transference of psychoses the victims would be relieved and the obsessing spirits could then be reached by the advanced spirits who would care for them and instruct them regarding the higher laws of life.

They claimed they had found my wife to be a suitable instrument for such experimentation and proposed that, if I

15

would cooperate with them by caring for and instructing these ignorant spirits, as they allowed them to take temporary but complete possession of my wife's body, without any injury to her, they would prove their assertions were correct.

Desirous of learning the truth or falsity of such important claims, which, if true, would have a great bearing on the cause of much that is otherwise baffling in criminology, as well as in psycho-pathology, we accepted what seemed a hazardous undertaking.

These Guiding Intelligences are sincere, unassuming individuals, thoroughly tested and dependable, whose identity has in many cases been verified, and during our forty years of research in normal and abnormal psychology and psychiatry they have abundantly demonstrated their assertions to be an important reality.

This research has proven conclusively that death is only a sleep and an awakening, the process of awakening depending largely upon the individual's mental attitude, such as religious bias, unreasoning skepticism or the wilful ignorance of and indifference to life's meaning, so prevalent among the multitude.

In the case of the open-minded, unbiased individual there is no protracted death sleep, for as transition from the physical draws near he will often discern the presence of waiting friends from the Unseen, bidding him welcome into the new life, thus verifying the statement of Jesus, "If a man keep my word, he shall never see death." (John 8:51.) Hundreds of departed spirits have manifested through Mrs. Wickland shortly after their transition, sometimes even a few days thereafter; these have described their experiences and evinced great joy concerning their new environment.

Others again may waken from the death sleep entirely oblivious of their transition and remain in such oblivion for many years as vagabond spirits. That these spirits are important *contributing* factors in many phases of mental aberration, pseudo-invalidism, crime, suicide and insanity has been indubitably proven during my many years of medical practice which has been particularly devoted to abnormal psychology and psychiatry.[1]

[1]See "Thirty Years Among the Dead," by Carl A. Wickland, M.D.

16

This phase of Psychic Research obviously should be of greatest importance to psychiatrists, criminologists, reformers and ministers. Contact with the invisible world is not limited to any particular investigators; facts concerning the inter-relationship of the two worlds can readily be obtained by earnest students who will enter this field as any scientist takes up a definite line of research.

One would expect a true scientist to maintain an unprejudiced and unbiased attitude of mind relating to all avenues of research. Scientists today are concerned almost exclusively with research in the domain of physical nature, the workings of the physical universe, relativity, with the question of whether the universe is running down or what is really happening in the great cosmic realms. All of which has undoubted value and interest, yet the most important theme of all, the why of existence and the question of the survival of the ego, is taboo.

If an individual scientist, whose acumen in other research work is fully recognized, tries to break away from the conventional indifference to life's problems and investigates psychic science, such an one immediately loses caste, his discoveries are discredited and he is suspected of being a victim of senility or softening of the brain, regardless of how logical or lucid his new findings may be.

This illogical attitude of the dogmatic and conventional scientists is most unfair, as well as most unfortunate, as it deters many from openly entering into this, without question, the most important of all fields of research, for fear of ridicule and ostracism of the conventional school.

Educational bodies are greatly at fault in retarding Psychic Research, for since the polity of the organizations prohibits such research, instructors who dare venture individually into this field immediately jeopardize their positions. Likewise ministers, many of whom are liberal minded, may not step out openly and declare their broader convictions for fear of losing their pulpits, owing to the limited nonprogressive attitude of their respective congregations.

"Without the training and development of the spiritualized instruments (psychics) in the world of mortals the thoughts that belong to the higher spheres of developed spirits cannot be transmitted, and the spiritual growth upon

17

earth is far less than what it otherwise would be. The people grow brutalized who fail to become spiritualized, and the world suffers and agonizes because of inability to understand that life has some other outcome than annihilation or living for the purposes of selfish gratification."

"There is no work in spirit life more positive in its importance than that of raising the grade of spirituality upon earth through the exercise and manipulation of the power of thought-transference. There is no limit to the development of spiritual powers of the mind that grasps the significance of this principle." ("Illuminated Buddhism," Siddartha, Sakya Muni.)

It is said that "where there is no vision, the people perish." (Proverbs 29:18.) It is obvious so long as the world's intelligentsia limit their research to the physical domain, ignoring the most vital of all problems, the meaning of life here and hereafter, so long, unquestionably, will the world remain in the quagmire of upheavals, distress and social unrest.

When scientists, educators, the dogmatic church and selfish interests discard the present befogging mental attitude and prejudices and give their earnest and scientific attention to the solution of the seeming mystery of existence and the question of the survival of the ego, then, and then only, will humanity usher in the new dawn of a broader civilization, one founded upon the understanding of the Science of Life and the ultimate practice of the Golden Rule, which a scientific religion implies.

CHAPTER II

Psychic Research

PSYCHIC RESEARCH is at present subjected to a great deal of criticism and ridicule, much of which is justified. It is often stated by opponents of Psychic Research that the greater portion, some claim ninety per cent, of the phenomena is fraudulent and that the remainder can be better explained on other grounds, such as personal idiosyncrasies or psycho-neuroses.

Anyone thoroughly versed in the various phases of Psychic Research is well aware that fraud is practised by unscrupulous individuals who enter the field merely for pecuniary gains while they themselves do not believe in the reality of spirits or spirit phenomena.

During a financial crisis in Chicago, a lawyer attended a seance where the medium, a man of questionable integrity, supposedly materialized the form of the lawyer's spirit wife. This spirit wife told the lawyer that his money was not safe in the bank and advised him to bring it to her at the next seance and she would take care of it for him in the spirit world. She also told him to bring her diamond brooch to her for safe keeping.

At the next seance the lawyer brought five hundred dollars and his wife's diamond brooch and gave them to the purported materialized spirit wife. Some time after this the lawyer saw the wife of the medium on the street and to his amazement, she was wearing his wife's diamond brooch.

Disillusioned, the lawyer hurried to the home of the medium to accuse him of theft but the man had left the city. The lawyer followed him, however, and had him arrested.

When the case came to trial the judge asked the lawyer, "To whom did you give this money and the brooch?"

"To my wife," the lawyer answered.

"Where is your wife?"

"In the spirit world," the lawyer admitted.

"Then you must find your wife," the judge said sarcastically. "The case is dismissed."

Another amusing instance of a designing medium and credulous victims came to our attention some years ago. Two ladies were attending, for development, a series of materialization seances where King Arthur (?) materialized and each lady claimed him as her own guide. To restore peace the medium dismissed one woman from the circle but the latter went to another circle where the medium, a man, also produced materializations, later proven to be fraudulent.

The lady told the medium of her longing to have King Arthur for her guide and the medium obligingly materialized King Arthur, who said to her, "It will be best if you and I are married. Buy a diamond ring and bring it to this circle. I will materialize, you can give the ring to me and we will be married. I will wear the ring in the spirit world and then I will always belong to you."

The lady followed instructions and this marriage to a spirit (?) so strongly appealed to four other romantic women in the circle that they also bought diamond rings and presented them to their materialized spirit (?) guides, to whom they were in turn married.

Later one of the "brides" accidentally met the medium and saw that he was wearing all the rings. She told the other women of her discovery, but when they attempted to bring about the arrest of the medium they found that he had disappeared and with him the rings.

Since physical phenomena, such as materialization, require darkness or subdued light for genuine manifestations, this phase is most easily imitated and therefore most exposes of psychic phenomena are chiefly concerned with physical or mechanical demonstrations. Owing to frequent exposes of such dishonest performances, persons who think "very little and very seldom" come to the conclusion that all psychic phenomena are fraudulent.

Psychic Research is no exception to the general rule; fraud and deception are common everywhere, in the busi-

20

ness world, in the Christian ministry, in the various professions. Yet no one will claim therefore that all is fraud, for it is well known that honesty is the prevailing practice. If one discovers a bogus coin he does not conclude that all coins are counterfeit. Likewise, while admittedly there are fraudulent practices in Psychic Research, to designate all such research as trickery or imposture is absurd. "The day a man's mind shuts is the day of his mental death," said Sir Arthur Conan Doyle.

Mr. Harry Price, Director of the British National Laboratory of Psychical Research, states, according to his reports in "The American Weekly," of the Los Angeles Examiner: "Probably I have had more experience trying to get to the bottom of these occult matters than any man in the world . . . though I have looked in vain for the faintest crumb of evidence that the soul, personality or ego persists after death."

"There is something at the bottom of Spiritualism, but it is not spirits. Though I have had more experience in Psychical Research than any other man, never have I found a shred of evidence that anyone survives the grave . . . There is no scientific evidence that the dead have ever communicated with the living, or that a person, once dead, has ever 'come back.' "[1]

Mr. Price then describes many mysterious, unexplainable occurrences, relating that objects sealed in air-tight glass cases were caused to move; a solid, wooden table was split into almost matchwood under his hands, etc. He also reports his observations of a young girl "possessed of a devil," a "poltergeist that inflicted bites and scratches on the girl which produced marks and brought forth howls of pain . . . As to the stigmata, they frequently appeared while I and other trained observers did not take our eyes from E. for a second. At one time they broke out on her face in such profusion that she looked as if tatooed."

"I placed her in a chair in the middle of a perfectly strange room which I had prepared in advance, marking the positions of movable objects, surrounded her with trained observers in broad daylight. She could not move a finger or

[1]For the harmful results of such pernicious assertions see Chapter IX, "Is there a God?" Page 178.

an eyelid without some one seeing it. Yet promptly things began to happen. Objects began to jump about the room and even a metal letter got out of the hands of some workmen who were erecting a sign outside the building, flew into the room and wrapped itself around a knife in the pocket of one of the observers."

Mr. Price reports many other experiences too lengthy to quote. To one who is thoroughly versed in the various phases of Psychic Research there is nothing mysterious in these occurrences. Through a trance medium, who would allow herself to be controlled by these activating forces, it could be readily ascertained that these activities were due to either mischievous, discarnated spirits or spirits who were eager to make their presence known.

Mr. Price states: "I have seen all sorts of things happen in a way that defies every possible scientific precaution against fraud and every possible explanation occurring to known natural laws." Since he admits that he does not know what the force is with which he is dealing, how can he claim that "it is not spirits"?

Mr. Price's assertion that he has had more experience in Psychic Research than any one in the world is, to say the least, an absurd assumption. How can he possibly know to what extent others are following research in both normal and abnormal psychology?

His statement that there is no scientific evidence that the dead have ever communicated with the living is beside the facts. There is no subject so well authenticated in ancient and modern history as the existence of spirits and their communication with mortals, for good as well as otherwise.

He is evidently obsessed with the idea that there is no spirit return and is laboring merely to substantiate that notion. Mr. Price seemingly fails to realize that there are dogmatic spirit forces that are doing all within their power to negate or prevent the truth of spirit return being known. These are the forces referred to by Paul in Ephesians 6:12: "The spiritual hosts of wickedness in the heavenly places."

The axiom, "No one is so blind as he who will not see," seems evident in Mr. Price's method of research since apparently he strives to disprove facts instead of seeking to obtain intelligent evidence of survival.

It may be of interest to relate an experience that occurred during Mrs. Wickland's early years of mediumship which undoubtedly proves survival. Mrs. Wickland had an intimate friend, Mrs. Lackmund, whose little girl, at the age of two and a half years, became an imbecile after one sudden convulsion. The mother was convinced that this condition was caused by spirit obsession, and together with Mrs. Wickland began to investigate the subject.

Mrs. Lackmund and Mrs. Wickland had made an agreement that the one who should first pass to the spirit side of life would try to return and communicate with the other, saying, as a test, "Spirit return is true."

A year after this Mrs. Lackmund died and two weeks later, early in the morning, she appeared to Mrs. Wickland, so life-like that the latter did not at first realize she was a spirit. Mrs. Lackmund touched her friend lightly on the cheek and Mrs. Wickland sat up, exclaiming, "Mrs. Lackmund!"

Then Mrs. Lackmund spoke. "Anna, spirit return is true. Go to Professor Lackmund (her husband) and tell him my diamond ring is in the bureau drawer."

Eager to ascertain the facts Mrs. Wickland went to the home of Professor Lackmund, related her experience and gave the message concerning the diamond ring.

Professor Lackmund then told Mrs. Wickland that he had been looking everywhere for his wife's ring but was unable to find it and had intended that morning to question the servants regarding the disappearance of the ring.

Looking in the bureau drawer, as suggested, Professor Lackmund found, in a corner, the ring wrapped in a piece of paper with a note attached: "Give this ring to Franz (four-year-old son) when he is sixteen years old."

This occurrence could not have been due to a trick of the subconscious mind since Mrs. Wickland had known nothing whatever of the circumstances of the missing ring.[1]

It is evident that those offering psychic phenomena,

---

[1] For further evidence of spirit verification see Chapter III, "Verification of Spirit Identity."

23

especially physical, should be carefully scrutinized in order that deception may be avoided. Of the various phases of psychic phenomena, the unconscious trance state is the most dependable since through a genuine trance psychic direct contact with discarnated spirits is facilitated and the identification of many of the communicators is made possible.

While there are many earnest students of the interrelationship of the two worlds and many excellent psychic intermediaries who do great credit to the cause of psychic research, yet there are also many individuals, nondescript and illiterate, who possess psychic powers but are dominated largely by designing and deceiving spirit entities. These entities, seeking to please the vanity of ambitious psychics, may assume the names of great personages, especially those of renown and fame, but their twaddle and inconsistencies are entirely foreign to the original characters they represent themselves to be.

Many such pretentious assertions have come to our notice. Some years ago we heard a spirit speak through a medium saying that he had lived before the Pyramids were built, and yet he spoke an excellent modern English, as did another spirit that controlled a woman and claimed to have been Queen Esther of biblical fame.

A certain medium, whose husband is declared to be Jesus Christ reincarnated, claims that she is the reincarnation of the Virgin Mary, yet she swears, smokes and drinks like a man. A young man of quite ordinary intelligence informed us that the great Socrates was his spirit guide, and we were recently invited to attend a circle to hear Jesus talk through a trumpet. (We did not, however, accept the invitation.)

At a dark seance conducted by some colored folk for materialization of spirits, a spirit presuming to be Jesus manifested and talked to the audience, saying, "I am Jesus of Nazareth, your Savior! King Herod was my father!" Spirits claiming to be Moses, Abraham and Elijah also materialized and spoke, asserting themselves to be the original biblical characters.

It seems unbelievable that intelligent persons who attend these meetings are completely blinded and fully accept the preposterous claims of such entities. One young man in particular, of whom one would expect better judgment, was so infatuated with these "divine (?) entities" that he could not be reasoned with, an attitude of fixed delusion which only too frequently leads individuals to the insane asylum.

When asked, "How do you know this spirit was Jesus?" the young man replied, "I *saw* him and *talked* with him."

"What language did he speak?"

"English, because that is the universal language in the spirit world."

It is evident that the personalities alluded to were the type of entities that John referred to in his admonition: "Believe not every spirit, but try the spirits . . . because many false prophets are gone out into the world" (I John 4:1), which experience has proven is as true today as it was in that period.

At a gathering of Spiritualists in an eastern city a woman medium arose, entranced, to address the audience and her spirit guide said: "I do not allow my medium to read anything, not even the newspapers. I am George Washington!"

Another medium then arose and her spirit guide announced through her: "I am John the Apostle! Many a time I have rested my head on the bosom of Jesus and that is more than any of you people can claim!"

Only a short time after this we learned that a highly cultured gentleman on the western coast, an occult student, declared himself to be the reincarnation of John the Apostle. Yet this gentleman had been born before the supposed John the Apostle spoke through the medium in the Eastern city.

Too many psychics ignore the admonition, "Believe not every spirit . . . but try the spirits." (I John 4:1.) As a result the investigator turns from the entire subject in disgust and Psychic Research is relegated to the domain of credulity, delusion and superstition by the superficial skeptic.

"In the spheres of spirit life thought may be said to be the light of the soul, and the grade of the ideas held by the spirit is a good index of its spiritual unfoldment." ("Illuminated Buddhism.")

Ordinary, intelligent spirits are never pretentious, but plain and simple; they talk intelligently concerning the relationship and condition between the two worlds. In other

25

words, they act intelligently and depart intelligently. Such will prove to be of greatest blessing to the investigator and to humanity at large, as they are ever eager to help human advancement and will be loyal friends, faithful, loving and kind.

As the radio receives every vibration, harmonious or otherwise, so the advanced Intelligences perceive human thoughts and actions. There is no admonition so powerful for right living as the knowledge that we are surrounded by spirits who are aware of our shortcomings, wilful or dishonorable conduct, since they discern our very thoughts. "We also are compassed about with so great a cloud of witnesses." (Hebrews 12:1.)

Maximus of Tyre, Greek rhetorician and philosopher, said: "God is the Supreme Being, one and indivisible though called by many names, accessible to reason alone, but as animals form the intermediate stage between plants and human beings, so there exist intermediaries between God and man, viz., daemons (spirits), who dwell on the confines of heaven and earth. The soul in many ways bears a great resemblance to the divinity; it is partly mortal, partly immortal, and, when freed from the fetters of the body, becomes a daemon (spirit). Life is the sleep of the soul, from which it awakes at death."

No subject from antiquity on is so thoroughly confirmed in sacred as well as profane history as contact with the unseen world. Through the ages the influence upon mortals of intelligent spirits for good, as well as the detrimental interference of ignorant and mischievous entities, has been recognized by mankind.

The spirits of former chiefs of primitive tribes became the ruling powers from the invisible world and were selfish and tyrannical beings, oftentimes posing as gods, acting through the "medicine men" who were required to be psychics before they were accepted as tribal leaders. Many of the characters referred to in the Bible as "a jealous God" were unquestionably just such legendary monstrosities parading as "Lords" who had to be placated by various offerings, even human sacrifices, to satiate their selfish, barbarous lust for power over their ignorant devotees. Similar practices are not entirely extinct today as there are still tribes and groups in some countries that are slaves to such fetishes and are held under the dominance of despotic spirit entities.

Is Psychic Research dangerous? This is a mooted question which may be answered both yes and no. Dr. William J. Mayo, internationally famous surgeon, stated in a paper contributed to a special volume of the American Journal of Surgery: "If (a person) wishes to devote his life to a study of so-called psychic phenomena, it is one thing, but as a side line, investigation of the occult carries distinct danger to integrity of thought."

A publication, "The Great Psychological Crime," which lays particular stress upon the dangers of mediumship, asserts among other statements: "Up to the present time there is a wide and prolific field of insanity which the medical fraternity find it necessary to classify under the general heading of 'Causes Unknown.' In this great class, generally speaking, will be found at the present time, for the most part, the various forms of Hysterical Insanity, Religious Insanity, Religious Mania, Emotional Insanity, and so-called 'Delusional Insanity' of all kinds and degrees. These, however, might all be included in one general class and properly designated as 'Mediumistic Insanity' or 'Subjective Insanity.'"

A noted English clergyman declared that there are millions of insane spiritualists in and out of the asylums. (He failed, however, to state the fact that among the inmates of the asylums are an overwhelming number of religious fanatics.)

Dr. Marcel Viollet, Physician to the Lunatic Asylums, Paris, wrote: "For the sake of the predisposed and the lunatics as well as for the sake of the normal participants (of a seance) and even for the sake of the future of spiritism itself, we utter the warning cry: Beware! Beware! Avoid all madness, and, at the same time, avoid the dangers of madness. Filter your assemblies . . . You, the predisposed . . . take care of the disintegration which is lying in wait for your brain . . . You—conscientious savants, well-balanced minds, and the inquisitive—do not let yourselves be encumbered with these perilous promiscuities. Spare them their madness, spare yourself the dangers, guarantee your doc-

27

trine and your pre-scientific facts. Establish a sanitary customs-house at the entrance to your seance-rooms, and, certain henceforth of being among healthy minds, disclose to us a new Science."

Before entering into the problem of the dangers of Psychic Research, it would be well to consider the dangers and fatalities resulting from all manner of research and experimentation. How many lives have been sacrificed to chemistry, the X-Ray, radium, the science of aviation, to medical research in its endeavor to discover hidden causes of diseases, in laboratories where scientists strive to unravel nature's secrets of electricity in the effort to control this force for the use of humanity? Countless have lost their lives in these various avenues of research, and yet where would the world be today were it not for these pioneers?

In the every-day walks of life dangers lurk on every hand; thousands and millions are continually losing their lives from one cause or another. As a matter of fact, our very physical existence is a matter of uncertainty, and, at best, of limited duration. Yet, regardless of the manifold disasters, research and experimentation go on unceasingly and humanity thereby continually evolves to higher stages of knowledge, progress and betterment. But for these pioneers of progress, wrestling to uncover nature's secrets, men would still be savages, dwelling in smoky caves.

No one with wide experience in Psychic Research can honestly deny or refute the assertions made by opponents of psychic phenomena, that psychic investigation is unsafe in the hands of thoughtless novices and the neurotic. That the various mental aberrations quoted above are often consequential to the impingement of discarnated spirits as contributing factors is no longer a mere hypothesis but a fully demonstrated fact which medical science ere long will be obliged to recognize and include in its diagnosis of mental abnormalities.

Our forty years of research in normal and abnormal psychology have fully proven that the foregoing statements have a foundation in fact. Herein lies the cardinal issue pertaining to Psychic Science, the Scylla and Charybdis, the danger which lurks about novices or those uneducated in psychic laws, those who "rush in where angels fear to tread."

Some years ago we knew an excellent trance medium, Dr. E., highly spiritually minded, through whom genuine slate writing, verifiable materializations and messages were given. But he did not understand obsession and when earthbound spirits impressed him he became greedy for money, began dishonest practices and sold worthless charms to poor working girls. His intelligent spirit guides withdrew from him and the earthbound spirits dominated him entirely, driving him to utter dissipation and finally suicide.

Later this spirit was attracted to one of our meetings and controlled Mrs. Wickland, begging pitifully for help. He explained that while he had been honest in his early work, the woman whom he had married proved to be a dishonest and fraudulent medium, dominated by selfish, mischievous spirits. Her invisible forces had encroached upon his sensitive nature and, unaware of spirit obsession, he became overpowered by them, hence his fall and tragic ending.

A young girl in Chicago, who came to us for help, had attended a seance where a woman, beside whom she sat, shivered and shook violently, explaining that these manifestations were due to spirit influences. This woman told the girl that the latter was psychic and invited her to come to her seances for development.

The girl did so with the result that she became obsessed by earthbound spirits to such an extent that she could hear their voices day and night and finally came to us for relief. While we were conversing with the patient a spirit controlled her, and I asked, "Who are you?"

"I am a little girl from the seventh sphere," the spirit answered.

"A little girl from the seventh sphere would not come and control a sensitive person against her will," I said.

The spirit finally admitted being a man and a vagabond. "But I am not alone; there are seven of us."

"You must all stay here," I replied. "You will be helped by Intelligent Spirits. Now you must leave the girl."

"I can't, unless you help me."

Whereupon I made certain passes over the patient, the spirit became disengaged and the girl left in great haste. Later this spirit spoke through Mrs. Wickland at our circle

29

and said that he and the other spirits had for some time been attached to the medium whose seance the girl had attended but they had left the medium and followed the girl.

Three years afterward we met the girl again; she had had no further trouble with spirits but assured us that she had never again gone to a seance. The medium herself came to one of our meetings and admitted that she had formerly been bothered by earthbound spirits and added, "But they are all gone now."

Many demonstrations are brought to our attention showing the unfortunate results of unwise psychic experimentation as well as the strange situations in which spirits often find themselves owing to lack of needed education in life concerning the simplicity of the change from the physical to the invisible state of being.

Mr. A., an elderly gentleman, was well situated financially and had everything to live for but subsequent to his attendance at spiritualistic dark circles he became afflicted with insomnia, melancholia and an indefinable depression for which there was no assignable reason. Being familiar with Psychic Research he came to our Institute to ascertain if his depression could by any chance be due to some outside interference. Static electricity was applied to the gentleman in the presence of Mrs. Wickland who became entranced by a foreign entity that strenuously objected to the treatment, saying: "I don't like that! (Noticing Mr. A.) Hello, pal! I like you so much; you're a nice man."

Dr.
Wickland Where did you meet this man?

Spirit I found him at a meeting. (Mr. A. had attended a trumpet seance.) I was so depressed. (Coughing and choking, evidently repeating his death struggle.) I took something. (Committed suicide.) Then I slept for awhile and after that I walked a long time in the twilight. It seemed like the desert. Then I came to a meeting; it was dark and they were singing all kinds of hymns. And there I saw my pal.

Dr.   How did you become his pal, John? Is John your name?

Sp.   No, my name is Philip Mendelsohn. Everything seems confused. This gentleman asked me how I became his pal. There was a gathering sitting in the dark; they were singing hymns but it was not a church. I looked around and I walked around; I had to push to get in. Some people were sitting in a circle but outside of the circle was a big crowd (spirits) shoving, pushing, pulling and crowding like at the stock market. I've never been in such a crowd.

Mr. A.   Most of them must have been in much the same condition as you were—in the twilight.

Sp.   You in the circle seemed like sane people; those outside seemed like crazy people. I was curious and wanted to see what was going on. After awhile there was a trumpet; they took hold of it and talked through it and the trumpet was flying around. They (spirits) were fighting to have a chance at the trumpet.

Some said, "I am father," or "I am mother." I wondered why they advertised themselves. Then I thought those in the circle must be blind. (To Mr. A.) After awhile I spotted you. I saw a dandy lady (spirit) come to you; she was a peach! I saw another; she was older. I thought, "You ladies are too nice to get into this crowd; you are too respectable." Then I looked at you and I thought you were too nice to be in that crowd. When the crowd was stampeding every one (spirits) went away—or up—or some place —just disappeared. The nice ladies were gone!

Mr. A.   Wouldn't you like to see them again?

Sp.   Yes, I would.

Mr. A.   I am strongly impressed that was my spirit wife and my dear mother. They would help you. Do

31

what you are instructed to do today. Look around and see whether you see some bright persons here.

Sp.   (Gazing about.) There is not such a crowd as that night; that was like the stock market.

Dr.   Are you familiar with the market?

Sp.   I made my money in the wheat pit. Then I lost my head and my money and had to suffer for it. That was in Chicago; I lived there for awhile. I had plenty of money. Money is a good thing to have but if you haven't sense with it, it is a detriment.

My father had money and I went through Yale; I thought I'd be a civil engineer. Life went all right for awhile but if you have too much money you don't like to be sent out into the mining country and have to walk miles and miles. It was too hard and I thought I didn't need to do it, so I gave it up.

I won money in the market and wanted more. Then the crash came and down I went. Then I began to worry and was always depressed.

Mr. A.   Now all that depression of yours you bring to me.

Sp.   I do? I'm sorry. When I come close to you I can have a little peace. But I always feel as if my hands are tied and I get down-hearted and think there is no use in anything. Did I make you feel that way?

Mr. A.   Yes, you did.

Sp.   (Emphatically.) Well, I wouldn't do that for the world. I had a good brain once but there was too much money. If you have children and have money, put the money in trust and let the children work. There, that is the story of my life.

(To Mr. A.) When you went home I followed you because you had such a bright light around you, and I became a pal of yours. The others (sitters at circle) at that meeting were gray and muddy; don't ever go there again.

Mr. A.   Now there will be others (intelligent spirits) with a much brighter light to help you.

Sp.   Did I do much detriment to you?

Mr. A.   Yes, you did.

(The spirit was then made to understand that he was a spirit, temporarily in possession of Mrs. Wickland's body, facts of which he was unaware. His attention was also called to the presence of invisible friends whom he could discern if he would look around carefully. He remained quiet for a moment.)

Sp.   Oh, look there! There's my dear old mother! She says, "Philip, your father and I have been trying to find you but you were too clouded in earthly conditions. You were lost in a cloud of ignorance; you did not pass to the spirit world but stayed near the earth." My mother thanks you for having helped me.

She says when those ladies (they were so bright and beautiful) saw I was lost they looked up my father and mother. My parents were Presbyterians, and they were still in the path of religion, buried in their creed—"bond servants" —although they were spirits. Your wife and mother brought them understanding of the laws of life and nature, so we have to thank you doubly.

Your wife says there are so many spirits in the earth spheres; very few go at once to the realm of understanding. After my parents were enlightened they looked for me, they say, and found me with you. But now I am free.

We all thank you. Your wife and mother are going to take us to the real spirit world. I thank you and I am sorry I bothered you.

Mr. A.   I am glad I suffered as I did, Philip, if I helped you.

Sp.   I was ignorant. It is easier to say "I believe" than it is to study. My mother looks so happy, but I feel as if I were nothing at all.

Mr. A.   You are just as valuable as anyone, in the sight of the Great Benevolent Father.

Sp.   My mother says my selfishness has been conquered. If I can ever do a favor for you, I certainly will. Now I will go with my people.

(The spirit departed and the gentleman afterward declared himself relieved of the depression.)

As all research has laws which must be observed, so also has Psychic Research governing laws which must be thoroughly understood and strictly followed to obviate disaster. Knowledge and careful observance of these laws will prevent any unfortunate consequences to the mentally and physically qualified psychic sensitives or investigators who may be interested in the furtherance of Psychic Science.

It is advisable to have trained, experienced researchers to give instruction pertaining to these laws; it is likewise of paramount importance that the group of investigators be harmonious, sincere, conscientious persons, exercising intelligence and reason. These conditions are necessary to attract intelligent spirits as guides and protectors.

In such research a thoroughly trained medium, one who is mentally and physically well-balanced and willing to make any sacrifice necessary in the interest of science, is fully protected by intelligent spirits, who are ever eagerly seeking for the co-operation of mortals in order to reveal the truth of continued existence, and particularly to make known the serious problem of impingement in human affairs by ignorant spirits.

Many mediums receive thought impressions emanating from some discourse given by intelligent spirits in the spirit world and mistake these spirits for "guides," claiming that Lincoln, Washington or other advanced spirits are their guides. Yet these mediums are merely tuned in like a radio on these particular thought waves.

Mediums who suffer writhings, convulsions and distress

34

in general when going under control are not fully developed, nor have the controlling spirits fully developed the process of control.

When there is firmly implanted in the mind of the medium a dogmatic, fixed idea, say, regarding religion, reincarnation, egotism, etc., this acts as a deterrent to the communicating spirits and often colors the communication.

A medium should be a free soul, neutral, without creed, dogma or ism, and should be able to relax completely, leaving the way open to full control by intelligent spirits. Thus will advanced, intelligent spirits be attracted, the process of control be easy, natural and comfortable, strength be given to the medium by the guiding spirits and truthful messages and communications be received.

Mrs. M. T. Longley, who devoted most of her life to Psychic Research, wrote in "The Spirit World": "The power of mediumship is deep and far reaching; its source is in the potential energies of the universe; the principle of all sentient life; it is divine. Mediumship is delicate, it is subtle, rooted in the spiritual structure; it may be easily put out of tune; it can be even perverted to base uses and brought down to ignoble ends." . . .

"It is possible for some of these delicately attuned instruments to be set ajangle by the wear and tear of conditions, to be unduly influenced by designing spirits in mortal flesh as well as by duping beings outside of this clay. The wonder is, that with the conditions provided them by careless, self-seeking visitors, curiosity-hunters—perhaps from both sides of life, not to speak of designing encroachers on their magnetic forces and environments—so many psychics are held to truth and probity in their line of conduct and of work." . . .

"The ancients understood the needs of their oracles; they knew that subtle vibrant forces must sway sensitives who could be susceptible to the forces of the unseen worlds sufficiently to receive and to register them correctly; so these sensible people removed their psychics from contact with the ignorant crowd; they built for them temples, and gave them beautiful surroundings, made them free from anxiety concerning the supply of bodily needs, brought them into the Sanctuaries of Silence . . . and provided the proper

35

conditions for the exercise of mediumship to its best and fullest extent."

"That which is gained by the good and pure medium . . . the sweetness, purity and beauty which come from the consciousness of helping, sustaining, blessing other human lives, create a happiness and spiritual wealth in the medium, or in any such ministrants, that belong to Spirit, and that is everlasting."

Psychic Research should be undertaken with the determination to ascertain conditions obtaining on the invisible side through contact with good, bad and indifferent entities, with charity for all. That sense of charity will increase with the realization that the often deplorable conditions of many discarnated spirits are due to erroneous doctrines, habits, wilful ignorance or unreasoning skepticism maintained in earth life.

"The dead know not anything" (Ecclesiastes 9:5) is a statement in the Bible which the theologian would apply to those who are supposed to be dead and in the grave, yet it is not the dead bodies in the grave that are alluded to. Spirits of those who were born in ignorance, squalor or evil environment hover about the earth plane in a twilight state, totally unaware of being spirits, knowing "not anything" of their situation. They are alive, but owing to their earthly-mindedness and lack of knowledge regarding spiritual laws it is often impossible for enlightened spirits to reach them or bring them to a realization of their condition.

Spirits unaware of their transition often find themselves wandering about like persons in a fog, usually alone, although now and then they may observe some other wanderer. It is a constant coming and going, a drifting to and fro, described by some spirits as a condition comparable to a vast ocean in which ignorant spirits float about, occasionally contacting each other, then passing on.

Thoughts of help sent out by enlightened spirits ("the spirits of just men made perfect," Hebrews 12:23) are not perceived by these denizens of the twilight plane, often because they do not realize that they are discarnated. Although possessing spirit bodies, these dwellers in the "gray spheres," as Sir Arthur Conan Doyle designated this realm, still retain their mortal habits of thinking and fail to discern the thought waves sent out by those who would help them.

Hence the enlightened spirits urgently request humanity to co-operate in this rescue work by establishing radio centers where psychic intermediaries may serve as the radio apparatus to which the ignorant spirits can be attracted and through which they can be made to realize their situation. Through such stations intelligent spirits can contact the ignorant ones and lead them on to the pathway of understanding.

When earthbound entities are allowed to temporarily control a mortal sensitive they generally show susceptibility to logical reasoning, are usually responsive to a spirit of charity and become highly appreciative of help received. Their attention will then be attracted to the intelligent spirits about them, of whose presence they have been unaware; the latter are therefore then able to assist them to progression in the spirit world.

The interference, in various ways, of discarnated spirits in human affairs has proven a factor which must be recognized. A fuller knowledge of the significance of spirit influence will explain many of the involved and perplexing situations in human lives. To relegate Psychic Research to the limbo of credulity and superstition will not solve the problem regarding causes of abnormal mental conditions so often occurring in individuals who know nothing whatever of psychic phenomena and do not believe in the existence of spirits. Experience has proven that such persons may be suggestively or actually obsessed and dominated by discarnated entities without being aware of it and while refusing to believe in spirit influence.

The obsessing entities may likewise be unaware of being spirits or of having interfered with anyone and may even not believe in spirit existence. "When these spirits come to a man they enter into his entire memory and thus into his entire thought . . . These spirits have no knowledge whatever that they are with him." ("Heaven and its Wonders and Hell," Swedenborg.)

The advancement of research in normal and abnormal psychology has shown definite evidence of utmost importance; of all sciences none is of greater importance than

Psychic Research as it deals with the condition of the "dead" and their influence for good or ill in human affairs.

Instead of being left, as hitherto, in the hands of the idly curious as a mere pastime and a butt for ridicule, this research, especially the abnormal phase which reveals the hidden causes of much that is obscure in many of the mental aberrations so prevalent on every hand, claims the fullest attention of science.

The editor of "Scientific American" declared in a recent issue: "Some day the fundamental nature of the causes of psychic phenomena may be discovered. The more precise sciences, such as physics, may then be able to fashion a tool to work with, and the investigation may be taken up in the manner science likes best and is most accustomed to."

Science wants psychic phenomena to harmonize with its preconceived notions; however, each problem in nature has laws of its own which must be recognized, for the laws of nature will not adjust themselves to any caprice of men of science.

Psychic Research does not lend itself to grab-bag methods, such as have often been used by skeptical investigators, and hasty conclusions, pro and con, must be avoided. This, of all scientific research, requires an open mind, a keen sense of discretion and patient effort in accumulating the requisite evidence.

Verification of these statements is readily obtainable through the co-operation of a highly trained trance psychic, developed for the purpose, who, under proper physical and spiritual protection, will permit herself, or himself, to be temporarily controlled by interfering spirits that have been dislodged from persons suffering from such influence, incidentally proving that the psychosis was not of physical origin since this could not have been transferred to a second person.

Appropriate treatment of the patient through the use of static electricity, hydro-therapy and suggestion greatly facilitates the transfer of the spirit, or psychosis, to the properly developed psychic sensitive. By this method the investigator obtains direct contact with the interfering entities who are usually unaware of being spirits or of being then in possession of another person's body. Direct conversation can be had with them and much discussion may be necessary to bring these ignorant spirits to an understanding of their situation, which many are loath to recognize.

They frequently offer all manner of argument in an endeavor to disprove the facts, and deny being spirits, deny having obsessed anyone or being then in possession of the body of another. Although it is sometimes a difficult task to convince such spirits of their actual condition it is generally possible for the investigator to enlighten them; advanced spirits will then take them in charge for further instruction.

The evidence obtained in our research work has chiefly been secured through the physical organism of Mrs. Wickland, the author's wife, who has devoted over forty years to this work without any harm to herself. Mrs. Wickland's mediumship is that of unconscious trance, induced by the Intelligent Invisible Co-Workers; her eyes are closed and after waking, as if from a deep sleep, from three or four hours of trance, she is utterly unconscious of what has transpired, and, instead of being fatigued, feels rested. Mrs. Wickland also has the gift of clairvoyance, which is a very important adjunct in diagnosing cases in which interfering entities are contributing factors in the various psychoses.

Mrs. Wickland has allowed herself to be temporarily controlled and possessed by intelligent entities as well as by all manner of spirits, many unaware of being dead but still dominated by various habits acquired while in the physical existence and still retained mentally.

The many-sided conditions prevailing in this latter class are almost unbelievable and actual contact with these spirits will convince the most skeptical of the serious nature of this problem.

39

CHAPTER III

Verification of Spirit Identity

URING contact with spirits the investigator is often able to learn the identity of the spirit, his name, something of his earth life and connections, and may frequently, by subsequent investigation, be able to verify the statements made. We have had many such experiences in our work.[1]

A young girl suffered from attacks which had been diagnosed by physicians as epilepsy. At times she complained of pains in the stomach or dryness of the throat and alternately had paroxysms of choking and spells simulating paralysis. The patient had been under our observation for some weeks, receiving electrical treatments and medical attention, when one morning Mrs. Wickland became controlled by the spirit of a woman that had been dislodged from the girl.

The spirit gave her name as Frances Dickinson and was very despondent. She said she had had severe stomach trouble and when she became paralyzed her husband had left her. Discouraged, desperate and unable to make a living for herself, she had committed suicide by turning on the gas in her room.

When her true situation had been explained, spirit kindred appeared to her and she was taken away to receive further enlightenment.

The father of the patient was greatly interested in the statements made by the spirit and decided to verify them if possible. Accordingly he made inquiries at the Coroner's office in Los Angeles and looked up the records of the Bureau of Vital Statistics, where he found the following entry:

"Frances Dickinson, age 71, native of Canada, committed

---

[1]See case of "Charlie Herrman," Chapter XI, "Reincarnation," Page 213.

suicide by turning on gas in her room at Number ——, South G—— Avenue, Los Angeles, June 13, 1922."

Obtaining the address of the undertakers in the case, he found their records showed Frances Dickinson had died from gas, and the body had been cremated June 20, 1922.

Further verification was received from the woman's place of residence and the added information given that she had suffered considerably from stomach trouble.

Mr. P. H., a contractor specializing in building greenhouses, had been afflicted for several years with a condition of paralysis agitans which caused his hands to shake constantly; he also suffered from mental disturbance and severe headaches. When his sister, Mrs. J. W., arrived from Europe, where she had read our book, "Thirty Years Among the Dead," pertaining to our experimental work, she brought Mr. H. to us for consultation and treatment.

After some weeks, during one of our circles, a spirit controlled Mrs. Wickland, whose hands immediately began to shake violently.

Dr. Wickland	Good evening. Who are you?
Spirit	I don't know who I am right now. Just leave me alone; it's bad enough to shake without talking.
Dr.	Why are you shaking?
Sp.	I don't know. I suppose because that man does. (Referring to patient.)
Dr.	Does he shake?
Sp.	Yes.
Dr.	Do you realize that you have been in a strange condition for some time?
Sp.	You bet I do, but what can I do?
Dr.	Get understanding.
Sp.	Where?

Dr.   Right here. You do not belong with that man, and if you listen we can help you realize your situation. Do you. know you have been bothering a man?

Sp.   No, but a man bothers me, and I don't like him at all.

Dr.   Any reason why?

Sp.   Because he won't let me work.

Dr.   Are you an active person?

Sp.   I am active if only I can get to do what I want. I want to do something, if the work is not too hard.

Dr.   What work did you do?

Sp.   Contracting for buildings and greenhouses for Howard Smith, Germain's and Paul Howard. (Nurseries in Los Angeles.)

Dr.   Did you know P. H.? (Patient.)

Sp.   Yes, he worked for me; I was the boss. But I haven't worked for some time now.

Dr.   You have lost your physical body and do not understand it. You drifted about and evidently got into this man's aura. Now you must leave him. He is sensitive to spirit influences and you are one of the spirits that bothered him. You have been an earthbound spirit without understanding that fact.

Sp.   Spirit! I don't care for such things.

Dr.   When you had your own physical body, did you ever think where you would go when you died?

Sp.   Wherever they all go. Where am I now?

Dr.   You are controlling the body of a woman; she is a psychic sensitive and allows spirits to use her organism so they may be helped. We are following research work to learn what becomes of the dead. Can you remember whether anything unusual happened to you?

Sp.   A couple of winters ago I was caught in a severe storm. I got wet through and took cold. I was sick and then I went to sleep. (Died.) When I woke up I felt all right but many queer things happened. I went to work but nobody took any notice of me. I would tell them to do things but they didn't care what I said. I got so mad I wanted to strike them.

Dr.   Even had you struck them they would not have noticed you.

Sp.   I sat looking at things for awhile and all at once I felt very strange. I seemed to have gotten closed up with some man (entered patient's aura) and I shook as if I had a stroke. I heard somebody say I was paralyzed. I wasn't, but I couldn't stop shaking. (Patient's condition.) It made me so angry.

Dr.   Now you have been taken away from that man and we can explain matters to you. Do you realize where you are?

Sp.   Not exactly.

Dr.   You are in Los Angeles.

Sp.   That is where I live.

Dr.   What is your name?

Sp.   Wagner.

Dr.   Now you must go with spirit helpers who will teach you how to progress and when you have learned how you can help the man whom you have been troubling.

The spirit was then taken away. When Mr. H. was asked whether he had known anyone named Wagner, he said, "Why, yes, I used to work for him and after he died I bought his business." These circumstances were entirely unknown to us.

Several weeks later, at our experimental circle, another spirit, shaking as if palsied, was permitted to control Mrs. Wickland.

Dr.
Wickland   What is the matter with you? Forget your old condition. You must realize you are now a spirit.

43

	Do you understand that you have lost your physical body?
Spirit	No. Where is P.? (Name of patient.)
Dr.	He is not here just now. Are you related to him?
Sp.	No, just a friend.
Dr.	Where did you know him?
Sp.	In Los Angeles. (Hands shaking as if palsied.)
Dr.	Did you always shake like this?
Sp.	I wouldn't shake like this if I could help it.
Dr.	How long did you do this shaking while in life?
Sp.	I am in life yet. I was very sick. Where is P.?
Dr.	He is out in the country.
Sp.	I want to go to work. Where is P.?
Dr.	I told you he is not here.
Sp.	Well, get him.
Dr.	That would take a couple of days. Have you been staying with P.?
Sp.	Yes.
Dr.	Did he ask you to stay with him?
Sp.	No. I worked for P.
Dr.	What kind of work did you do?
Sp.	We built greenhouses, but I got hurt.
Dr.	Through an accident?
Sp.	Yes; I got hurt in my neck. (Pain in the neck was one of the patient's symptoms.)
Dr.	What were you doing at the time you were hurt?
Sp.	I was up on a ladder building a greenhouse. I was working for P.
Dr.	How long ago was that?
Sp.	I don't know, but it was some time ago.
Dr.	What is your name?
Sp.	Ivar Johnson. I am a Swede.
Dr.	What have you been doing lately?
Sp.	Shaking. I can't do anything else.

Dr.	You evidently passed away through an accident and got into P's. aura. Do you know you are not shaking your own hands? Look at these hands. (Indicating hands of medium.) Do they look as if they could build greenhouses?
Sp.	(Examining Mrs. Wickland's hands in amazement.) No, they couldn't!
Dr.	Look at the shoes you are wearing. (Pointing to Mrs. Wickland's shoes.)
Sp.	What in a thousand devils is this? I'm not a woman!
Dr.	Now the shaking has stopped.
Sp.	How did that happen?
Dr.	It slipped from your mind.
Sp.	I was just going to look at these things I'm wearing. It's a miracle! In the name of a thousand devils, where did I get all these things? Me, a man! I guess I'm not a Swede any more. Oh, gosh! Oh, gosh! Why in the world have I these things on?
Dr.	You have lost your physical body, but you are not dead. You say you had an accident; at that time you must have become disengaged from your body.
Sp.	I fell from the scaffold on a pile of lumber and struck my spine. I got paralyzed and I began to shake. The doctor said some nerve got struck. I couldn't work after that. (Hands beginning to shake.)
Dr.	When you think about shaking you begin to shake.
Sp.	I have been locked up; I guess it must have been in a prison.
Dr.	No, it was with P. himself. He has been shaking like this for a number of years. You have been influencing him.
Sp.	Couldn't I get a pair of trousers instead of this dress? Give me a pair of overalls. I feel so ashamed to sit here in this dress with all these ladies looking at me.

45

Dr.   You are talking through the body of a lady. We do not see you.

Sp.   How in a thousand devils did I get in here? (This was said in Swedish.) Excuse me, but when everything used to go wrong, I forgot myself. Someone (spirit) just told me I cannot swear when I am in this company.

It is strange, but when I get real mad I have to swear in Swedish. Not everybody understood me, but that was all right. You know, I did not get into trouble by swearing, because whenever I got awful mad I swore in Swedish, and when they asked me what I said, I always said I was not feeling well!

I always talked English except when I got real mad. I just had to get it out of my system. Then everybody used to laugh.

Swear in some other language and you don't get into trouble. You people who talk a foreign language, just remember that.

Dr.   It sounds like good advice. But you must understand that you have been a spirit for some time.

Sp.   Spirit! What do you mean?

Dr.   Just what I say. The mind is not the body.

Sp.   You mean I am a soul?

Dr.   Yes, soul, or mind, or individual.

Sp.   But they say when you die and are a ghost, people are afraid of you.

Dr.   We are not afraid of you.

Sp.   Will I have to go back to that prison? (Patient's aura.)

Dr.   No, you will be free now. Did you have any unusual experiences lately while you were in that "prison?"

Sp.   Yes, all kinds. Some were terrible.

Dr.   What were they?

Sp.   Well, I don't know what you would call it, but fire from Heaven rained down on me. (Static

46

treatment given patient.) I didn't know what to do; I thought it must be the Last Day.

(Suddenly seeing another spirit.) Why, there's my mother! That's strange. How did you get to America, mother? You died in Sweden.

My mother tells me that I must go with her as she has a home in the spirit world.

That will be very interesting—to go home to my mother again! The world is peculiar—very queer.

I'll go with you, mother, if you have a cup of coffee. You always had the coffee pot ready.

Dr.   Now you must go with your mother.

Sp.   I'll go, but I can't go in this dress. I want a coat and trousers. What will I do?

Dr.   You will have to leave the clothes here; they do not belong to you. This body is not yours either.

Sp.   Why, you don't think I can go with my mother without any body, or without clothes, or anything, do you?

Dr.   Has your mother a body?

Sp.   Yes; and she is all dressed up.

Dr.   She has a spirit body and you will also have a spirit body. You have lost your physical body without understanding it. No one ever "dies." The personality leaves the physical body and then has a spirit body. You remember, the Bible says, "There is a natural body and there is a spiritual body . . . first . . . that which is natural then that which is spiritual." (1 Corinthians 15:44, 46.) Most persons do not understand this and do not realize it.

Sp.   I don't realize it myself.

Dr.   You yourself did not die when you had that accident. You merely left your physical body. You liked P., you thought of him and entered his aura. Then you conveyed your shaking condition

47

Sp. to him and he came here to have electrical treatments.

Sp. So *he* got the treatments! It seems as if nothing is my own!

Dr. He took the treatments hoping to get rid of any spirits that might be attached to him, and you were one of them. You must understand your situation and take things more seriously. Think yourself with your mother and you will be there instantly. Go with your mother and be open-minded.

Sp. So, you want to get rid of me! All right, I'll go. Thank you for getting me out of that shaking business. Good-night.

Interrogating Mr. P. H. later as to whether he had known such a person as Ivar Johnson, he said that a man by that name had worked for him, but he had had an accident, from which he died.

The patient, in addition to his physical ailments and mental disturbances, had spells when he would fall on the floor and make facial grimaces, strongly indicating that some outside influences dominated at such times. After being rid of these influences, the disturbances ceased, the patient's mind became entirely cleared and he was able to attend to the details of his own business, which previously he had been unable to do.

Mrs. P. and her husband, who resided in a village in Canada, were visiting in California; having read with much interest our book "Thirty Years Among the Dead," they came to us for an interview to learn more of our experimentations in abnormal psychology.

Mrs. P. casually complained of being greatly distressed by a throat difficulty and said she had suffered from this since childhood. Medical treatments had not changed the

48

condition and an operation which had been performed upon the throat had given no relief.

Mrs. Wickland clairvoyantly discerned the spirit of a man with Mrs. P. and sensed that he had passed out with throat trouble, evidently cancer. From the description given of this spirit Mrs. P. recognized him as her father who had passed out forty years before with cancer of the throat.

It may be of particular interest to state that at that time Mrs. P. was ten years old, was a favorite child of her father and that she had been present at his death.

It was evident, since her throat trouble had had its origin from that period, that at the death of her father his spirit had inadvertently become attracted to his daughter and locked up in her aura. Unaware of his true condition, or of being a spirit, he did not know how to free himself from her and, believing himself still ill, had thrown the condition of his former sickness upon her.

Such occurrences have been frequently observed in our experimental work and verify the Bible statement, "Where your treasure is there will your heart be also." (Luke 12:34.)

Several static electrical treatments were applied to Mrs. P. in an endeavor to dislodge the spirit and at a subsequent circle which Mrs. P. attended a spirit took control of Mrs. Wickland and attempted to speak to some one in the circle but was at first unable to talk.

Dr.
Wickland Is there some one to whom you wish to speak?

(The spirit turned with outstretched hands to Mrs. P., moaned and breathed heavily, then placed hands upon throat.)

Dr.   Forget your sickness. You are not sick any longer. You are carrying the habit of sickness in your mind. That condition has gone.

Mrs. P. My father used to act just like this spirit is acting. That breathing is just how my father reacted to his doctor's treatment.

Dr.   (To spirit.) Forget your old trouble. Your sickness belongs to the past.

49

(The spirit coughed with great effort and in a peculiar manner.)

Mrs. P.   That is just the way my father acted. This is wonderful!

Dr.   (To spirit.) You need not cough. You are a free spirit. This is not your body; you are now talking through another body which is healthy. You carry this habit of coughing in your mind. You came in contact with your daughter and threw your condition on her. You caused her much trouble.

Sp.   Lizzie, I did not know that, but I have suffered and I made you suffer also.

Dr.   (To Mrs. P.) Is that your name?

Mrs. P.   Yes, my name is Elizabeth.

Sp.   I did not understand and I could not get away from you. I threw my sickness on you.

Dr.   You will no longer do that. It is only your mind which is troubled.

Mrs. P.   Now you must help me to keep well.

Sp.   I will, when I get stronger. I see that I got into your magnetic aura and I could not get out. I am very glad you came to this doctor because he has helped you, and me too. You will now feel better and stronger every day.

God bless you, and give my regards to all at home. I love you, my dear, and God bless you! When I am stronger I will help you.

Dr.   You no longer have your old trouble.

Sp.   No, I do not have that throat trouble now! I thank you, Doctor, for freeing my daughter and also for freeing me. I was in great torment myself. Now I must say good-night.

The spirit was then taken away. After this experience Mrs. P. was entirely relieved of her distress. Three years later she wrote us from her home in Canada: "I want to tell you that I have never once had a sore throat (referring to experience as related) since I had the treatments. I think it is simply wonderful; remember, I suffered with my throat from childhood."

A young musician had been "meditating" and "sitting for development" in dark psychic circles, striving to attain "mastership," in consequence of which he had become sensitive to spirit interference and was tormented by spirit voices.

The young man's disposition became entirely altered, necessitating his being placed in a sanitarium. He was greatly emaciated, labored under various mental aberrations, also, complaining of great distress in his stomach, refused to eat, his behavior requiring forced feeding.

His brother and a friend, who knew something of obsession, were convinced that spirits were interfering with the young man and brought him to us for static electrical treatments. During three weeks nine spirits were removed from the patient, each being in turn allowed to control Mrs. Wickland. One of the first of these controlled at a seance when the patient's brother and friend were present. The spirit was greatly bewildered by his situation.

Sp.   Where am I? (Bending forward as if in pain.)

Dr.
Wickland In Los Angeles. What is your trouble?

Sp.   I have such pain here. (Stomach.) I cannot eat anything. (Moaning.) I am so sick.

Dr.   Forget all that; it belongs to the past. You have lost your physical body.

Sp.   (Pointing to brother of patient.) Oh, I know you! Don't you remember Reuben? (Reuben had been a colored butler employed in the patient's family for thirty-five years; he had died in the patient's presence after a lingering illness, of cancer of the stomach.)

Brother   (Recognizing speech and mannerisms of spirit.) Is that you, Reuben?

Sp.   (Excitedly.) Yes, yes! (Eagerly extending hands.) I'm so glad to see you! I'm so sick. What is the matter with me? Oh, help me! You were always so good to me.

Dr.   You must realize your condition. You must forget your old trouble. You are a spirit now and have no physical pain.

Sp.   What is the matter?

Dr.   You have lost your physical body and are temporarily controlling another body. When you leave this body you will be free.

Sp.   I am so sick.

Dr.   Were you sick?

Sp.   (Appealing to patient's brother.) You know I was sick, don't you? For a while I suffered awful. (Stomach cancer.) Thank you for all you did for me. You were always good to me; you did all you could for me.

       We both had a good time together when you were a little boy. You were such a good boy; I liked you. Where is your brother? (The patient.)

Brother   He has been sick, but he will be better now.

Sp.   You remember how sick I was; you know how I suffered.

Brother   You will be well now.

Sp.   Help me, please! You will not leave me, will you?

Brother   No, indeed. We are all going to help you.

Dr.   Do you know that you have lost your physical body?

Sp.   You mean I died?

Dr.   You left the physical.

Sp.   (Frightened.) You do not think I am going to die? I'm pretty sick. I don't think I went to church enough, you know.

Brother	That makes no difference. You were honest and sincere. That is enough.
Sp.	Yes, I was always honest.
Brother	Any one that led the life you did is going to come out all right.
Sp.	How is your mother?
Brother	She is very well.
Sp.	God bless her! She is a lovely woman. Where is your brother? Did you say he is sick?
Brother	He is going to be better now.
Dr.	Evidently you have been attached to him so closely that he complained of suffering just as you did before you passed out. You were ignorant of the fact. Now that you are away from him he will gradually improve.
Sp.	(To the brother.) You know I got so I could not eat. I was so sick here. (Stomach.)
Dr.	You are no longer sick. Take your mind off that condition. You must progress now.
Sp.	Am I going to Heaven?
Dr.	You will go to the spirit world, where you will find your kindred.
Sp.	Do they take colored folks there?
Dr.	Color does not count on the other side of life.
Sp.	Was I good?
Brother	Sure you were.
Sp.	Do you like me?
Brother	Certainly.
Sp.	I felt sorry I could not do much lately, but you gave me a good home.
Brother	We did all we could for you.
Sp.	How many good times we had when you were little and how I carried you around.
Dr.	(To the brother.) Did he do that?
Brother	Sure he did.
Sp.	We had nice horses, didn't we?
Brother	That is true.

Sp.	Why, my pain is all gone!
Dr.	That is because you put it out of your mind.
Sp.	(To the brother.) God bless you! Tell your mother that I thank her for being so good to me. I will never forget her. What was the matter with me lately? I felt so shut up. (Obsessing the patient.)
Dr.	You have been interfering with this gentleman's brother. He had been studying the occult and became sensitive. You contacted him without realizing it and caused disturbance.
Sp.	Did I do that? Please forgive me.
Brother	Don't worry about that now.
Sp.	God bless you!
Dr.	Intelligent spirits will help you to learn about your new life.
Sp.	They want me to go with them. Good-bye.

One of the spirits dislodged from the patient gave the name of Ada, who had for years been the family nurse and was so recognized by the patient's brother; the symptoms of the nurse's last illness had also been impressed upon the patient.

Two other entities claimed to have been students of Yoga under Vivekananda; the first, Hugo Schiller, said he had left New York for the Vermont mountains "to study nature and higher philosophy" in order to acquire creative power and become a "Master."

The second declared his father had been an English General in India and that he himself was born in Calcutta; he asserted that after studying Hindu philosophy he had become a "Master" and assumed the name "Swami Wonvar." "I teach people to sit in the silence," he said, "for the development of the spirit and to get power from nature."

Both these spirits were unaware of their real condition and said they had been "floating around" until they found "a young man sitting in the dark," (patient sitting in the silence, meditating for mastership). Deciding to become his "teachers" they had become attached to him and were unable to free themselves.

These entities were brought to an understanding by seeing the spirit of Vivekananda, who said in part:

"You cannot teach Yoga in the western world as it is taught in the eastern world; the life is different and the vibrations are different. If you study Yoga it must be under proper conditions—in quietude. There is a wrong way and a right way to teach Yoga; you must know the laws and have spiritual understanding."

"Many Swamis go from India to America and fool people for the money they get from them. Often they go wrong because they use forces that do not belong to physical conditions or this mundane sphere."

"People sit in dark circles and 'look' for something, and do not know what they are looking for. That should not be done in the western world, for they open the psychic door and become obsessed. 'A little learning is a dangerous thing.'"

A gradual improvement was discerned in the patient after the removal of each entity; the young man regained his mental balance, resumed his normal activities, playing tennis and driving an automobile, and in a few weeks returned to his home. Five years later we heard from a friend of his that he was entirely well and had again taken up his music.

During an informal communication from the invisible side through the mediumship of Mrs. Wickland, at the home of Sir Arthur Conan Doyle several years ago, among other intelligences the spirit of Harry Houdini, the great magician, took control of Mrs. Wickland.

The spirit complained bitterly of his dark surroundings and referred to the great mistake he had made in ridiculing psychic phenomena, which he knew to be true.

Asked about the code agreed upon between himself and his wife, he declared that in his present mental confusion he could not even recall what the code was, and that he

55

must first acquire more understanding of his new condition, for he had a very great deal to learn and undo.

At the time, I was rather surprised regarding his seeming familiarity with Sir Arthur, but learned later that Houdini, while in life, had had many discussions with Sir Arthur anent the problem of spirit return, and also that Houdini had expressed a leaning toward the reality of spirit communication.

Readers are familiar with the recent successful decoding, through the mediumship of Mr. Arthur Ford of New York, of Houdini's secret code agreed upon between his wife and himself, at the time acknowledged by affidavit of Mrs. Houdini to be authentic.

Three years later, during a private seance at our home, the spirit of Houdini again controlled Mrs. Wickland. He expressed great regret at the stand he had taken while on earth against the truth of spirit return and communication, and declared he was now trying to do all within his power to right the wrong, speaking as follows:

"It seems cruel that a man in my position should have thrown dust in the eyes of people as I did."

"Since my passing I have gone to many, many mediums but the door is closed to me. When I was on earth I closed the door with double locks by ridiculing psychic phenomena and mediums. I have been able to open the door once or twice, but only for a little while. When I try to tell people of the real truth they say I am not the one I claim to be, because when I was on earth I did not talk that way."

"I ask you here to give me good thoughts, strength and power to undo my mistakes. I cannot progress until I have acknowledged the truth. I must, I must do it!"

"I found an avenue through that most wonderful medium, Arthur Ford, and gave my wife the code we had agreed upon."

"I have done great harm to many mediums. How I wish I could go to every one and tell them that I did a wrong thing, that when they worked for the good of the cause I tried to expose them to the world as humbugs. God help me for having done that."

"I see my mistakes but I cannot get out of my present

56

condition until I do good to the ones I ridiculed. I try my best to correct my mistakes but it is very hard."

Dr.
Wickland Do you recall the talk you had with Sir Arthur Conan Doyle shortly after you passed out? You spoke then through this same instrument.

Sp. "I tried my best to get through the opening but at that time I was so bewildered I did not know where I was."

"In my own soul I am so convinced of the wrongs I committed. Many do not know what awaits them on the other side of life, what the sleep of death is. When one has an understanding of death, there is no waiting, no hindrance."

"At first I was so confused that everything which belonged to memory was forgotten for quite a long time. (A common complaint of many spirits in their first efforts to communicate after transition.) Later, things came clearly to me, the things I had promised to do, and I tried very hard to get a message through. I wanted to tell the truth and undo my former error."

"I found a wonderful instrument in Mr. Ford. I talked through him and my wife was in a receptive spirit to accept me. I was very happy but suddenly the door was shut."

"How I also wish I could say a few words to another very wonderful medium, Margery. (Mrs. Crandon, of Boston.) I did much harm to that poor woman. How she has suffered because of my antagonistic thoughts."

"I tried to upset her and once I nearly killed her, but I did not think much of it at the time. I wish I could undo the wrong I did her. She is a very wonderful medium."

"I lectured and charged money—for what? To blind the eyes of the people. They would pay to hear me lecture and run down poor, honest mediums. (Covering face with hands.) Oh, it is awful!"

57

Dr. Wickland	Do not carry on that way, friend. You are controlling a medium and must be more careful. Do not over-excite yourself.
Spirit	I see things so differently now. Everything I did stands out before me.
Dr.	Change your attitude and look for the intelligent spirits around you. Do not think of your troubles all the time. Work you way out of them.
Sp.	But it is as if I am in a prison and cannot see anything.
Dr.	You will see in time. Ask the intelligent forces to give you strength and power to overcome so you can carry on.
Sp.	(Features brightening.) Thank you! I can see more clearly now. Standing here is a very beautiful little lady (spirit) and she says she will help me. (To spirit.) You say you will take me to your home?
Dr.	Does she say who she is?
Sp.	(Addressing an invisible.) What is your name, pretty little lady? She says her name is Miss Dresser. (Former member of our circle.) And you say you will take me and help me? I knew better in my heart than to lecture as I did. I did it, however, for money, money! I was so selfish.
Dr.	You can overcome that.
Sp.	Beautiful lady, will you really help me? How peaceful your soul must be. You are like a transparent angel!
Dr.	Her mind was occupied with higher ideals while in the physical body.
Sp.	She seems to float, not walk, and here I am, as heavy as lead.
Dr.	You must not think of that all the time. You made mistakes, but from now on determine to see the better side. Do not be so discouraged.
Sp.	You will give me your help, little lady?

Dr.   Of course she will. That is why she came here tonight. Until recently, she met with us in this little circle.

Sp.   Will you all send thoughts to me for strength? I know I did wrong, and I knew I was wrong at the time. If I had done what my conscience urged me to do, I would not be where I am now.

I was a psychic, and I knew it. I was helped in my work by the spirit forces, but more by the materially-minded forces, those who could work magic. But I shut the door to the higher intelligences.

Little lady, you who are so beautiful and bright, will you help me? Another one comes to me now.

Listen! Listen to that beautiful music! This little lady has brought two others who are now singing. Such music! At last my soul is at peace and I can go on. I have much work to do to right the wrongs of my past.

But listen, such beautiful music! Heaven is opening! I cannot describe this music because I never heard anything like it before.

And see those most beautiful flowers! Never, never, have I seen such beauty. Heaven is surely opening for me!

Dr.   You will find many wonderful things in your new life but you will have to work your way out of your present condition. Realize your mistakes and profit by them. Life is a school.

Sp.   Can you hear that wonderful orchestra playing? They tell me it is an orchestra that plays to open the eyes of those in darkness so they can see the beauty of the spirit world.

Oh, how I do wish I could tell my wife that I can see! It would make her so happy to know that I have found peace.

Dr.   We will all send you helpful thoughts.

Sp.   One thing I must ask all of you, and that is, do

59

not be doubting Thomases as to my identity. I
have enough to combat now. I am Houdini.
What place is this?

Dr.   This is The National Psychological Institute in
Los Angeles, established for research in normal
and abnormal psychology to ascertain the condition of spirits after transition.

Experience has shown that intelligent spirits
play an important role for good in human
affairs; on the other hand, many spirits, owing
to ignorance, often unwittingly act as contributing factors in many mental aberrations.

This is also a clearing-house where intelligent spirits, in co-operation with mortals, can
enlighten the perplexed spirits who are often
unaware of their transition.

Sp.   Now they tell me I must leave. But before going
I want to thank you for the help I have received.
God bless you all! Good-bye.

A report of this communication from Houdini was published in an eastern magazine and ten days later the spirit
of Houdini again controlled Mrs. Wickland.

Spirit   I have come to thank you for the help you have
given me.

Dr.   Did we help you?

Sp.   Yes, and I am much happier now. I had denied
facts which I knew in my heart were true. I
wanted to be original and have everybody think
I was scientific so I denied facts and criticised
others.

"When you have the truth, acknowledge it.
Now I have acknowledged my mistakes and I
want to ask forgiveness of the ones I tried to
harm."

"I thank you for publishing that article and
letting the public know that I came back. I am
glad it was given out to the world that I con-

60

fessed I wanted to ruin that little medium, Margery, (Mrs. Crandon) who lives only for the truth and sacrifices her life to demonstrate her work."

"I tried trickery with her but Walter (Mrs. Crandon's spirit brother) found me out beforehand."

"God bless the Crandons and God bless you! I am so glad that article was given out to show that poor Mrs. Crandon was persecuted. That is now known."

Dr.   Many believed that you were a wonderful medium yourself and that spirits helped you in your work. Was that correct?

Sp.   Yes, but I would not acknowledge it. Whenever I was going to do something spectacular, if I did not hear a voice telling me to go ahead I did not dare go on. Many times I did not perform my tricks because I did not hear the voice. When I heard it I knew that everything was all right. I cannot tell you exactly how I did my tricks because I do not know myself. I was in a semi-trance when all that took place.

Question   I should like to know how you got out of the tank of water and came up on the stage from the front. I claim that could not have been done without spirit agencies.

Sp.   I do not even know myself how it was done. When I was in the tank of water I could hear the voices talking but I could not hear what was said. Up to a certain point I was myself, but not after that.

From the time I was tied and locked up until I was free I did not know what took place. But I could not have told that. People would have wondered what was the matter with me and that is the reason I did not dare say anything. I wanted them to think I was doing the tricks myself, but the spirits were the ones who acted through me.

61

Dr. You are making progress now, are you not?

Sp. Yes; I have progressed far enough to give enlightenment to some and I do all I can to help the unfortunate ones. I have certain duties to do to help others before I can progress to new development. I am happy but in a way I am restricted because I have to find those who are in trouble and help them and give them strength.

    I do work now that I should have done in earth life. If I had stood for the truth and given credit to spirit power, the world would have been more enlightened, because the spirits did wonderful things through me.

Dr. Have you contacted the spirit of Sir Arthur? (Sir Arthur Conan Doyle.)

Sp. Yes, and I have also asked him to forgive me. I said many unkind things about him. I was down on all Psychic Research and on every good medium. If I had happened to know you, Dr. Wickland, and your wife, you would also have gotten something. Those who escaped only did so because they had not come under my notice.

    I thought I knew it all and that there was nothing more to learn. I want to tell you, whenever you reach that state of mind where you know it all, ask God to help you out of it. When you feel you know everything and condemn everybody and have the idea that you are the only one, it is very bad. There is always something to learn. The more you learn the better it is for you.

    I am more than glad that the world knows I came back and have asked to be forgiven. That means more to me than I can explain. I thank you for the light you gave me.

    Now I will not take up any more of your time but I thank all of you.

Dr. We all wish you well.

Sp. Thank you and Good-night.

Intelligent Spirit Forces ask for human co-operation in diffusing a rational understanding of the relationship between the two spheres; they earnestly implore scientific minds to set aside prejudice and skepticism, which lead nowhere, and co-operate by establishing institutions for careful, unbiased research, centers to which ignorant spirits can be brought and enlightened from the mortal side.

For this purpose The National Psychological Institute was organized and incorporated as a benevolent association to carry on experimental research in normal and abnormal psychology as a nucleus to disseminate knowledge relating to the problem of Life and Death and the Science of Religion.

Maintaining no allegiance to any sect, belief, ism or cult, the Institute especially desires, so far as practicable, to encourage, and offer advice to, hospitals, asylums, educational associations and religious institutions to follow up similar research in the hope that the fact of survival will ultimately be placed on a rational, scientific basis proving "It is not all of life to live, nor all of death to die."

CHAPTER IV

Death and the Future Life

NTELLIGENT Psychic Research proves survival of the spirit and that the physical, objective world is of greatest importance as a part of the plan of the Over-Soul, the directing Universal Mind.

The spirit of the infant first enters the physical world in a state of unconsciousness, to slowly develop through varied experiences in the physical journey the faculty of consciousness and other mental and soul qualities requisite when ultimately entering the spiritual realm.

Lack of understanding of this fundamental law, and failure to train human minds in these particulars are among the greatest causes of apparent wrongs in the world.

The average individual thinks little regarding the why of life but lives in the objective and the physical. In other words, he is only mortal-minded, concerning himself very little, or not at all, with the meaning of existence.

Seeing that persons die on every hand and that their bodies go to the grave, many conclude that is all there is to life and hence expect that when their own time comes they will have a like ending and become lost in oblivion. These judge only by appearances, not by conclusions drawn from reason or mental analysis.

Such individuals live merely in an animal sense and, as a matter of fact, they are dead even while yet alive. The quickening process, or the spirit of truth, the desire to discern the meaning of existence, has not yet risen to the surface of consciousness, for the spirit of understanding still remains in an embryonic state.

The spirit, while in the body, absorbs erroneous ideas of many kinds, then enters the next life oblivious, for a longer or shorter time, of its reality and, in so many instances, of his very transition.

"Death does not change the character of a man, but simply strips off his masks and compels him to stand forth as he is, and he becomes after death the image of his own character." (Andrew Jackson Davis.)

During the three days of sleep which usually follow transition the spirit is unaware that his physical body has been cremated or removed to the cemetery and when he wakens he fails to comprehend the new situation since he still occupies a body, although one of finer substance, and still retains old habits, desires and ideals. Being as alive as ever it does not enter his mind that anything unusual has happened and he may remain oblivious to his condition for years.

Countless such spirits hover about the mortal sphere constantly conveying their various mental attitudes to mortals who may be impressed with all manner of delusions and false ideas.

Many spirits, unaware of their transition, linger about the scenes of their former earth activities, and, being very material, sometimes succeed in making themselves heard, as is evidenced in cases of haunted houses.[1] We have had a number of experiences with such spirits.

Mr. and Mrs. M., of Hollywood, were for some time greatly disturbed by inexplicable occurrences in their home; knockings and rappings were heard everywhere and each morning the clothes which had been carefully hung up in the closets the night before were found scattered about on the floor. One evening when Mr. M. fell asleep while reading in his chair he was suddenly awakened by a loud noise as if bricks had been thrown down beside him. Mr. and Mrs. M. were unable to go out for an evening as no one would stay with their children because of the mysterious sounds in the house.

At the request of Mrs. M., Mrs. Wickland and I, with three friends, and Mr. and Mrs. M., held a circle in the home of the latter to ascertain, if possible, what was causing these annoying disturbances.

---

[1]For further reports of Haunted Houses see our book, "Thirty Years Among the Dead."

Mrs. M., a psychic sensitive herself, was convinced that the house was haunted. She had learned from neighbors that the bungalow had been built for rental purposes by an eccentric recluse who lived alone in the garage in the rear and had died there. After his death the house was sold and rented, but tenants invariably left after a short stay, being driven away by the strange and unaccountable noises.

When the circle was singing Mrs. Wickland became entranced by a spirit who complained of being very cold.

Dr. Wickland	Tell us who you are.
Spirit	That's none of your business. I'm so cold! (shivering.) I'm cold—cold! I'm so cold I don't know what to do.
Dr.	Why are you so cold?
Sp.	Because I am so sick. Give me something to drink; I'm so cold.
Dr.	We want to help you.
Sp.	Leave me alone; I want to be by myself. I don't care to have any one around me. (Authoritatively.) I want you all to get right out of here!
Mrs. M.	We rent this house and have paid our rent, so we shall have to stay here.
Dr.	Do you own this place?
Sp.	I should like to know it if anybody else does. I'm so cold. Give me something strong to drink so I can keep my stomach warm. Give me something warm! I think I am dying.
Dr.	You "died" some time ago and are now a spirit. Let us help you to an understanding.
Sp.	What is the matter with me? I feel so strange. What is the matter with me, anyway? I try to do all I can to let people know I am around but they never pay any attention to me.
Mrs. M.	My husband and I paid attention to you because you made so much noise around here. What is your name?
Sp.	I don't seem to know. (An experience common to bewildered earthbound spirits.)

66

Mrs. M.   Were you a crank?

Sp.   That's nothing to you. You attend to your business and I'll attend to mine. No one needs to interfere with me. If I want to do anything, I'll do it! If I don't want to do anything, then I will not. All I want is to be let alone and go to my place to sleep. It's home to me.

Dr.   Where is your home?

Sp.   Right here. I wish you would all get right out of here. I wish I could get my hands on something, you would soon get out! Give me some whiskey; I am so cold.

Dr.   Don't you realize that something happened to you when you were so cold?

Sp.   I don't feel well. I was very sick and I didn't have any whiskey. (To Mr. and Mrs. M.) You folks took possession of my place. What right have you to do that?

Mrs. M.   We rent this house from a lady.

Sp.   I can't understand it. I never had anybody pay any attention to me before and I don't see why you are doing it now. Either you folks want whiskey or money out of me, I don't know which.

Mrs. M.   We do not want anything of the kind. We all want to help you.

Sp.   I haven't asked anybody for help. This is my house and here I am going to stay. I will chase you out whether you want to go or not.

Mrs. M.   I don't see why you should do that.

Dr.   "Dead" people have no use for material houses.

Sp.   Dead people! Dead people!

Dr.   Understand, you yourself are not dead, but you have lost your physical body, probably at the time you were so cold.

Sp.   I heard some people talking (spirit helpers) and they said if I came in here I could get help. I don't want any help. All I want is to be by myself.

67

Dr.   That does not make you happy.

Sp.   Every day I was by myself. Why didn't I get help when I needed it? Nobody ever said, "How do you do?" I lived in that place (pointing to garage) like a dog. People didn't come to see me when I was sick, and they don't need to bother me now.

Dr.   Perhaps you were too crabbed. Your disposition was wrong. You shut yourself away from everybody and were not friendly. Search your own conscience. We want to help you realize that you are now a spirit. If you look around you will see spirits who will be glad to help you. They will take you with them to the spirit world.

Sp.   When I die I shall go to Heaven or hell.

Dr.   Do you know that "heaven" is a condition of mind, not a place?

Sp.   This house is mine but I don't get the rent for it. It is always somebody else that says what is to be done.

Dr.   Spirits have no use for earthly houses. You were very sick and probably died when you were so cold. Apparently you lived only for yourself and by yourself.

Sp.   Why can't I live back there again? (Garage.) I fixed it up as my home.

Mrs. M.   You died there; they found your body and afterward this property was sold for taxes.

Sp.   (Excitedly.) Who sold my property?

Mrs. M.   The city sold it for taxes. Now a lady owns it and we rent it from her. When we came here I knew there was somebody in the house beside ourselves.

Sp.   I have chased two or three other families out. They got scared, I made so much noise. You were too tough. The others did not dare tell what they heard.

Mrs. M.   I felt glad there was some one in the house we could help.

Sp.	I am old enough so that I don't need any help. I want to know why they dare take my house from me. Are you going to stay here?
Mrs. M.	Yes; we like it and the children have a nice yard to play in.
Sp.	I fixed it up all by myself. I don't want to live right in the house—it's too nice for me.
Dr.	You do not need any material house. You have lost your physical body and are a spirit. This body you are talking through is not yours. Mrs. Wickland is so constituted that spirits can talk through her. She allows them to use her body so we can help them.
Sp.	If any one drives me I can be very stubborn. If you are stubborn to me, I shall be stubborn to you.
Dr.	Try to understand, friend, that you have lost your physical body and are a spirit.
Sp.	I never was a spirit and never will be! Give me something to drink, or something to smoke!
Dr.	You must get rid of your old habits. You have gone through the change called death but do not realize it.
Sp.	Things are queer. I tried to get people to understand me but that lady over there (Mrs. M.) is the only one who understands me, in a way. She pays attention to me. I made things pretty hot for the other people who came here. (Former tenants.)
Dr.	Did you ever hear of haunted houses?
Sp.	In olden times we did.
Dr.	You have been haunting this house as a spirit. Do you remember the Bible says we have a natural body and a spiritual body? (1 Corinthians 15:44.) "First that which is natural then that which is spiritual." (1 Corinthians 15:46.)
Sp.	I have been here looking after the property. I always kept things up. I had no other home. Wouldn't you do the same thing?

69

Dr.	Now you must go to the spirit world.
Sp.	I want to think things over. I want to know what I am going to do. What is the matter?

I got cold and had chills; I wanted something to drink and I drank all I had. I couldn't get warm. I think I went to sleep (died) and slept for awhile.

I know I was an old crank. I was afraid that everybody would steal everything from me. I kept everything to myself and no one knew my business. I didn't meddle with anybody. People thought I was queer and I let them think it.

All at once I took an awful cold and started to shiver. I shivered and shivered and couldn't stop. How I suffered! After awhile (after death) I started to walk but it was all so dark. (The condition in which ignorant spirits often find themselves.) This woman (Mrs. M.) was like a light. She understood. |
Mrs. M.	What is your name?
Sp.	Charlie Wells.
Dr.	What year do you think this is?
Sp.	I don't really keep track of dates. This place was a field and some trees, mostly oranges, when I came here. That was a long time ago.
Question	Did you know anybody by the name of S.? (Old settlers in same locality.)
Sp.	Yes, yes! I know those people. They had a big farm. They were well to do and had a big family. (Verified by two of the sitters.)
Mrs. M.	Do you realize that you have died?
Sp.	You say so.
Dr.	Intelligent spirits are here, waiting to help you.
Sp.	Something strange takes hold of me now and it seems my eyes are opening. (Astonished.) I see things now! (Spiritual vision.) The house is full of people. (Spirits.) There is my mother! She says she is glad to see me. There's my wife and my son, Edward! My wife says she has been

70

	waiting for me for a long time. I never thought they would wait for anybody after they died.
Dr.	Now you must go with your kindred.
Sp.	They say if I follow them and try to do the best I can they will all help me. I thank you for helping me to see, and you (Mrs. M.) for your help. (To Mr. M.) You will not be mad at me for scaring you, when you jumped in the chair?
Mrs. M.	You scared my husband when you dropped those "bricks." (Mr. M. explained there had been a sudden noise as though bricks had been dropped on the floor.)
Sp.	I wanted him to go to bed. He was sitting up too late; he was trying to read and fell asleep. I thought he had better read or else go to bed; he might have caught cold sitting there.

Now they (spirits) tell me I must go. My mother and all the others want me. I want to say, thank you all very much. Good-bye.

After this experience the M's. were not troubled by any further disturbances in the house.

Many years ago in Sweden a brother of mine witnessed psychic occurrences during which physical objects were transported from one place to another. My brother was then a young boy of sixteen, staying at an uncle's country home, when one day some gypsies drove by in a wagon. Stopping, they asked for some straw which was given them, but as it was not the kind they wanted they became disgruntled.

They were about to drive away when one of the children of the household, a boy of seven, with the curiosity of a child, looked into the gypsies' wagon and this caused the gypsies to turn their ill-will against the child. As they drove

71

away one of them shouted to the boy, "Oh, you want to see things! All right, you will see!"

From that day astonishing events occurred and continued for some nine months, as for instance, whenever the workmen returned from logging in the woods and entered the farm premises, the logging chains would jump from the sleds without any visible agency and land some distance away in the snow. Crowbars, likewise, would leap into the air to become buried in some deep snowdrift, where my brother often had to climb to recover them.

One day the boy told his parents that he could see some one moving around in the storehouse, a building near the residence, where foodstuffs and winter clothing were kept. Although the parents could see no one they immediately investigated; no one was found in the storehouse yet the clothing had all been thrown in a heap on the floor and a jar of preserved fruit turned upside down on top of the pile of clothes.

Before leaving school the boy usually placed his books in his desk but upon arriving at home the books would now frequently be lying on the doorstep of the house. One day, under the teacher's personal supervision, he placed his books carefully in his desk and walked home, accompanied by the teacher, and when they reached the house the school books had already arrived and were waiting on the doorstep!

In the kitchen, towels often flew into the fireplace, apparently by themselves, and, most annoying of the unaccountable events, the barrel, filled with water laboriously carried in from a near-by spring and always kept covered, would again and again be filled with an assortment of clothes and other articles.

The parents at first accused the children of playing pranks and punished them, although the children denied any knowledge of the occurrences. My brother was convinced that the children were wrongfully accused and to prove their innocence suggested, one evening after the children were in bed, that he and his uncle examine the water barrel to be certain it contained only water, replace the cover and remain in the room to await developments.

No one entered or left the room, nor was any unusual

72

sound heard, but later in the evening, when the lid of the barrel was lifted, the barrel was again filled with clothes, on top of the clothes lay a wooden spoon and in the spoon was —an onion!

Seeing this the uncle exclaimed, "Shall I believe the devil is loose?"

Determining to put an end to the trouble, he called in a Lutheran minister, but the minister got his nose severely pinched by the invisible tormentors and left the house in great haste.

As the disturbances continued, a Baptist minister was called in and while he was standing in the living room with an open Bible in his hand my brother entered with an armful of wood which he deposited in the wood-box as the minister placed the open Bible on the table.

The Bible was immediately closed, as if by magic, and several pieces of the wood were thrown on top of it. This minister's nose, however, was not pinched and devout Baptists declared this proved the devil could not play any tricks on a Baptist minister!

It was observed that when the boy was away from the premises nothing unusual occurred; everything was then normal and quiet, but as soon as the lad returned the mysterious annoyances began again.

The parents then took the boy to a near-by city and consulted a physician who was reputed to be wise in occult lore, having studied occultism in Wittenberg, Germany. While the parents remained in an ante-room the boy was taken into the physician's private office; although the relatives were unable to distinguish what was said they could hear, through the closed door, the voice of the physician speaking very sternly and authoritatively (no doubt commanding the obsessing spirits to leave the tormented child).

The boy could never be induced to tell what the physician had said as he had been forbidden to do so. After this, all disturbances ceased.

It is readily discernible that in this world we have all kinds of personalities, from the evil-minded and selfish, the indifferent (constituting the majority), to the more reasoning, intellectual type. Through physical sciences and Psychic Research it is becoming more and more self-evident that the unseen world is largely similar to this objective world.

All, both good and bad, pass out of the visible ken, but, paradoxical as it may seem, after leaving the physical untold numbers do not realize they are discarnated spirits and remain ignorant of their real situation. Swayed by their earthly training and its beliefs, creeds and skepticism, they are held in the mortal environment for a longer or shorter time by these imbibed notions and beliefs until they become aware of their true condition.

Then the advanced spirits are able to reach them and they are taught to drop their old erroneous ideas; when they become willing to be instructed in the new school of life they are taught how to progress.

Had these spirits been enlightened and educated regarding the simple facts concerning the progression of the spirit from the invisible through the visible and onward into the invisible again, the transition into the next school would have been a natural and happy event.

"The wisest men are glad to die; no fear of death can touch a true philosopher. Death sets the soul at liberty to fly." (T. May.)

The teaching that, no matter how ignorant an individual may be concerning the Science of Life, when he passes from this life he will enter a dogmatic heaven as a full-fledged saint if he has belief and faith in orthodox doctrines, is only an error promulgated by dogmatism. This causes untold numbers to enter the next life totally unprepared for the actual conditions in the new sphere and leaves them wandering in a twilight state, the "outer darkness" of the Bible. (Matthew 8:12.) "Blessed . . . is he that hath part in the first resurrection: over these the second death hath no power." (Revelation 20:6.)

There are many blind religious spirits whose minds are saturated with the belief that after death they will imme-

74

diately find themselves in the presence of a visible, personal God. Such concepts are illogical since God is Spirit, not a spirit, (see John 4:24, Revised Version Margin,) and is at no time visible either to mortals or spirits.

"God is love; and he that dwelleth in love dwelleth in God." (I John 4:16.) "The kingdom of God is within you." (Luke 17:21.) "There shall no man see me and live." (Exodus 33:20.) "No man hath seen God at any time." (I John 4:12.) "Ye are the temple of God, and the spirit of God dwelleth in you." (I Corinthians 3:16.)

It should always be borne in mind that life, intelligence and all that belongs to life are always invisible, although perceived through material manifestations.

Sir Oliver Lodge, in an address at London, stated in effect that "we cannot appreciate electricity or magnetism or even light except by their effect upon matter. Our eyes do not tell us about light itself, but about the material body which is illuminated. Our knowledge of light is an inference from the behavior of matter. The function of matter is to manifest and display to our senses activities which themselves have an existence apart from it. All we see of each other is the body organism; all the rest is inference—not by the brain but by the mind. Reality is in the region of the unseen."

Of the thousands of spirits we have contacted in our many years of research, not one has seen God. Spirit, like intelligence, is invisible. All advanced spirits describe an all-pervading Power expressed through lofty, inspiring ideals and indescribable harmonies permeating all things. Such harmonies or spirit vibrations are not discernible to blind, religious devotees who have not added understanding to their faith.

Faraday writes, in the spirit communication, "Origin of Religions": "No mind emerges from the darkness of superstition so long as it adopts the errors of faith as truth. When a knowledge of the truth is obtained the mind advances, and by a steady acquisition of truth becomes wise and freed from the superstitions that belong to the primitive condition of mentality."

We are told that "God is Spirit; and they that worship

75

him must worship him in spirit and in truth." (John 4:24.) Also, "Faith, if it have not works, is dead." (James 2:17.) Faith alone is only a prompting from within, a key with which to open the door to understanding. Only by adding knowledge will understanding be acquired; only knowledge will replace ignorance of life's problems by understanding.

A person may have faith in himself and may believe that he can accomplish anything he may undertake, say, learning a profession or becoming a musician, yet he cannot accomplish his aim by mere faith alone. It is necessary that he strive by effort to acquire the necessary knowledge in order to become proficient in that in which he has faith. "Add to your faith . . . knowledge." (II Peter 1:5.)

Millions accept as sufficient mere faith pertaining to conditions hereafter. Some assume that at death the individual goes to the grave and remains there until awakened by the blast of Gabriel's trumpet at the Resurrection. Others believe that death liberates the soul from the body and the soul then goes directly to "God who gave it."

So there are many other faiths founded on mere beliefs, which Psychic Research, when carried on free from preconceived notions and theories which the investigator is determined to prove, demonstrates to be false and misleading concepts.

The ministrations carried on in the churches touch chiefly upon one phase of these truths, namely, the moral side of life, which unquestionably is of greatest importance. But the most essential phase, that of definite knowledge of the continued existence of the ego after transition, is totally lacking.

The early church recognized the inter-relationship of the two worlds. The prophets of old were seers, such as the clairvoyants and mediums of the present day, and had communications with the invisible world.

It is evident to every thoughtful, analytical mind that we are spirits springing from the invisible, manifesting through this physical organism for a time. Entering the physical domain, we build up vehicles or bodies through which our minds obtain experience, unfoldment of consciousness and the faculty of understanding. In due season our

76

spirits vacate the physical forms and enter the invisible realm wherein wider opportunities are afforded for fuller and broader discernment of life's meaning.

In a spirit communication, "Development of the Spirit after Transition," given by Faraday, this growth is described. "In the realms of purely spiritual existence the experiences . . . are analogous to a condition in earth life where every desire of the mind is supplied without opposition, and where the development of the powers latent in the personality is unchecked by any adverse condition. The spirit in such a state becomes divine in beauty of expression . . . and feels no inclination to injure itself or others by departing from the principles of truth and righteousness."

"When spirits have attained to this degree of unfoldment they can explore the inmost principles of wisdom. They range at will in the spheres of causation and become conversant with the basic principles of being."

"Physical nature is the laboratory for the production of living organism which becomes the basis for an animated spirit world, where plant life and animal life together form a paradisical condition for the soul's next abode. Therein still greater soul vistas become discernible ultimating in the soul's realization of its oneness with the soul of the Great Architect of the Universe, which is Love and Wisdom."

"As far as mind extends, so far extends heaven." (Brihad Aranyaka Upanishad.)

"Life eternal is a condition where thought-power is the great motive agent in action and spiritual perfection consists in the cultivation and acquirement of those mental states that produce the most perfect happiness in either world . . . The whole life of the soul is in learning the lessons that teach the spiritual nature the principles that produce a perfect mental balance . . . The spirit can go forward upon the plains of wisdom and intellectual unfoldment forever." ("Illuminated Buddhism.")

While conversing with our Invisible Co-Workers regarding the subject matter of our book the spirit of Sir Arthur Conan Doyle unexpectedly controlled Mrs. Wickland and spoke, in part, as follows:

"There is only a journey between earth life and spirit

77

life—like the water one crosses between England and America. The Spirit World is the real life. No one can progress until he is willing to learn life's lesson and use reason."

"Intelligent men who should have knowledge fail to use reason when they take up Psychic Research. They begin to investigate phenomena with the thought in mind, 'There is nothing in it.' "

"They know nothing of the subject. How could one take up any science without knowing the laws? Many such investigators do not want to be called 'spiritualists'; they want to be called 'scientists.' Many have had countless, genuine manifestations yet deny the facts."

"I am sorry to say, intelligent men who call themselves scientific do not study this subject of Psychic Research in the right way. England has many excellent mediums, but also very excellent skeptics who do not know how to investigate."

"If you go to a medium in a neutral mental state you will have good results, but if you are skeptical you cannot receive much. If investigators are earnest and sincere in taking up Psychic Research they will have wonderful revelations."

"We have many problems to solve in the Spirit World as well as you have in earth life. Since I came to spirit life I have studied and learned a great deal as to what is right and wrong in psychic work. In a few years there will be marvelous spirit demonstrations."

"I cannot describe my own experiences in the Spirit World; these cannot be described any more than one can explain college subjects to a child in kindergarten. I have learned much since I have been in the Spirit World—the world of Understanding, Harmony and Love."

"On earth all minds are mixed, no two alike, and you are surrounded by temptations of all kinds. In the Spirit World you go where you belong because you enter the place you built while on earth."

"If you have studied and learned to overcome all desires and have acquired understanding while here, you pass through the Sphere of Ignorance to the Sphere of Enlightenment."

"Having had an understanding of the after life while on earth, one progresses after death to a higher understanding and the marvel of understanding God."

Intelligent spirits, in describing the wonders of the Invisible Side, assert that vegetation and flowers are living in the world of spirit and seem to express a degree of intelligence. To a doubter, these assertions would seem fanciful and absurd but, contemplating vegetation in its activities we find therein a process similàr, on a lesser plane, to mankind's evolution, an underlying, inner, intelligent process, ever evolving from lower stages to higher and higher, forever becoming.[1]

Jacob Boehme, the great German seer, wrote: "There are objective products in that celestial world which appear there as 'natural' as ours appear on the terrestrial plane; but as the celestial world is far more refined, glorious, and beautiful than the terrestrial world, those products must also be superior to any that can be found upon this earth."

"The celestial powers, by their interaction, generate trees and bushes, whereon grows the beautiful and lovely fruit of life. Likewise, by means of these powers, there arise various flowers of beautiful celestial colors and exquisite odour, in a similar manner as in this perverted and dark terrestrial valley various kinds of trees, shrubs, flowers and fruits grow, and as the earth produces beautiful stones, silver and gold."

St. Martin says: "There in the higher world all things are more closely related with each other. There the light is sounding; melody produces light; colors have motions, because they are living, and the objects are all at once sounding, transparent, moving, and can penetrate each other."

"Letters from the Spirit World," written through Carlyle Petersilea, state: "Within everything that lives and moves and has being is the spirit that lives and moves within it; this life or spirit covers itself with matter and whenever that matter is cast aside the life or spirit rises and takes its place within the spiritual world, and this principle holds good with everything that has the power of growth or has form." . . .

---

[1]See Chapter XIII, "The Great Designer," Page 260.

79

"The spiritual spheres of the earth are fed from the earth. The earth is the great reservoir or feeder of the realms which rise above and surround it . . . The spirit world is a real and tangible world filled with life and beauty . . . The spiritual world is not an intangible nothingness but real, filled with real life and the living souls and spiritual bodies of men, women and children, with its homes, its colleges, its institutions for knowledge of all kinds, and as rapidly as the errors and mistakes of earth can be purged away, peace and purity reign supreme—wisdom and love go hand in hand, and an eternity of joy and gladness await the soul of man."

"In my Father's house are many mansions." (John 14:2.) Religious devotees conclude that this statement implies more or less permanent houses or homes which await us when we step out of the physical. However, it should be discerned that this does not refer merely to abodes but more particularly to mental states in the Spirit World, or the condition of attainment of understanding. "Spiritual things . . . are spiritually discerned." (I Corinthians 2:13, 14.) The broader our mental concept the greater our progress on the journey to perfect understanding.

The homes in the Spirit World have often been described by intelligent communicating spirits, but it should be understood that these homes cannot be made for us by someone else. Our acts in this life determine the kind of abode we shall have hereafter. The individual who has groveled selfishly and ignorantly in gross acts and thoughts in this life without any interest in the problems of existence, and without any kind acts for others in his favor, will find a corresponding situation in the spiritual world and his home may be a mere hovel since he has failed to "lay up . . . treasures in heaven" (Matthew 6:20)—treasures of kind acts and intelligent discernment of the nobler meaning of life. Or he may find himself a mere vagabond spirit without any abode whatever if his earth life has not produced the proper material for a home.

Beautiful homes and scenes in the Spirit World, as described above, are often perceived by earthbound spirits as their spiritual vision opens; however, they realize they cannot enter therein until they have acquired an understanding of the new situation and cheerfully taken up the duty of service. There is no "forgiveness of sins"; wrongs committed in the physical, as well as erroneous mental attitudes, must be transformed by service into a "newness of spirit."[1] (Romans 7:6.) To enter heaven we must take heaven with us.

From the lowest strata to the higher, the attainment of loftier spiritual altitudes depends upon the degree to which minds and intelligences have been applied in acquiring an understanding of life's meaning. "The City of Happiness is in the State of Mind." Homes in the spiritual world correspond to the degree of unselfish efforts put forth by the individual while here and depend upon his thoughts, acts, love of truth and his realization that life means more than is apparent in the objective world.

Mediums sometimes inform inquirers regarding friends or kindred who have recently passed out, "They are very happy and are now in the Seventh Sphere." Such statements imply lack of knowledge concerning the nature of spheres. "Spheres" are not localities but grades of development or attainment. Many enter the Spirit World with a one-sided development and such cannot progress until the qualities necessary to balance this lack have been developed.

As one cannot pilot an airplane until the governing laws have been learned so a spirit cannot progress until he understands and complies with the laws governing spiritual advancement.

Spiritual "spheres" are not places, they are degrees of attainment of understanding and may be compared with grades in various schools. As realization is attained of the nature of spirit, of the Spirit World and its laws and of Universal Intelligence, understanding and a soul-sensing of the qualities of the Infinite unfold and the individual gradually progresses.

Dr. J. M. Peebles wrote: "Spirit life is an active life, a social life, a retributive life, a constructive life, and a progressive life; and reason, affection, conscience and memory go with us into the future state of existence . . . There are schools and lyceums, massive libraries, and everything to

[1]See "Nine Ingredients of Love," Chapter X, "Christian Science," Page 191.

81

charm, educate and unfold the soul, and the light of their love is the sunshine of their world."

The truth of the above statement has been verified in communications received through Mrs. Wickland from the spirit of Dr. Peebles after his transition, as well as in communications from many other spirits.

Schools in the Spirit World are of particular importance for infants and children who have passed to the Invisible Realm lacking development of their latent faculties. Such schools are also a necessity for those born with defective physical bodies and organs which prevented their mental unfoldment, as well as for children and individuals whose development has been retarded through interference by ignorant or mischievous discarnated spirits, which frequently causes such individuals to behave as idiots or imbeciles, as our research work in abnormal psychology has fully substantiated.

In Psychic Science lies a vast field for research whereby understanding is obtainable concerning the future life. The Bible, especially the New Testament, contains many scientific precepts regarding the inter-relationship of the two worlds which are not yet understood by those who presume to be representatives in this world of the truths pertaining to the future life.

These facts should be understood by the churches and should be as much a part of their teachings as their precepts for moral conduct and right living.

The waking intelligence of today is not satisfied with mere theory and blind belief but demands a rational understanding and knowledge of the meaning of life, both here and hereafter.

These principles should be the foremost teachings inculcated in human education; they are so simple that a child can readily comprehend the essentials if properly instructed therein.

If death ends all, as many materialistically-minded individuals hold, then life would indeed be a mockery, a meaningless phantasmagoria. But "There is no Death! What seems so is transition." (Longfellow.)

Shortly after passing from the physical life, a spirit, Mrs. H. R., sister of one of the members of our psychic circle, was brought to an understanding of her new condition while controlling Mrs. Wickland and gave an enthusiastic description of her first spirit vision.

"Oh, look at that picture! A beautiful walk, with beautiful flowers on each side. There are verbenas and forget-me-nots as far as you can see, then yellow daisies with black centers, and in another row white Shasta daisies that come up like a wall. There are lilies, maidenhair fern, all kinds of dahlias and honeysuckle."

"All these make the wall on each side of the road. Across the road is a gate which is made of three statues, a lady on each side and in the center another lady holding out her hands over the other two."

"The statue on one side is Love, on the other Truth, and the one holding out her hands is Wisdom—Wisdom gained through Love and Truth—the Understanding of Life beyond the Gateway. The gate is beautiful scroll work of roses."

"Now they open the gate and here is my sister, bringing beautiful flowers! She says, 'Come with me to the Everlasting Home, where there is no sorrow, no sickness, only joy and happiness.' Such a beautiful home!"

"My sister says, each one has a home of materials made of the good he has done in earth life. 'Your home is made of your good deeds,' she says."

"Oh, this is so new! There is my home and my mother is there! There are so many friends and they say they will help me."

"I am going with them but my sister says she will bring me to you again."

Mrs. E. M., a friend of ours, was a highly-trained musician, numbering many great artists among her friends. While playing on her organ, which was to her a great inspiration, her soul became liberated from the mortal and was

83

wafted into the Life Immortal. Later she described her experience while in control of Mrs. Wickland.

"My passing over was very wonderful. I was sitting at my organ and as I played before I realized it I was playing in the spirit world. It was most beautiful. I heard the last note played, then I was gone. I heard more music and as I opened my eyes I saw around me friends who had passed out."

"I said, 'Why, I was just playing, and I am still playing, but this music is so different.' "

"Then my friends gathered around me and congratulated me, but I said, 'Why do you congratulate me? I do not play as well as formerly.' "

"I did not realize that I had gone over to the other side of life. Many of my former friends appeared; Modjeska came to me and she said: 'You dear little soul, now you are with us.' "

"Carlyle Petersilea (you remember I was one of his pupils) played for me, and such playing! Such beautiful music, music I had never heard before."

"After I had seen my friends and heard the wonderful music, I slept for a time. It was a refreshing sleep; it seemed as if all trouble and care were forgotten. When I awoke I felt stronger. I was in a most beautiful home where my father and mother held a reception for me. The music and the flowers were lovely. Many friends welcomed me."

"You cannot realize what happiness it is to die when you have understanding. People should be taught how to die. It is all so beautiful when you step from the physical and find your friends waiting to receive you."

A musician of note, Miss C. D., who had attended our psychic circles for years and had carried on extensive individual Psychic Research, had in her youth studied with Carlyle Petersilea, one of the organizers of the Boston Conservatory of Music.

This gentleman, in his later years, became interested in Psychic Research and received communications from his spirit father, who in earth life had been a fatalist but in these communications proved to his son the error of his former belief.

Professor Petersilea also wrote a number of books pertaining to the invisible world which were received through automatic writing from his spirit father and mother, namely: "The Discovered Country," "Oceanides," "Letters From the Spirit World" and "Mary Anne Carew," the last inspired by his mother, describing her entry into the spirit world.

After Miss D.'s transition, the spirit of Carlyle Petersilea, while controlling Mrs. Wickland, described this lady's entry and reception into the new life.

"I have come here tonight to gather another of my flowers. This is Carlyle Petersilea. You know I call all my pupils 'my flowers' and I want them gathered together so they can join my beautiful orchestra."

"I have been watching for this flower for a long time and I have come now to gather her to be with the rest of us. She was one of my early pupils; one upon whom I could depend. She was faithful in her duties and she was always ready, never making excuses."

"Now she will be taken to the banquet we are having for her; there she will meet her dear friends and be with them. Our festival for her will be a joyous occasion."

"We have waited for her a long time, helping her, and now we are ready to take her to the beautiful home in the spirit world which she has prepared for herself."

"I wish you could all hear the singing and see the flowers and the banquet table. Two of her friends take her hands and lead her to the reception. She is now seated and receiving her friends and relatives who have gone before. She is the guest of honor in the banquet hall."

"She realizes now where she is. How beautifully her face is illuminated; she feels so happy to see her old friends. They all come to congratulate her."

"I am pleased that I can be the one to bring my flower to the banquet hall. I have many flowers, but she also has many that she has developed in the musical world in the past. They are here to greet her and welcome her to a happy home in the spirit world where she will continue her musical career."

"She is dressed in a shimmering white gown and has a lily-of-the-valley wreath on her head. There is also a very pretty token, a lovely little wreath of rosebuds, which her dearest friend has placed above the lily wreath."

"I wish you could see those who are gathered in this Inner Hall; she had so many friends. All is music; everything is radiant, with brightly colored lights decorating the Hall."

"After the banquet we will take her away to her new home. When she returns she will be stronger and will tell you herself of her experiences in the spirit world."

The spirit of Miss D. has many times communicated through Mrs. Wickland, telling of her reception and the wonders of the Life Beyond.

That the visible and invisible realms are closely inter-related is sometimes evidenced in a most interesting manner.

Some years ago, in Los Angeles, there passed suddenly from the physical life Mr. R., a great orchestra leader. He had been director of the Philharmonic Symphony Orchestra for some years and had, a few days previous to his sudden death, directed with great success Brahms' First Symphony and was to have been the leader of a great Beethoven festival the following week.

Thousands attended the impressive funeral rites which were reported in one of the daily papers, in part, as follows:

"While the Philharmonic Orchestra played the allegretto of Beethoven's Seventh Symphony at R.'s funeral today, the director's stand was vacant, but the great conductor's spirit seemed to direct."

"The conductor's stand on the stage was empty to the eyes of the orchestra—but to their hearts, it still contained the commanding presence of R."

"The obsequies were opened by the string section of the orchestra playing the Andante Cantabile of Tschaikowsky's string quartette . . . as finely shaded and polished in performance as if the baton of R. hovered above them . . . After the eulogium had been delivered the orchestra, as orderly and collectedly again as if the iron will and guiding hand of R. were on the conductor's stand, played the allegretto of Beethoven's A Minor Symphony, of which R. had often said: 'It is the last expression of peace for me.' "

"These words must have dominated the orchestra today for it played the selection as it has seldom been performed . . . Only an orchestra drilled and disciplined to the highest point could have played like this, without a leader in the flesh. And only a leader of superlative personality and force could have directed such an orchestra from the mysterious land of death."

Five days later, at a private circle held in the home of a friend in Santa Ana, the gathering was singing when a spirit assumed control of Mrs. Wickland. At first bewildered, the spirit listened a moment, began lightly beating the rhythm of the song, then, with a sudden look of intense concentration, directed the music with the uplifted hands of a master conductor. When the singing ceased the spirit again seemed bewildered.

Spirit   What *is* the matter with me? I was leading the orchestra—don't you know I am the leader? (Seized by a sudden cough.) I worked a little too hard. I was going to consult the doctor about my heart, but there was so much to do. I worked nearly day and night on that wonderful masterpiece we were going to play this spring—the Beethoven number.

(Gazing in amazement at some spirit vision.) Why, there he is—Beethoven! I must be losing my mind! Beethoven! (Ecstatically.) I loved him! Somehow, when we played his music, I always felt his presence there. But now—I see him!

87

But no—impossible. (Utterly confused, then coughing.) My heart! Once or twice my heart bothered me when I was leading; I could not conquer it lately.

Dr.
Wickland   Forget that now.

Sp.   (Gasping, smiling.) The symphony! Listen! (Clasping hands.) Oh, let me take it down. One great orchestra — Beethoven, Wagner, Liszt, Mozart—all in one orchestra! Can't you hear it? I have never heard such music, never. I can't describe it. What grandeur—what grandeur! What music! I cannot describe it.

(Intensely uplifted.) It is life! There is no death; all the great musicians are there. The wonderful, wonderful music!

I thought we could play but I feel now that I do not know anything. (Humbly.) I am a child; I must learn.

I could die in that music. I do not care to live; I want to die now. I would have that memory. (Listening raptly.) This is a dream, a vision!

Dr.   What are they playing?

Sp.   I have never heard it before. The grandeur—the music is life! There are flowers; the music has coloring. The colors pass from one instrument to another; they are blending into one beautiful harmony. Let us be quiet and listen to the music.

(It was then explained to the spirit that he had very suddenly passed out of the physical the preceding Saturday while driving his automobile.)

Sp.   I felt so sick; I felt I must go out and get fresh air. I became dizzy and stopped for breath.

Dr.   Then what happened?

Sp.   Nothing. But since then I have been leading the orchestra. I never heard them play as they did Monday (the day of the funeral).

Question	Did you hear the Tschaikowsky and Beethoven numbers?
Sp.	I was delighted with them. It was heaven. I think they did their very best. After that I went to sleep.
Dr.	The orchestra played in memory of Mr. R. (Explaining more fully regarding the funeral and memorial services.)
Sp.	After that wonderful playing I went to sleep until somebody called, "Wake Up!" Then I saw Beethoven and Wagner! It must have been a dream.
Dr.	That was not a dream; you were given a glimpse of the spirit world. (Further explanations of transition and spirit life followed.)
Sp.	I saw Beethoven many times when I was playing his music; he seemed to be there and I saw him, but I thought it was a dream.
Question	Did you ever speak to any of your orchestra men about the spirit world, perhaps to Mr. K.? (A student of the occult.)
Sp.	Some; I was not a disbeliever. But I had little time to study anything but music. All my dear fellows who worked so faithfully with me—how they stood by me. Send them my love. The last time we played, on Monday (Memorial Service), was wonderful.
	(The spirit at last comprehended that he had left the physical and had been listening to spirit music.)
Sp.	Why am I here?
Dr.	Spirit friends must have brought you here to obtain an understanding of your condition. The revelation you had was real; it was not a dream. When you understand and progress in the spirit world you can be with the masters of music.
Sp.	I cannot realize it yet. They are all so young— Beethoven and the others. They look as they did on earth but younger and happier.

89

Question Beethoven is not deaf any longer?
Sp.   No. Poor fellow. But he says he does not need
          to starve in the spirit world. Why is it that
          genius always has such a struggle? (Brushing
          forehead thoughtfully.) Many things in life are
          hard to understand. But I lived in the world of
          music.
              Now some one tells me I must go with friends
          and I will learn more of music and life and
          harmony.
              I thank you all for your kind interest.

   This spirit had lived so completely in music that it was
his very world and life, therefore, upon leaving the physical,
he contacted at once the spirit realm of music.

   The mortal man is prone to think and believe that conditions on the Invisible Side must be as he postulates, ideas
which, in most instances, he finds entirely erroneous upon
arriving on the spirit side of life.
   The new arrival often finds himself like a mariner, without chart or compass, stranded on an unknown coast. How
could it be otherwise? The average man lives only for the
mortal, disinterested in the tomorrow after death. Here,
what we do not know we must learn, in order to obtain
understanding; likewise over there we must acquire knowledge of the new conditions, by degrees.
   The spirit of Thomas A. Edison, the great inventor,
according to the daily press, spoke through a medium in a
seance to Dr. Miller R. Hutchinson, for years his chief engineer, saying: "Well, Hutch, I've had to revise my ideas
about life after death. I'm on the other side of the river.
But I don't know where I am going from here."
   So also the spirit of Edgar Wallace, English novelist and
dramatist, is reported in the "Psychic News," of London, as

having described, by automatic writing through a medium, his life since passing, dedicating the script to Hannen Swaffer, English dramatic critic. Among other statements he is quoted as declaring: "What is to be my destiny? I do not know. What of me? I must still live on unto when I do not know."

This communication, according to reports, caused great resentment on the part of Mr. Wallace's son, who designated the same as "spiritualistic platitudes, revealing nothing."

Mr. Wallace's description of his situation after transition is, to one versed in Psychic Research, but a repetition of hundreds of similar descriptions of the state in which many spirits have found themselves when first entering the Invisible World.

While Mr. Edison and Mr. Wallace were brilliant concerning mortal things, both, as reported, were disinterested in and even scoffed at the idea of obtainable knowledge pertaining to a future existence and therefore found themselves temporarily in the situation alluded to.

That there is a natural progression should be understood; progression is the law of our being. The ignorant child could not understand university problems nor could it understand heavenly problems except through slow mental evolution. As a child progresses through kindergarten, the grades and High School to the University, so, step by step, does the mind broaden in its progression in the next school of life, the Spirit World.

If, upon entering the invisible school, the individual has been fortunate in obtaining some degree of understanding and discernment of the stages of the mind's progression, he will have a wonderful advantage. "As he thinketh in his heart, so is he." (Proverbs 23:7.)

The first requisite is gradual attainment of an understanding of fundamentals. "There is no royal road to knowledge." Knowledge cannot be given to us; to have value it must be acquired by each individual for himself. This is the law in the physical world and the same law obtains in the realm of spirit. "However learned or eloquent, man knows nothing truly that he has not learned from experience." (Wieland.)

91

These are elements requisite for the soul's advancement and the unfoldment of the mind; without them there can be no progression. Only when the world at large will recognize these facts and put them into practice will we attain a rational millennium and the wished-for "Peace on earth, good will toward men."

CHAPTER V

Obsession

RANSITION in itself does not necessarily change the mental attitude since death is only a sleep and an awakening. As patients, suffering from some ailment, may have periods of sleep during which they are unaware of their condition but waken to find themselves in the same state of sickness, so also may sick individuals when they sleep out of the physical body through "death" waken and, at first unaware of their new situation, still retain the habits of their sickness and continue in the same mental attitude as formerly for an indefinite period until enlightened.

Such entities may in their wanderings become attracted to mortal sensitives and unwittingly convey their thoughts to these individuals. The victims, unaware of the source of their impressions, may suffer physical agony corresponding to the disease from which the spirits had passed out. Permanent relief in some cases can only be attained by dislodging the spirits.

Mrs. B., of Kansas City, had for many years been an invalid, suffering from an unaccountable heart trouble and swollen feet. Failing to secure relief from the medical profession she had taken up Christian Science, but to no avail, and finally she came to California for a change of climate.

While she was in an hotel here, a friend, without telling Mrs. B. of her intention, asked us to do what we could for the invalid, and after concentrating for her Mrs. Wickland became controlled during a circle by a spirit who said she had been through a very severe sickness but had become well again; she was now with a lady who traveled a great deal and it seemed she had to go with her.

She stated she had been troubled with a heart affliction, suffered from swollen ankles and severe pains in her legs and could never get shoes which fitted properly. The doctor had told her she could not live long and her family, understanding she was frail and sickly, had let her have her own way and did not interfere with her.

She claimed she had always had all the money she wanted and could go wherever she pleased but had to be very careful on account of heart trouble. Lately she had traveled a long way and since then had been living in an hotel.

She said she had studied Christian Science for some time, hoping to be relieved of her aches and pains but, although she understood a great deal about it, she had not been helped, therefore she had come to the conclusion that she was not in the right understanding.

She gave her name, Paulina French, saying she was born in Liverpool, England, and was twenty-seven years old, June 7, 1909.

She lived in New York and St. Louis; when she became ill she decided to go to a sanitarium near Kansas City, but could not remember whether she ever reached the sanitarium as she was taken so seriously ill on the train she seemed to sink into a coma state.

Then she suddenly became well (died) but seemed to be a double personality, sometimes being herself and at other times another lady, whom they called Mrs. B.

When told she was at that moment controlling the body of another she asked where the lady was whose body she was occupying and what had become of her mind.

Explanation followed that the mind of the psychic was in a state of abeyance during the time her body was controlled by an invisible entity, that mind is invisible, intangible and unlimited and when the spirit is permanently withdrawn from the body, the body dies, but there is no death for the spirit.

She was told that higher intelligences would help her attain knowledge and wisdom, and the entity then departed.

A few weeks later Mrs. B. was relieved of a second entity after which she fully regained her health and returned home, where she resumed her social activities. During our fifteen years of correspondence, her letters have been happy

94

and cheerful with no allusion to any recurrence of her former ailments.

Many persons who receive impressions foreign to their own normal way of thinking believe something is wrong with the brain, and, in fear of becoming insane, commit suicide, whereas, if the fact of spirit interference were known, such mishaps could be prevented.

That this inter-action between spirits and mortals is not a mere hypothesis but a serious reality and of frequent occurrence, can readily be ascertained by the medical scientist who will with unprejudiced mind follow up requisite research.

Spirit influence ranges from mere impression to actual possession, as happens in many cases. Purity of life and motive, or high intellectuality do not necessarily offer immunity from obsession; recognition and knowledge of these problems are the only safeguards.

Regarding such invisible influence Mrs. M. T. Longley wrote in "The Spirit World": "To say that no spirit can obsess or annoy, or in any way seriously discommode or injure a mortal, is to talk with foolishness. Those who persist in such statements are blinded to the very forces of nature, to the operations of the elements of human life, to the condition of human beings in every nation upon the globe. They are blinded to facts which can be readily perceived if they will only lay aside their preconceived opinions and prejudices and come to a close study of the subject."

"If a spirit obsesses a mortal for any length of time it may be difficult for a spirit teacher or a physician on either side of life to immediately disengage that parasite, and why? For this reason: That all the forces and elements directed by the persistent will of the spirit entity have imbedded themselves in the magnetic aura of the (mortal) —the aura is permeated by them—and to rudely tear away (so to speak) the encroaching spirit would be to injure, most fatally perchance, the sensitive."

"Such a procedure might destroy the physical body, or it might very easily drive the mortal sensitive insane. Therefore the work must be done . . . with systematic order . . . in such manner . . . as will help to . . . eliminate the coarse and objectionable foreign elements from the aura

95

of the sensitive, and thus . . . detach the spirit operator, and draw him from the sensitive, leaving the latter in a condition by which he may be strengthened and brought up to a state of happiness, health and peace."

Dr. Tomlinson, while Superintendent of the St. Peter Insane Asylum, St. Peter, Minnesota, stated, in a report to the Annual Convention of the American Medical Association, that of sixty cases which had there been given special observation, in forty-three cases auditory hallucinations occurred; in eighteen cases, visual; in fifty-one, ideas of persecution distorted the mind. Confusion was the early symptom in nearly all cases, accompanied by suspicion, dread and fear. Religiosity was practically always present.

"In thirteen cases," he reported, "the persecutory ideas led to aggressive resentment toward those to whom the voices heard and the acts anticipated were attributed. In twenty-two cases, on the contrary, the voices heard and the things seen, prompted seclusion instead."

The symptoms quoted by Dr. Tomlinson clearly indicate interference by discarnated spirits, the "auditory hallucinations" being due to clairaudience, the "visual," to clairvoyance. "Ideas of persecution" are caused by the patient being tormented by ignorant, mischievous spirits; in "confusion, suspicion, dread and fear" the patient's thoughts are impregnated by thoughts emanating from spirits; "religiosity" is due to the presence of spirits that are fanatical regarding religion. Research has shown that interfering entities seek "seclusion" in order to maintain their hold on the victim.

When psychiatrists will recognize the above stated agencies in mental aberrations and will follow up the necessary sincere and unprejudiced research they will then be able to obtain positive evidence that discarnated spirits are definite contributing factors in insanity, and, incidentally, will also prove the survival of the ego.

Professor C. E. Turner of the department of biology and public health, Massachusetts Institute of Technology, in a report to the American Physical Education Association, stated: "At the present rate, more public school children will go to insane hospitals than will go to college. In the hospitals of the United States there are more patients suffering from mental disease than from all other diseases combined."

A recent report issued by The Human Betterment Foundation, of Pasadena, California, summarizes statistics regarding insanity as follows: "This, then, is the situation which America faces now: 18,000,000 persons who are or at some time during life will be burdened by mental disease or mental defect, and in one way or another a charge and tax upon the rest of the population. It challenges every thoughtful person. The misery resulting from this insanity and feeble-mindedness provides the first reason for grappling with the problem. No stratum of society is immune from such suffering."

Rodney H. Brandon, director of the Illinois State Department of Public Welfare says: "The mentally unsound and delinquent in Illinois institutions are increasing far faster than the population; already they number 25,000; and about 50 per cent of all general property taxes collected by the state is used to care for them. . . . Mental unsoundness in Illinois heads the list of all those causes which bring unhappiness to the general public."

While it is true that wonderful advancement has been made in the science of psychiatry yet psychiatrists are still amiss in their refusal to recognize the impingment of ignorant, discarnated spirits in the various psychoses, a knowledge of which would greatly enhance the number of cures and establish a scientific understanding of what becomes of the dead and of their activities in human affairs.

A man, aged fifty, was brought to us in Chicago, from Minneapolis, by his brother, a son, and a doctor. The case had been diagnosed as senile dementia and pronounced incurable by the physician in charge, who considered it folly for us to undertake to do anything for the patient, saying the proper place for him was the asylum, as he was hopelessly insane.

While the condition of the patient seemed to warrant the doctor's prognosis, the history of the patient's former practices indicated to us the possibility of spirit interference. In the hope of receiving a message from his wife, who had died a short time previously, the patient had resorted to automatic writing, a practice which is, from our observation, a dangerous procedure for a novice who is ignorant of the laws which must be followed in order to avoid mishap.

Interested in the case from this angle, we determined to see what could be done for the patient. He proved very unruly, used coarse, vulgar language and attempted to run away at every opportunity, having to be watched very closely.

In the evening a bath was administered, first warm then cold spray, which acted as a shock to the patient, or rather to the entity controlling him; he swore and shouted, "What in hell are you trying to do?"

With this, the entity lost control, the patient became his normal self and asked in great surprise, "Where am I?" He remained normal until four o'clock the following morning when he was again controlled by a spirit who endeavored to jump through a window and run away. He was forced to lie down and the condition again changed.

The symptoms then presented were those of a person in a drunken stupor. The controlling entity said, "I am John; I'm thirsty. Get me a drink!"

This spirit had been known to the patient in life and had died of delirium tremens. He had communicated with the patient through the automatic writing experiments, demanding that he get whiskey for him, but the patient, being a temperate man, had refused to do so.

"He would not get whiskey for me," the spirit said, "but now I've got him!"

We reasoned with the entity and he finally departed, after which the patient slept quietly. However, when he came to breakfast the next morning he seemed speechless; mild static electricity was applied but without effect. After increasing the current, the patient began to utter guttural sounds and make motions with his hands, as if he were a deaf and dumb person.

This spirit being dislodged, the patient once more became himself and identified the spirit as a distant relative who had been deaf and dumb; he also had communicated with him through automatic writing.

The patient remained normal throughout the day and

enjoyed a social gathering in our home that evening. The following day he showed an ugly disposition, attempted violence and made a desperate effort to run away. A static treatment was applied, the spirit was dislodged and the patient regained his mental poise. There were no further disturbances by interfering entities; the patient experienced great fatigue but during a month's stay, fully recuperated.

After his return home, while attending a ball game, he met the doctor who had declared him incurably insane and the latter was amazed at the patient's recovery.

The last letter received from the patient, ten years later, stated he had had no recurrence of his former trouble.

Another case brought to our attention in Chicago was that of an imbecile, a girl of twenty-two, who was unruly, obstinate and destructive, could not speak coherently, was unable to conform to customary table manners, opposed so strenuously being bathed that four persons were required to administer a bath, and required constant observation and care.

When strangers visited the family, the girl would stamp her feet and swear, although she had never heard swearing as her parents were religious and lived in the country where the girl had no occasion to hear such profanity as she used.

According to the early history of the case, the girl had been normal until the age of two and a half years and could walk and talk. At that time she had one severe convulsion after which she was not able to talk coherently, was unable to walk again until seven years old, cried a great deal and needed constant attention. During the intervening years there had been no improvement, her development remaining in abeyance.

After a period of medical attention and electrical treatment, an interesting experience occurred. During a concentration circle, attended by two sisters of the patient, Mrs. Wickland became controlled by a spirit who gave his name and stated he had been a friend of the girl's father in the latter's birthplace, a foreign country; in later years he was a neighbor of the family in Wisconsin.

The spirit explained that, unaware of being dead, he had unwittingly been attracted to the child and could not free

99

himself from her. When anyone visited the family he wanted to make his situation known but could not express himself, hence he would stamp his feet and swear.

He also stated he objected to baths when they were administered by women, saying, "Would you expect a man to allow himself to be given a bath by four women?"

The patient's sisters confirmed the statement of the spirit concerning his name and their father's birthplace, as well as the fact that he had been their neighbor in Wisconsin, where he had died many years before.

After freeing this spirit there was a decided change in the girl for the better.

No education had been possible during her years of obsession therefore she had to be taught much as a child. She became very observant, learned correct table manners, took her own bath, helped with the housework, learned to talk, played with children and could be sent on errands. Where previously she had objected to treatments and medical attention, she was now eager to come to the office.

Altogether a marked improvement was shown in the case, incidentally verifying the fact that discarnated spirits may be a contributing factor in imbecility and other cases of feeble-mindedness.

In a recent convention of the American College of Surgeons at Chicago, Dr. George Crile, of Cleveland, is quoted by the press as saying: "We may confidently expect that science will disclose the nature of life and with it the physical nature of mind and personality." Such an hypothesis intimates that when the body ceases to act, mind and personality become non-existent.

If the modern skeptics, who maintain that death means annihilation and therefore ends all, could realize the serious consequences of such teachings they would indeed hesitate before coming to these rash conclusions.

Death does not end all; transition is only like stepping out of an old garment; it does not in any way change the mental attitude or condition.

The "death ends all" doctrine encourages many perturbed persons to conclude that the easiest way out of their difficulties is to plunge over the brink of the supposed

100

"unknown" by committing suicide with the idea that by this act their troubles will be ended forever. But suicide does not do this; it only plunges the person from light into darkness, much as an individual is left in darkness when he loses his physical eyesight. The suicide merely shuts himself out from contact with the external; his mind is more disturbed than before.

Many remain in this condition for years, ignorant of spiritual laws and even unaware of being spirits, since they find themselves in possession of a spirit body which they mistake for a physical one. Nor does this free the spirit from an accusing conscience, if his life has not been right; the new conditions only add to his mental torment.

Such spirits, hovering about the earthplane, may often be the indirect cause of unpremeditated suicides, for, not realizing that they have already succeeded in separating themselves from their physical bodies, they persist in striving to "end their lives" and becoming enmeshed in the auras of mortal sensitives, they convey to the latter their own gloomy thoughts and a sudden impulse to "end it all." Many a person who suffers from such strange impressions, (the "confusional" symptoms listed by Dr. Tomlinson) concludes he is going insane and determines to commit suicide.

Were abnormal psychology thoroughly understood, a person receiving such impressions would be able to analyze the absurdity of his impulses and, realizing that they were due to some discarnated entity who had transferred, perhaps unintentionally, his own disturbed mental condition to the sensitive mortal, he would avoid committing any rash act.

Such spirit influence is illustrated in the following case, contacted through the psychic instrumentality of Mrs. Wickland during an experimental seance.

The controlling spirit was in great anguish and confusion, which is to be expected consequent to an act such as she described. For obvious reasons full names of persons and places have been omitted. The conversation held with the spirit follows:

Dr.
Wickland   Tell us, friend, where you came from. You evidently do not understand your condition. You

101

	have lost your physical body but do not realize it. You are now a spirit, temporarily in possession of a body not your own. What is your name?
Spirit	B. K.
Dr.	How long have you been dead?
Sp.	(Hysterically.) Forgive me, A.! Oh, forgive me!
Dr.	Calm yourself and we will help you understand your condition.
Sp.	Oh, I didn't mean to kill myself!
Dr.	Did you take your own life?
Sp.	Yes. (Crying distractedly.)
Dr.	You did not destroy your spirit, you only destroyed your body. You are now a free spirit but you need understanding. Do not doubt what I tell you. This is not your body.
Sp.	Forgive me, forgive me, oh, A.!
Dr.	Where was your home?
Sp.	In S. P.
Dr.	How long since you passed out of your own body?
Sp.	Oh, what is the matter?
Dr.	You are in the dark.
Sp.	I can see my mother crying all the time.
Dr.	On what street did you live in S. P.?
Sp.	F. Avenue.
Dr.	What number?
Sp.	I can't remember. (Crying.)
Dr.	Calm yourself. We can help you. Tell us everything.
Sp.	I didn't do it.
Dr.	Who did it? What happened to you?
Sp.	I can't tell.
Dr.	I am asking in your interest. What did you do? You must know something about it.
Sp.	I was so muddled. Now I don't know what to do. Mother! Mother!

Dr.	Try to collect yourself and listen to me. We can help you if you will become quiet.
Sp.	Poor A.!
Dr.	Who is A.?
Sp.	He's my husband. I love him so. If I could only get to him.
Dr.	What did you do?
Sp.	No, no, I did not do it! There were so many people (obsessing spirits) and I was so muddled. I was sick. I don't know why but I see only strange people.
Dr.	What do they do?
Sp.	I don't know.
Dr.	Do they talk to you?
Sp.	I was so tormented by them (earthbound spirits) that I could not stand it any longer.
Dr.	What did you do?
Sp.	I was so sick. My poor husband and mother! They are mourning and mourning. I got free, and now I can't tell them I am free. I am so sick and worried.
Dr.	All this excitement does not help you. Be calm and we can help you.
Sp.	Why do these people (spirits) around me drive me away from home?
Dr.	What do they say?
Sp.	They torment me. They stand there and laugh and laugh at me. They say all kinds of strange things. (Spirit became hysterical.)
Dr.	Friendly spirits have brought you here and you must do your part. Try to understand your situation.
Sp.	I didn't do it! I didn't do it! Those people around me made me do it.
Dr.	What did you do?
Sp.	I shot myself. (While controlled by earthbound spirits.)

103

Dr.   You are not dead; you are still alive. No one ever actually "dies." You only drove yourself out of your body.

Sp.   They haunted me so!

Dr.   Who?

Sp.   All those people.

Dr.   They are ignorant spirits. Would you like to remain in this condition?

Sp.   Oh, no!

Dr.   Do you want to be helped?

Sp.   Yes.

Dr.   Then be quiet and calm yourself.

Sp.   Oh, A.! Mother! I was so sad and so sick!

Dr.   You threw yourself into the invisible world and not having any understanding you are now in the dark. You must be willing to attain understanding of the laws of progression in the spirit world. Are you listening?

Sp.   Yes, but I am so weak.

Dr.   Determine to be strong. Listen to the intelligent spirits who will gladly help you. They will take you to the spirit world and teach you better things. Do you understand?

Sp.   Yes.

Dr.   Look around and you will find kindly spirits who will teach you how to overcome your present condition.

Sp.   Will those people go away? (Earthbound spirits.)

Dr.   They will not bother you any more. There are many others who will help you. Look around for Silver Star, a little Indian girl, (spirit) who helps spirits in trouble.

Sp.   Look at that beautiful light! God help me and give me understanding and light! I did not mean to do it. I love my husband and my home. But I went away into the hills. God help me!

Dr.   You will receive help but you must not become

	so excited. You saw a beautiful light a moment ago. God's messengers are here to help you.
Sp.	I have suffered so. I have constantly seen my husband and mother, both very sad and crying. Oh, God help me!
Dr.	Spirit friends will show you better things.
Sp.	I want peace of mind. I want peace!
Dr.	You will find it.
Sp.	Why should I be tormented so terribly?
Dr.	You were evidently a psychic sensitive but did not know it.
Sp.	God help me!
Dr.	You must understand your condition. Spirit friends are the messengers of God and they will help you. They will teach you how to attain an understanding of God.
Sp.	(Psychic vision opening.) Look at those beautiful things! Look! Some one says I will have to serve others.
Dr.	We cannot live for ourselves alone. You feel that in your heart, do you not?
Sp.	Yes.
Dr.	Now you must go with the spirit friends.
Sp.	I see such a beautiful girl (spirit) and she says, "Come with me."
Dr.	She will help you.
Sp.	Can I have peace in my heart? I was so notional.
Dr.	You can, if you control that excitement. Learn the meaning of life.
Sp.	My conscience hurts me so much. See the sorrow I have caused. I go home but they cannot understand that I am suffering.
Dr.	Obtain understanding in the new life, and progress.
Sp.	My conscience bothers me.
Dr.	You must appease your conscience by serving others. Invisible friends will help you.

105

Sp.	Can I go with them? I am so tired; I want to rest.
Dr.	Go with these kind friends. You will be taught to overcome self and you will find the light.
Sp.	Will you ask my husband and mother to forgive me?
Dr.	Perhaps we can communicate with them.
Sp.	Now I will go. Thank you for helping me.

The spirit then departed. This entity and her history were entirely unknown to us but her story was afterward fully corroborated by her husband.

A warning against the folly of self-destruction was given through Mrs. Wickland by the spirit of a young woman who had ended her earthlife while extremely despondent. In the physical this young woman had refused to believe in obsession although her mother frequently warned her of the danger of spirit interference. This spirit spoke at a seance which the mother attended.

Spirit	Mother, I wanted to come to you today to let you know I am with you to help and guide you. I can help you so much better now than I could when I was here with you because I have learned the lesson of overcoming selfishness and jealousy.
	"Those were my worst faults but now I have learned to understand what love, true love, which each one should have, means. But I had to go through trouble and sorrow to understand that. Since I left you I have gone through much suffering in overcoming my difficulties."
	"You realize, Mother, that I did not commit that act. (Self destruction.) Some spirit did the deed through me."
Mother	I knew, my dear, that it was caused by obsession.

106

Sp.   I was not myself; I was obsessed but I did not realize that until it was too late.

(To the audience.) "Do not let any influences whisper to you to commit such an act. Be strong and overcome."

"Do you know the consequences of taking your own life? I wish I could impress them firmly on your minds."

"When you have committed suicide, you stand there, looking at your own body and you cannot, cannot, control it again. You thought you were in trouble before, but now—!"

"What misery to see your body lying there and realize that because of your own deed you can never control it again!"

"You see people in great distress standing around your body; your relatives are crying and you are helpless. You are left alone, in darkness, because you took your own life. You are alone with your thoughts."

"There is no death; the spirit lives on after dissolution takes place."

"I wish to emphasize that if troubles come to you, do not shun them; face them. Be brave and do all you can to meet them. Do not destroy your physical body. Do not be a coward and run away from trouble."

"Learn to live rightly. Your sorrow is only a phase through which your are passing. There is beauty around you if you will only look for it."

"Today, Mother, I am very happy, for I have overcome much. Good-bye."

Only an understanding of the laws pertaining to the life here and hereafter can relieve the distorted minds of suicide spirits and enable them to progress in the spirit world.

107

"Except ye . . . become as little children" (assume the child-like spirit, eager to learn) "ye shall not enter into the kingdom of heaven." (Matthew 18:3.) These spirits must cease acting according to self-will and apply themselves to obtaining knowledge of the laws of life. A self-centered mental attitude prevents intelligent spirits from reaching them; these are eager to help and they may in some instances be able to shorten the misery of the suffering ones.

A comprehension of the various phases of the next life while here would train humanity to go through earth life patiently and by so doing, the entry, at the appointed time, into the World Beyond will be one of happiness leading to progression.

A PSALM OF LIFE.

Tell me not, in mournful numbers
    Life is but an empty dream!
For the soul is dead that slumbers,
    And things are not what they seem.

Life is real! Life is earnest!
    And the grave is not its goal;
Dust thou art, to dust returnest,
    Was not spoken of the soul.

Not enjoyment, and not sorrow,
    Is our destined end or way;
But to act, that each tomorrow
    Finds us farther than today.

Art is long, and Time is fleeting,
    And our hearts, though stout and brave,
Still, like muffled drums, are beating
    Funeral marches to the grave.

In the world's broad field of battle,
    In the bivouac of Life,
Be not like dumb, driven cattle!
    Be a hero in the strife!

Trust no Future, howe'er pleasant!
  Let the dead Past bury its dead!
Act, act in the living Present!
  Heart within, and God o'erhead!

Lives of great men all remind us
  We can make our lives sublime,
And, departing, leave behind us
  Footprints on the sands of time;

Footprints, that perhaps another,
  Sailing o'er life's solemn main,
A forlorn and shipwrecked brother,
  Seeing, shall take heart again.

Let us, then, be up and doing,
  With a heart for any fate;
Still achieving, still pursuing,
  Learn to labor and to wait.

HENRY WADSWORTH LONGFELLOW

Michael Faraday, distinguished English physicist and chemist of the Royal Institute, had refused, while in earth life, to recognize Psychic Research but upon entering the Spirit World realized his error and became interested in the inter-relationship of the physical and spirit worlds. In a spirit communication from Faraday, detailed observations on obsession are given from the spirit viewpoint.

"Not one in ten thousand enter the spirit realm with any true ideas of its realities. Thrown upon its shores like ship-wrecked mariners upon an unknown coast, without information or conception of its conditions, they drift in their thoughts and feelings to the only state of life in which they have ever perceived sensation and find themselves within the atmosphere of the earth to which they cling with nearly as much tenacity as though living in the physical body and seek no other pleasure than to still live there." . . .

"This tendency to gravitate to the earth plane is the primary cause of the phenomena of obsession . . . fraught with consequences of grave importance to those still living in physical life. The mental vibratory action of these spirits is transmitted with great energy upon the brains of . . . mortals." . . .

"The involuntary transmission of power through electric action compels spirits out of or in the body to influence each other, according to the grade of atomic action of the elements composing the different organisms. Here is a power which the will of the strongest cannot always control, even when he knows of its existence. How much less then, one who has no knowledge of its true nature and who is involuntarily exerting his will through it, upon those whom he has no idea of affecting as he really does!"

"The involuntary action of the will of the spirit affects the recipient of earth through the electrical force. . . . All organisms are the result of certain combinations of the elements and that motion of the atoms comprising them is ever subject to electric energy; in fact electric action itself is this motion transmitted from one combination to another. Consequently if the same degree of atomic action can be induced in two different organisms the thought evolved will be identical; and as thought is a manifestation of the real force of the spirit in its action in either world, it follows the law of equilibrium when two minds approach each other."

"When spirits intensely desire to accomplish their wishes, the influence of such desire reaches some sensitive mind, awakening a like desire with an intensity proportionate to the will force exerted. If the spirit is ignorant of truth or destitute of moral principles, his will power is directed subject to the ruling motive of his mind and the victim will be impressed to do and think differently from his own better judgment. The only effectual remedy for such delusions is to instruct the victim as to the nature of the source of his ideas."

"The recipient of these influences . . . never dreams that he is obeying the will of unseen beings who may often unconsciously act upon his mind for the accomplishment of their desires. When people are swayed by an irresistible

110

impulse to commit unlawful acts and to express irrational ideas at the command of a supposed voice of God, they are victims of deceiving spirits whose thought impulses affect them, whether they are aware of them or not."

"The world is subject to the influence of mental conditions which must ever act and react upon its inhabitants with inevitable results. There can be no escape from the influence of minds who dwell in the realms of spiritual darkness except by their elevation and instruction in the laws of spiritual progress; and even then their power to influence is not lost but changes its direction to the production of happiness instead of misery."

"Because of this law, advanced spirits have for centuries striven to reach earth with truth concerning the nature of spirit. They have been thwarted in their efforts by those upon both sides of life who, for selfish purposes, are desirous to propagate old ideas as truth, and on account of their position as leaders have refused to recognize the true source of evil."

"The Principle of Spirit Obsession is so little understood that the involuntary phases of it are generally misunderstood or denied by those who are its victims. To obtain a correct, or even partial comprehension of its nature, the world must first be instructed in the basic principles of spiritual science. Man must learn that mental powers are transmissible between the two realms (spiritual and physical) and that the mental status of spirits or mortals is never higher than its natural development."

"Hence to expect that spiritual ideas are necessarily truthful because their source is traceable to those living beyond the mortal state, is a grave error. The myriads who have passed to the world of spirits can no more transmit ideas of a higher, or even of a different character, from those evolved in their own mentality, than a child in mortal life can comprehend the problems of the advanced sciences before he has learned the alphabet."

"Superstitious spirits are great obstacles to a correct understanding of the Spiritual Philosophy and the importance of Spiritual Phenomena. They have not advanced to the plane of mental action, they exert a powerful influence

111

... and shadow the earth with a power of will indescribable in earthly language." . . .

"A serious error of mankind has been to regard ideas coming from a spiritual source as emanating from the Deity. Hence the delusions of religion, politics, and often of business and social life which sway the minds of many, to their discomfiture if the results are contradictory to the promises made."

"Should it be well understood by the earth people that spirit intercourse is not of a religious nature the delusions which arise from it would pass away. This result is so much feared by those minds who wish to retain their control over the superstitious that they oppose the dissemination of this knowledge upon earth while multitudes of ignorant victims, both on earth and in spirit life, are so much under their will power that they offer little opposition."

"Besides the involuntary psychological power of those spirits who believe knowledge of spirit life is detrimental to mankind is added the hostility of designing spirits to such an extent as to largely prevent truthful ideas from the spirit world from exerting much influence on earth." . . .

"God has made no law forbidding mankind to know of its destiny . . . Obsession is the result of a natural law which exists in the relationship of spiritual and mortal conditions, its effects will ever be manifested whether understood or not. Humanity on earth will suffer and persons in spirit life will excite their malign or benign influence in direct proportion as their own development enables them to rise above the plane of deception or error."

"Truth alone is the remedy for all forms of evil and knowledge of truth the only panacea for the woes of a spiritual nature."

That ignorant or mischievous discarnated spirits play a serious role as contributing factors in insanity, unaccountable crimes, immorality, invalidism, suicides and other mental aberrations is no longer a theory or hypothesis but may easily be verified by unprejudiced scientists and truthseekers. Investigators should be willing to make such research unhampered by any preconceived notion, beliefs or disbeliefs, but determine to ascertain facts and with open

112

minds allow the Invisible World to carry out its own revelations. Findings may then be analyzed according to reason.

By a system of transfer, under the guidance of intelligent co-operating spirits, obsessing entities may be attracted from a victim and allowed to temporarily control a properly trained psychic intermediary and through direct contact with the entity evidence may be obtained proving that some discarnated spirit, whose identity can often be verified, has been a contributing factor in the psychosis.

This transference is facilitated by the use of static electricity which, while harmless to the patient, is an important adjunct, for the obsessing spirit cannot long resist such electrical treatment and is dislodged.

After such transference of psychoses the victims will be relieved and the obsessing entities can be reached by the advanced spirits who will care for them and instruct them regarding the higher laws of life.

It is not to be understood that the transference of a spirit to a psychic sensitive is necessary as a general means of procedure in treating all cases of mental aberration but only where it is desired to obtain scientific data relative to spirit interference, although a good psychic is of great importance in assisting in diagnosis.

If state and other mental institutions would follow up this line of research, much that is at the present time mystifying and perplexing in psycho-pathology would be revealed.

These statements are not a matter of mere belief but facts learned from the observations of more than forty years of research, carried on independent of ism or cult, to ascertain the underlying causes of what are often baffling conditions in psychological and psychiatrical research.

CHAPTER VI

Multiple Personalities and Psychic Invalidism

THAT the average physician is poorly versed in insanity and psychiatric problems is indeed unfortunate since he is usually the first to meet the mentally disturbed patient but the psychiatrist is largely at fault in this situation, as the following aptly illustrates:

"Medical societies do not study the question of mental disease," states Dr. James H. Hutton of Chicago, in the "Illinois Medical Journal." "If a psychiatrist is billed to talk before a medical society he is apt to address empty benches. The reason is not entirely the fault of the doctor."

"For the most part the psychiatrist speaks in a language of his own that the ordinary medical man does not understand any better than if the psychiatrist spoke Sanskrit."

"Some years ago," relates Dr. Hutton, "I discussed this with a very high-grade secretary of a county medical society. He said that he would be glad to have a psychiatrist talk to their group but it would do no good. After the first half dozen sentences none of their members would know what the psychiatrist was talking about, and when he finished the net result would be some badly disturbed naps on the part of most of the members. I recounted this conversation to a man who had had considerable training in psychiatry. He said the county secretary was absolutely right but very conservative, that if half a dozen psychiatrists got together they wouldn't understand each other."

At the eighty-eighth annual meeting of the American Psychiatric Association in Philadelphia in 1932, in a series of Encephalographic Studies in Schizophrenia (Dementia Praecox or Multiple Personalities), a report was given of sixty cases in which the cerebro-spinal fluid was removed and air replaced with the purpose of utilizing "a safe method whereby such pathologic changes that may be present in the brains of schizophrenics can be demonstrated in the living subjects," yet the statement was made, "however, it is not implied that the procedure is of therapeutic value."

Considering the findings in Encephalographic Studies and the comprehensive research already made in this branch of psychiatry, the remissions and cures so far obtained are, according to the above report, comparatively negligible.

W. Spielmeyer, author of "The Problem of the Anatomy of Schizophrenia," declares, "There is no *known* anatomic or histologic basis discoverable at the present time for Schizophrenia."

While psychiatrists are to be commended for their efforts in the study of underlying causes of the various phases of mental aberrations and insanity from a physical and biological standpoint, and their Encephalographic Studies are undoubtedly of importance in the case of the insane yet, if the same studies were carried out on the brains of normal-minded, physically suffering patients, might not similar brain findings be discovered, therein negativing the brain findings as a cause of insanity?

The unscientific attitude and aloofness of the medical fraternity toward any research that suggests discarnated spirits, due to fear of ostracism, of jeopardizing professional standing, or owing to the fallacious notion that it is unethical and beneath the dignity of science to follow such research, is today a serious obstacle to advancement of knowledge pertaining to contributing causes underlying mental aberrations and insanity, and is a hindrance to neurological and psychiatrical research.

The merest tyro in Psychic Research today often understands more correctly than the average psychiatrist the cause of mental disturbances, as he recognizes discarnated spirits as an active factor.

When the professors of psychology in the colleges and universities will earnestly take up Psychic Research as it pertains to all manner of mental aberrations they will discover such research to be of far greater value to humanity than the study of "Rat Psychology" now so prevalent, since few homes are exempt from the ravages of mental disturbances

115

in which, as experience has clearly proven, ignorant discarnated spirits are a serious *contributing* factor.

Psychiatric research is clearly indicative of spirit impingement, yet in the study of cases of "Multiple Personalities," "Dissociated Personalities," or "Disintergrated States of Consciousness," modern psychologists and psychiatrists disclaim the possibility of foreign intelligences on the ground that these personalities give neither evidence of supernormal knowledge, nor of being of spiritistic origin.

Our experience has indubitably proven that the majority of such intelligences are oblivious of their transition and hence it does not enter their minds that they are spirits, and they are loath to realize the fact.

In the well-known case of Miss Beauchamp, as recorded by Dr. Morton Prince, in "The Dissociation of a Personality," reporting four alternating personalities, no recognition was given by Dr. Prince that any outside intelligences were responsible for the various personalities, and yet "Sally" (personality 3) insisted that she herself was not the same as Christine (Miss Beauchamp, the patient), that her own consciousness was distinct from that of Christine, and told of Christine's learning to walk and talk. "When she was a very little girl just learning to walk . . . I remember her thoughts distinctly as separate from mine."

The case of Mrs. X., as reported by Dr. Cornelius C. Wholey, in "The American Journal of Psychiatry," is designated by Dr. Wholey as one of "Multiple Personality" or a "psychogenic adjustment similar to a conversion hysteria" in which "parts of the mind are split off and the parts become egos, each in its turn presiding over the organism . . . the normal or original personality is pushed aside or held in abeyance and is replaced by an independent grouping of the elements of consciousness on a lower, simpler, more childish plane . . . The subject of multiple personality . . . is capable of an easy backward, or regressive shift even to earliest childhood."

From the standpoint of research in psychic phenomena as it pertains to abnormal psychology, the case of Mrs. X. would prove conclusively to be one of interference by ignorant discarnated human spirits. That the seven "split-ups" observed were different foreign entities is clearly evidenced

116

by the variance in personality and activities and their assertions of being spirits.

For example, the "Susie" personality said she had been shot by her husband while in a jealous rage at her secret lover and asserted, "I was a girl from New York when I was a living person but since I was a spirit I was put right in Hattie (the patient). I have been in Hattie for twelve years. Hattie is the girl that the body belongs to." Susie said she "took Hattie's spirit, pulled it down and then came up" herself.

The patient could often hear Susie talk to her; the former complained of pains innumerable but Susie never had an ache or pain. Susie was childish, carefree, mischievous, flirtatious and irresponsible, delighted in posing before a camera, while the patient had a fear of having her picture taken.

The patient's husband stated that astonishing changes had taken place in his wife's behavior after the birth of her first baby. "At times he would come home to find her domestic, interested in her house, taking all a normal mother's fond care of her child. Again he would return to find the baby neglected, apparently forgotten, the mother would be out aimlessly parading the streets, gazing into shop windows and carrying on with strange men." (The baby later died of neglect.)

"The husband would upbraid her and take her home where often she would suddenly change from this frivolous person into a serious, conscientious mother-type. She would vehemently deny her escapades or even any absence from home. The husband believed she was lying, and finally resorted to beating her as a "cure" for her unwifely escapades. This procedure served but to augment the personality dissociation."

At this time a neighboring family (Mr. and Mrs. F.) befriended the couple and took them into their home. Dr. Wholey states: "The reason for the interest of the new friends was a fanatical superstitious belief that in these 'spells' the girl was possessed by devils, and that it was their mission to cast out these evil spirits . . . In her fainting spells, the man of the befriending family resorted to incantations and gestures to drive out the devils."

117

"Mrs. F. said, 'We thought we would pray to cure her . . . We started to pray and coax . . . and gradually got Lucille' (one of the "split-ups") 'so she would talk . . . so we kept on coaxing . . . and she would beg to be forgiven for her sins.' "

The Lucille "personality" asserted she was a Chicago cabaret girl, poisoned by a jealous girl friend. She often danced on her toes with her eyes closed, while the patient could not dance at all. Just before leaving, Lucille said to the patient, "I have seen light and I never want to go back into darkness again. I am going to leave; there is a better place for me. Well, Hattie, I am going and God bless you." She left and was never heard from again.

Mrs. F. said, "The others would fight us and we had the whole trouble over . . . coaxing again."

Another entity, who always cried, said her name was Pearl, that she had lived in Kent, Ohio, and was the daughter of a rich manufacturer. She claimed she had been kidnapped when sixteen and placed in a house of prostitution and later committed suicide by jumping out of a window.

Four male "personalities" were reported: A German; an Italian, who fought with a knife; a Pole, who swore and spoke Polish (the patient could not talk Polish); and Jack, who said he was an American. Jack had a masculine posture and hand grasp, also a heavy voice, and removed earrings and shoes, being uncomfortable in woman's clothes.

A shock was sustained by the patient when told of the death of a beloved friend; she fainted and upon recovering was unable to speak for some time. When shown a trunk containing the clothes and toys of her dead baby she looked these over carefully "paying particular attention to those things which the baby had appreciated most . . . then gradually changed . . . became a baby of one year in her attitude." She clapped her hands in glee and played with a ball and a doll. She had to be taught to talk, to use a spoon, to put on her clothes and how to walk.

Dr. Wholey reported that in this condition the patient was taken to a movie, became excited and ill, after which she returned to her normal self.

(The baby episode was undoubtedly the spirit of the

patient's "dead" baby temporarily acting through its own mother and actually playing with its own toys.)

After Lucille and Pearl were gone the various men personalities left. Susie finally said she had seen the light and before leaving wrote a farewell letter to the family. The patient stated that she was very weak after Susie left.

Dr. Wholey reports: "In a later interview with the patient, husband and Mr. F. we asked how the patient was and all replied that she was cured."

What was lacking in the case quoted was the presence of a genuine trance psychic to whom these supposed "split personalities" could have been temporarily transferred, proving them to be independent personalities whose identity could, in many instances, probably have been verified, thus showing the fallacy of the "split personality" hypothesis. If the "multiple personalities" were a part of the patient's own mind they obviously could not be transferred to another individual.

Another case in point, as reported by Dr. Mandel Sherman and Blake Crider, of the University of Chicago, in "The American Journal of Psychiatry" (quoted in "Science News Letter"), is clearly indicative of the influence of discarnated spirits.

"Time turned backward for a young married woman, Mabel Ruth, twenty years old, who after an accident in which she wrecked the family automobile was subject to severe attacks sometimes diagnosed as epileptic seizures, in which she would be insensible to pain. Following these attacks she would literally become as a little child."

"One such turning back of time took her almost to infancy. She spoke in typical baby talk, and could neither write nor draw pictures. Although she (patient) is an inveterate smoker, she had no idea of what to do with a cigarette. She did not recognize her own name . . . she smiled and played just as would a child about two years old. She was greatly amused by the ticking of a watch, reached for it and held it first to one ear and then the other, and then would toss it into the air as though it were a ball . . . Within a year she became apparently normal."

This patient evidently was a natural born psychic; the shock of the automobile accident brought out this psychic susceptibility to the impingement of spirits, each entity showing its own characteristics through the patient.

All manner of apparent changes in personality may occur following shocks, accidents, worries, etc., resulting in various psychic manifestations and changes of individuality; relatives may be disowned, personal identity denied and claims made of being someone else.

Experiences similar to the foregoing are of frequent occurrence in Psychic Research. These statements are not mere assumptions nor unproven hypotheses, but are based upon some forty years of serious research in this abnormal field.

Mrs. Wickland has proven an unusual psychic sensitive and in the interest of this important science has permitted herself to be temporarily controlled by all manner of discarnated spirits, ranging from spirits of adults to spirits of children, attracted from individuals and patients suffering from various psychoses and aberrations.

To explain our experiences on the theory of the Subconscious Mind and Auto-Suggestion, or Multiple Personalities, would be untenable, since it is manifestly unreasonable that Mrs. Wickland should have multitudes of personalities, some often speaking in a language unknown to her, and since it is so readily possible to cause transference of psychoses or mental aberrations from a patient to Mrs. Wickland, relieving the victim, and in this way discovering that the disturbance was due to a discarnate entity, whose identity can often be verified.

A case of the type known to psycho-analysts as "Double Personality" came to our attention some years ago. Mrs. Elizabeth Byrd, when a girl, had often heard spirit voices calling her name, and at the age of eighteen had been subjected to a severe shock which resulted in a coma that lasted for many days.

She seemingly regained her health, married at twenty-one, but the birth of her first child left her an invalid for three and a half years. During this period the death of her mother-in-law occurred and soon thereafter articles were moved about the house by some invisible power with such persistency that finally Mr. and Mrs. Byrd consulted a medium, who gave them unquestionable proof that the spirit mother was still in the house and moving articles about.

In time, Mrs. Byrd's health improved, but after the birth of two more children and undergoing several major operations, her physical condition again became critical, she suffered extreme depression and was finally completely prostrated. Before the end of the week she became conscious of a conflict going on between herself and some power, or intelligence, that seemed to be trying to force her out of her body.

Suffering excruciatingly, she resisted this force until one day it conquered and she found herself, helpless and out of her own body, in a corner of the room while some person who called herself "Stella" took possession of her body.

"Stella" spoke to the husband and said she had lived in "Betty" (Mrs. Byrd) all of the latter's life; that she had been cheated and was never allowed to express herself, while Betty had all kinds of opportunities.

The expression of the face changed completely, as well as the pitch of the voice, and the body had strength and activity which Betty had never possessed even when in the best of health. Stella would raise Betty's sick body up in bed, place her hands in the middle of the bed and vault over it with all the agility of an athlete.

Stella could walk or run tirelessly while in control of the body but she was able to remain only half an hour at the most. Mrs. Byrd was refined and intellectual while Stella had no profundity of thought and apparently no conscience, was extremely profane and very humorous. Her handwriting, to her great chagrin, was entirely different from Betty's.

Stella detested Betty's husband and children, and wanted to do the very things Betty never did—smoke cigarettes, ride on the scenic railway, shoot the chutes, go swimming, and wear a yellow petticoat. She hated Betty and called her "a damned fool," saying she had no taste in clothes and was much too good.

Stella was full of pranks and if she could create a scene in public she was extremely delighted with the resulting annoyance and mortification caused Betty and her husband.

Stella said she knew all about Betty and everything she did, but that Betty did not know anything about her, although sometimes she could make Betty do as she wished.

From the time Stella first took possession of Mrs. Byrd's body, Mrs. Byrd suffered from severe pains on the right side of the neck. However, when Stella took possession of the body she did not have this pain. When Stella came in, Betty dropped to the floor as if in a faint, and when Stella left, which she did only after a struggle, she also dropped to the floor.

In an effort to find help the family doctor called in, from a near-by city, a noted physician who was also a psychoanalyst of the Freudian school. This physician diagnosed the case as an example of "Dual or Split Personality," but Stella swore angrily at him and declared stubbornly she was not a part of Betty and that they had entirely different interests.

The physician asked Stella to write for him something Betty was interested in and Stella obligingly wrote:

> "The moving finger writes, and, having writ,
> Moves on, nor all your piety nor wit
> Shall lure it back to cancel half a line,
> Nor all your tears wash out a word of it."

"There," snapped Stella, "that's what Betty would write, the damn fool!"

The physician then asked Stella to write something for herself and she promptly scrawled, "Hello, Doc, how's the old boy today?"

The physician, however, insisted that Stella was a part of Betty's own mind and told her she would not be allowed to retain entire control but might stay with Betty and influence her at times to a certain degree. Stella was then "hypnotized" by the physician and after struggling desperately she relinquished control of Betty's body.

That Stella was an obsessing spirit did not seem to occur to anyone until some years later when Mrs. Byrd, who had improved in health, being troubled only occasionally by attacks of amnesia and coma but no successful attempts of control by Stella, investigated spiritualistic phenomena and

122

was told by several mediums that she was suffering from obsession.

However, little attention was paid to the matter until some years later when, after a severe nervous shock Betty again became prostrated and sank into a coma condition which lasted a month. Greatly discouraged, Mrs. Byrd was brought by a nurse to us in Los Angeles.

Diagnosing the case as obsession, I gave the patient an electrical treatment and she returned with the nurse to her hotel. During the entire night she was kept from sleeping by Stella's attempts to gain possession of her body. Mrs. Byrd heard Stella swearing at "that Doctor" and vowing she would not be put out.

The following day, while Mrs. Byrd was being given another electrical treatment, Stella took full control and swore at me, saying she had caused all the trouble in Betty's life, had always lived with her and intended to remain. Quite a struggle ensued but I reasoned with Stella and eventually she was dislodged and taken in charge by our spirit co-workers.

Mrs. Byrd then rose from the chair saying she felt as if a heavy load had been taken from her shoulders, a load she had always had to drag along. She said that she had "stood on the outside" and been partly conscious of the struggle which had taken place and knew when Stella left.

Mrs. Byrd continued the treatments for several weeks until she had entirely recovered her strength, then returned to her home in the northern part of the state. We visited her there two years later and found her in the best of health and spirits, actively engaged in varied and exacting executive duties and traveling about to lecture on subjects on which she was a recognized authority.

At a recent meeting of the American Psychiatric Association, Dr. Jacob Kasanin of the Rhode Island Hospital for Mental Diseases made the following assertion: "One type of a common mental disease, Schizophrenia, develops very insidiously from early infancy on . . . At a very early age . . . the child is considered by his associates to be queer, different or odd. He doesn't mix well with others . . . The peculiar personality increases as the little patient grows older, gradually and insidiously developing into the mental disease."

Many cases of the above described character have come under our observation and proven to be due to the impingement of discarnated spirits. Disturbance from a shock or convulsion in early infancy has usually been the focal point of the first impingement of an insinuating entity and the beginning of changed characteristics; vagaries of mind and behavior slowly revealing themselves, become more and more pronounced during the years, ultimating in various degrees of psychoses.

A patient had been brought to us by Dr. S., a girl twelve years of age, who had failed to respond to regular medical treatments. She had been an invalid for about three years, was without muscular control and remained in a dazed semi-stupor, often sitting for days in bed, bent over like an aged person, refusing to talk to anyone and seeming to suffer from stomach trouble.

Surmising some obsession in the case, static electricity was administered with the idea of dislodging any possible obsessing discarnate entity. This surmise proved afterward to have been the correct diagnosis, verified by the following experience.

At our regular experimental meeting Mrs. Wickland became entranced by a spirit that sat with the body bent forward and the arms held rigid.

Dr. Wickland	Who are you?
Spirit	I am an old woman.
Dr.	You are not old and stiff any longer. Forget that habit. You do not need to sit in that position. You have lost that stiff body and have evidently been controlling a young girl, making a slave of her for many years. She acts exactly as you are now doing.
Sp.	(Moaning, with hands over stomach, and coughing violently.) I have been very sick. I have a broken back.
Dr.	You no longer have your old body. (Raising medium's body to erect position.) Now you are sitting erect.

124

Sp.   (Bending forward again.) My back! Oh, my poor back!

Dr.   Hold your head up; your back is all right.

Dr. S.   (Patient's first physician, also among sitters in circle.) Did anyone ever call you J.? (Name of patient.)

Sp.   Yes, they always call me by that name, but that is not my name. My name is Samantha Ann Reed.

Dr. W.   What year do you think this is?

Sp.   I have no memory of the past; I can't remember. (Spirits, unaware of being so-called dead, are often in a confused mental condition.)

Dr.   Who is President?

Sp.   Why, I have even forgotten that. When you are sick and in bed, sometimes you don't even care who is president. I never saw the President, and if I had I should not have paid any attention to him. What is there for me to speak to a President about?

Dr.   (Holding mirror before medium's face.) Have you ever seen that face?

Sp.   That is not my face!

Dr.   But when you speak, the lips move. How do you account for that?

Sp.   That face doesn't have that big nose of mine. Have I got a new nose?

Dr.   Everything is new. You have a new body.

Sp.   Never!

Dr.   Look at this dress you are wearing and these flowers on your shoulder.

Sp.   All foolishness! Why wasn't the money that was spent for these things given to the church?

Dr.   To what church did you belong?

Sp.   The real church—the Moody Church.

Dr.   Moody, the revivalist?

Sp.   Yes. I got saved. The people of that church are the only ones God talks through. When they

	begin to roll on the floor they are all controlled by the Holy Ghost. I gave myself to God.
Dr.	Have you seen God?
Sp.	You don't see God, you give yourself to Him.
Dr.	What did you think would happen when you died?
Sp.	When I die I am going to Heaven to see God.
Dr.	Why have you not seen Him? Apparently you have been dead a long time.
Sp.	I have been traveling around. Once in a while I seem to go into a sleep. Why! (Startled at sight of a spirit.) There's my old mother!
Dr.	Isn't your mother dead?
Sp.	Yes, of course; she died a long time ago. I never thought of that. The very last time I saw her she was in her coffin. But she looks nice.
	Mother, have you seen God? (Listening.) What do you say, Mother? Are you not in Heaven? (Again listening.) She says "heaven" is a condition of mind. I don't understand that.
	Mother says that I can go with her to her home. Where is your home, Mother? She says, "In the world of spirits."
	Oh, my, my, no! Do you mean you have become a Spiritualist?
Dr.	You are a spirit yourself. You have lost your physical body and are now a spirit.
Sp.	(Greatly agitated at sight of another spirit.) For land's sake! Have you come to save me again? I gave you all the money I had. I gave it to you to save me.
Dr.	To whom are you talking?
Sp.	To that man, and he says—Oh, my, no! I don't believe it!
Dr.	What don't you believe?
Sp.	He says he has found that things are different from what he taught when on earth, and now, when his followers come to the other side, he

126

Dr.	has to preach to them and explain their condition. He goes into the lower spheres to help and to try to make people understand the new life. Now he has to serve, and he says, so do I.
Dr.	Who is "he"?
Sp.	Moody. He says he has to find as many of his followers as he can and show them all the right way to understanding; he has been doing this work since he got understanding of the real life.

But I have to be saved!

Dr. No one else can save you; you have to do that yourself. Try to understand God in the right way.

Sp. Moody says teaching the truth is his work now. What? Oh, my, no! He says he is in the spirit world; that is the world of understanding. He was hypnotized in his belief but after he got the right understanding on the other side his duty was to correct the false beliefs he had taught and to find bewildered people and help them.

That is quite an argument—he found me. (Listening.)

Dr. What does he say to you?

Sp. He says, "Now, Samantha, come with me. You have held in your mind the thought that you had a broken back, and no one could convince you differently. You got into the aura of a little girl (the patient) and at times you acted through her, although you could not control her all the time. We tried to wake you up but could not get you away from her. So many need help after they reach the spirit side.

Moody talks very different than when I heard him last. He says I will have to serve and help.

Dr. When you acquire an understanding of the real truth, you will have to be one of the helpers to serve others and waken them from their ignorance to a higher life.

Jesus said, "God is love, and he that dwelleth in love dwelleth in God." (I John 4:16.) You never thought of that, did you?

127

Sp.   I was always taught that God sat on a throne and we sat at His feet.

Dr.   That was not the teaching of Jesus.

Sp.   But Jesus died for our sins.

Dr.   No, he did not. Ask your spirit adviser about that.

Sp.   He says, "Selfishness kills Truth."

Dr.   That is true.

Sp.   Moody says, when he was on earth he wanted the easy way of belief. He says so many of the Christians want to do as they please, then pray to Jesus to take away their sins, but sins are our mistakes and through them we grow wiser and start to reason and think.

           (To Dr. W.) Please tell that little girl (patient) that I will never bother her again. God bless her, and you. I just woke up to understanding. Now I will go with all these people (spirits). Good-night.

A few days later another spirit was removed from the patient, after which there was a distinct improvement in her condition. A rapid recovery followed and some years later the girl called upon us, a picture of health and buoyancy, to express her gratitude for the help she had received.

Dr. Mandel Sherman, of the University of Chicago, reported to the American Association for the Advancement of Science: "A form of insanity is the delusion that you have serious bodily illness."

Such conditions are frequently due to the interference of ignorant discarnated spirits who suffered physical ailments in life, and after transition, usually ignorant of being spirits and still retaining in their consciousness the habit of their former ailments, may become attracted to a mortal sensitive and unknowingly convey the pseudo-symptoms to the victims. These symptoms can be so real that the victims mistake them for their own condition.

During our experimental work many such spirits have been attracted from pseudo-invalids and allowed to temporarily control Mrs. Wickland, after which the symptoms of the patients have disappeared.

The following cases will demonstrate the reality of such conditions. A young married woman, while pregnant, suddenly developed paralysis of the lower limbs and was unable to stand on her feet or walk. Attending doctors surmised that the condition was caused by nerve pressure due to pregnancy, but paralysis still persisted after birth of the child.

Mrs. Wickland clairvoyantly discerned with the patient a spirit who had been paralyzed in life and after death had unconsciously become attracted to the patient. This entity later controlled Mrs. Wickland and gave clear evidence of having been the cause of the pseudo-paralysis. After this, the patient was relieved of her suffering and during ten years has had no recurrence.

A lady, after a slight fall, became dominated by the delusion that both legs were broken. She could not be induced to leave her bed and had to be carried about as an invalid, yet no symptoms of fractures could be found.

Mrs. Wickland and I were called in consultation and Mrs. Wickland perceived that the spirit of a man was the cause of the delusion. This man had been killed in an accident in which both legs had been fractured. The patient was a natural psychic sensitive and the shock of her fall was the predisposing cause of the spirit's interference.

After attracting this spirit from the patient the latter sensed a change in her condition, immediately left the bed and walked without any difficulty.

A striking case of physical possession came under our attention recently, that of a lady whose symptoms suggested serious pathological disturbance yet without any direct physical ailment being discernible. There was absence of any pain, the temperature was normal but pulse over one hundred, suggesting tachycardia; the patient's back was bent and she walked with great difficulty, as though carrying a heavy weight. She could not raise her arms, was unable to articulate, speaking only in a whisper, and, being unable to swallow, she refused food, yet her mind was unaffected.

Medical efforts were unavailing and her vitality was ebbing rapidly, threatening collapse, when one day Mrs. Wickland clairvoyantly discerned the presence of an entity who was evidently conveying this condition to the patient.

Static electrical treatments were resorted to and the spirit of an old lady was transferred from the patient to Mrs. Wickland. This spirit gave an interesting account of herself, claiming she was ninety years old, that her name was Lena Rosenbaum and in 1895 she had been in a hospital in Chicago, where the attending doctor said she could not live. She had suffered from decrepitude owing to her age and had a complication of ailments—could not eat because unable to swallow, had Bright's disease, stomach trouble, was very weak, could take only a small quantity of food and that very seldom, and was so old the entire body seemed disjointed and worn out.

When controlling Mrs. Wickland this entity acted in every way as the patient had done, was bent over, spoke in a whisper and repeatedly stated, "I am so sick, I am so sick."

After this psychic experience the patient rapidly recovered and in a few days was herself again.

Countless other cases could be quoted of persons who suffered from all manner of ailments which appeared to be of actual physical origin. A number of cases of apparent paralysis proved to be due only to interfering spirit entities, after the removal of which the symptoms disappeared and the patients recovered.

The cause of these conditions is ascribable to individuals who actually were paralyzed and passed out; ignorantly still maintaining their idea of being paralyzed they contacted mortal sensitives to whom they conveyed these pseudo symptoms.

Mr. Thomas had been suffering some thirty years from excruciating pains in the back from which he was unable to obtain any relief. During this period he had also been clairaudiently annoyed by the voice of a discarnated entity, that of a man who was unaware of being a spirit.

Mr. Thomas came to us seeking relief. After the application of a few static electrical treatments—which, as above stated, are perfectly harmless to the patient but very efficacious in dislodging obsessing entities, who, unaware of the nature of the static current, often refer to it as "fire" or "lightning"—Mr. Thomas attended our meeting for concentration when Mrs. Wickland became controlled by the spirit of a man who proved to be the entity that had troubled Mr. Thomas for so many years, and the following conversation ensued.

Dr. Wickland	Who are you, my friend?
Spirit	My back! My back! I don't want that lightning and fire on my back. (Referring to the static electric treatment which had been applied to the patient.)
Dr.	Have you been in a fire?
Sp.	I should say I have—fire and lightning on my back!
Dr.	Who put it there?
Sp.	I don't know. That is what worries me. Things are getting worse and worse. (Stretching arms toward Mr. Thomas.) I want to go to that man again. Don't you know me? We always have a backache together.
Mr. Thomas	Oh, yes, I know you all right.
Sp.	Well, I am your old friend. I want you.
Mr. T.	I don't want you. I'm glad to get rid of you.
Dr.	That is the reason he took what you call "fire" on his back. That was a static electric treatment. He wanted to get rid of you.
Sp.	(To Mr. T.) Don't you like me any more?
Mr. T.	I do not want you to stay with me.
Dr.	He says he does not want you to bother him any longer.

131

Sp.   If he doesn't want me, where shall I go?

Dr.   To the spirit world, where you will get understanding.

Sp.   (Laughing.) I suppose you think I am a fool. What do you know about any spirit world? (To Mr. T.) You know you told me to go and I said I would not leave you. You can't keep me away from you long. Anyway, where could I go?

Mr. T.   Learn to progress. You are ignorant. Go where you belong and get understanding.

Dr.   You are ignorant of your condition. Can you remember whether anything unusual happened to you?

Sp.   The horse I was riding jumped and I fell off his back. I was hurt in my back and I went to sleep for awhile. (Died.) After that I woke up.

Dr.   Did anybody pay any attention to you after the accident?

Sp.   Yes, that man over there. (Mr. T.) He is going to help me; I asked him to.

Mr. T.   You have been taken away from me now and you can't come back.

Sp.   Why did you have that fire (static) put on you and me?

Mr. T.   I took those electrical treatments to get rid of you. To my knowledge, you have been with me over thirty years and I surely am glad to get rid of you.

Dr.   You cannot blame him for that, can you? What is your name?

Sp.   Morris O'Brian.

Dr.   Where did you live?

Sp.   With that man. (Pointing to Mr. T.) I have lived with him for many years. Now, when I have nothing, he shakes me!

Dr.   That is for your own good.

Sp.   How can that be when he chases me out of his house and home?

Dr.	Who invited you to go there in the first place? You invited yourself. Do you not realize your condition, that you are a spirit and have lost your physical body?
Mr. T.	I remember when you first came to me; it was in 1894. You must have died and lost your body around that time.
Sp.	You're crazy. You don't know what you are talking about. What place is this?
Dr.	This is Los Angeles, California.
Sp.	I won't stand for all this nonsense! To think that man doesn't want me around when I have lived with him all these years.
Dr.	Would you want him to attach himself to you for years?
Sp.	(Bewildered and distressed.) I don't know where to go.
Dr.	Go to the spirit world and get understanding. There are many spirits waiting to help you. You lost your body a long time ago, but you yourself are not dead.
Sp.	You bet I'm not dead!
Dr.	No one ever "dies." But you have lost your physical body. You are now temporarily in control of the body of my wife.
Sp.	There's lots of room for discussion in that statement.
Dr.	You say you are a man, yet just now you are speaking through a woman's body.
Sp.	Then let me be a man right away!
Dr.	You are a spirit, invisible to us.
Sp.	That's a great mystery to me. But the greatest mystery is how that lightning could strike me down and down and down until I could not stand it any longer, and here I am!
Dr.	That man (Mr. T.) had to take a snappy treatment to get you out.
Sp.	If he took it, I felt it just the same.

133

Dr.   The purpose of the treatment was to make you feel the electricity and to get you away from the man you were bothering.

Sp.   (Angrily to Mr. T.) I'll have no more to do with you after this!

Mr. T.   (Laughing.) I'm very glad of it. I'm glad to get rid of you.

Sp.   You were always a decent sort of a fellow until you took that fire on your back.

Dr.   You have bothered this man for many years.

Sp.   I just lived at his house.

Dr.   He did not want you there.

Sp.   Then why didn't he tell me to get out and hustle for myself?

Mr. T.   I did tell you that, many times.

Sp.   But you never let me go.

Dr.   Those sparks were given you to help you get away.

Sp.   Lots of times I wanted to go, but he held me to him.

Dr.   He did not do that intentionally, for he wanted you to go.

Sp.   I could not go until I had those sparks.

Dr.   We had to drive you out. You are a spirit, free now to roam wherever you choose. That man wanted you to go, but he could not get rid of you and you did not know how to leave by appropriate thinking.

Sp.   That man doesn't like me any more, and now I don't want to be with him. He has told me lots of times to go to the spirit world and get understanding, but he never said where that place is, so how could I go?

Dr.   Now you have an opportunity to acquire understanding. Your spirit eyes will be open, and spirit friends will take you in charge and show you things you have never dreamed of.

Sp.   If I go with them will I be happy?

Dr.	If you are honest and sincere.
Sp.	Have I been a bad man? I didn't mean to be.
Mr. T.	No, you have not, but you bothered me.
Sp.	I was ignorant of doing so. I did not want to bother you, but I had to be with you all the time and it made me very irritable. Sometimes I did not know what to do with myself. There were always the two of us.
Mr. T.	Friend, we have both suffered.
Dr.	Now you will not suffer any more. If you look around you will see friends you have not seen for some time.
Sp.	Two people (spirits) stand right there but I can't see them very plainly. Why, one of them is my father! He says he has come to help me and that I can go to his home. There are so many of my old friends coming to meet me, and there's my mother among them!
	(To an invisible.) Father, I understand I have been bothering a man, but I did not know it. I have lived with him for many years, but he has chased me away. Now that I can go with you, I don't mind. Will you help me, Father?
	Father says I can go with him, but before I go I want to ask this man if he will forgive me.
Mr. T.	Yes, I forgive you.
Sp.	God bless you, and I thank you.
Dr.	Think yourself with your father and you will be there instantly.
Sp.	Good-bye.

With the removal of this spirit the disturbances which had troubled Mr. Thomas for so many years entirely ceased.

Mr. S. consulted us about his brother, Mr. E. S., an invalid, who for many years suffered from intense pain in the back and stomach, was unable to walk without support, could not turn over in bed without help, get in or out of an automobile unassisted or help himself in any way. Yet the patient had an abnormal appetite, especially for beefsteak, and also drank heavily. Specialists in America and Europe disagreed about the diagnosis, some attributing the condition to cancer of the liver, others to internal hemorrhages or chronic nephritis.

Mr. E. S. had for many years traveled about to watering places and health resorts in various countries seeking in vain for relief. Mr. S. had just received a cablegram from the Orient informing him that his brother was dying.

Mrs. Wickland clairvoyantly saw that the condition was due to spirit interference and we placed the invalid's name on our list for concentration, knowing that our Invisible Co-Workers, the Mercy Band, would do all within their power to help.

At one of our psychic circles the guiding spirits allowed Mrs. Wickland to become controlled by a spirit who had been removed from this patient and the next cablegram received by Mr. S. stated that his brother had unexpectedly improved and was on his way to the United States and his home in an eastern city.

Mrs. Wickland suggested that Mr. S. bring his brother, while in Los Angeles, to us for a few electrical treatments in order to enable us to come in closer rapport with the case.

Accordingly one morning Mr. S. arrived with his brother, who was carried from the automobile into the office and placed in the chair on the platform for a static electrical treatment, although Mr. S. asked that nothing be said to his brother regarding spirit obsession.

"Doctor," said the patient, "if you can take away my backache it would be wonderful."

Mrs. Wickland clairvoyantly saw that the patient was influenced by the spirit of a crippled old man who had died from disease complications of the back. She said, "When the old man goes, you will be better." The patient assumed

136

that she referred to his helpless condition but his brother understood her meaning at once.

Presently the patient was asked to rise but said, "I cannot." Mrs. Wickland then stepped upon the platform beside him and, placing his hands on her shoulders for support, he rose and stood leaning on her while I applied the static electricity to his back.

Immediately the spirit of the old man was disengaged and attempted to control Mrs. Wickland but she would not permit this, knowing the patient would not understand the situation.

Mr. E. S. then stepped from the platform unaided and exclaimed, "I can walk alone! My backache has gone! Doctor, what have you done to me?" And without his cane he walked alone to the automobile.

The next morning Mr. E. S. returned for another treatment, reporting that he had slept the entire night, turned over in bed without help and had walked around the room alone, which he had not been able to do for years.

"See, I can stand on one foot," he said, "and swing the other foot! I feel as if something had been taken away from me."

In a few days Mr. E. S. returned to his eastern home; however, we continued our concentration for him and the Mercy Band dislodged three more spirits and these were allowed to control Mrs. Wickland at our seances.

The one was the son of a nationally prominent wealthy merchant who had lived in the city where the patient resided. This spirit said: "My father is rich and I am a gentleman. I do not have to work. I live only to eat and drink and have a good time."

He said that while he had been at a well-known club he was shot in the abdomen by a girl; to conceal the facts his father and physicians announced that he had appendicitis.

Ample corroboration of his statements was easily obtained, as the case had received wide publicity some years before.

The second spirit had been in the real estate business in the same city, but having lost his money, had become a heavy drinker and, while suffering from delirium tremens, had taken an overdose of sleeping powders. His one desire was highballs, gin, whiskey and beefsteaks.

The third spirit, a broker, had been a friend of the other two and remembered having had a severe sickness.

"The doctor said I would die but I only went to sleep and when I woke up I was with my friends. I knew they were dead and it was very strange, but there we were, all cramped up together." (In the patient's aura.) "We all had to travel with a strange man (patient) and we made him eat three or four steaks, one for each of us."

It is often found that discarnated spirits, while yet ignorant of their situation, and before enlightened, maintain their old earthly habits and convey them to a mortal victim, causing the latter to involuntarily carry out their suggestions by excessive gourmandizing, drinking, drug addiction and many other unaccountable vagaries of thought and action.

All of these spirits were unaware of their transition from the physical to the spirit world but after being enlightened were eager to do everything possible to atone for having interfered with the patient.

Mr. S. later informed us that his brother had been restored to health, ate normally and had stopped drinking; in fact, at a dinner where cocktails were served he asked for tomato juice. He also resumed his business activities and each day walked to his office, a distance of two and a half miles.

Spirit interference is indeed a problem for social scientists, sociologists, physicians, ministers, lawyers, judges, educators and welfare workers. The medical man, who is usually the first to contact mental cases, will be enabled to do more than at present, which is usually to assign a certain name to this or that symptom while remaining largely ignorant of the actual cause of the aberration.

This research will enable him to discriminate between the patient's actual physical condition and mental attitudes or idiosyncrasies and the exciting, contributing factors interposed by discarnated entities, oftentimes not an easy thing to do by one inexperienced in psychic diagnosis. The investigator will often find intricate combinations of the

138

person's individual peculiarities and characteristics and those of the impinging entities.

Hence the importance of setting aside preconceived ideas and the need for diligent and patient experimentation. Accumulating data will thoroughly prove the hypothesis of spirit obsession to be fundamentally correct and demonstrable.

It is commonly maintained that mental disturbances, from whatever cause, are a disgrace to the individual and his family. Such an attitude is most unfortunate as mental aberrations, whether due to physical causes or the impingement of discarnated spirits as contributing factors, are no more a disgrace than are fevers or any other physical conditions.

Interference by ignorant discarnated spirits is not necessarily an indication of feeble-mindedness; experience has shown that such interference can often occur with individuals who are very strong-minded or self-willed. Rather, spirit interference is more to be ascribed to a natural psychic susceptibility of certain individuals than to any weakness of mind or will.

That mental aberrations and insanity are hereditary family taints is also generally held, but such family tendencies are, I am convinced, better explained by the theory of an inherited natural psychic susceptibility to spirit interference.

When the probability of outside influences being the real cause of mental aberrations is scientifically established through research, the fear of such inherited tendencies will be greatly obviated, since relief from these disturbances is possible through dispossession of the intruding entities.

Our research work is carried on in co-operation with the Mercy Band of Spirit Forces under the leadership of the spirit Dr. Root. The latter, when speaking through Mrs. Wickland, constantly emphasizes the great need of an understanding of the complex problem of spirit obsession, and the following is quoted from one of his communications.

"Those who are troubled by spirits suffer greatly and need much sympathy. As soon as persons say they hear voices or see spirits the doctors declare they have hallucinations. But their suffering is a reality; they are clairaudient or clairvoyant and this should be understood."

"However, doctors place these poor sensitives in asylums. This is a living death for the spirit as well as the mortal. Many years may pass and they must live in that terrible commotion."

"Help these unfortunate ones; do not call them insane and send them to the asylum. Help them, because they are obsessed by spirits."

"Do you realize the spirit often suffers as much as the patient? When you help one, you help the other. Let mediums do this work and empty the asylums."

"Why should people doubt that insanity is spirit obsession? Christ drove out spirits. If you study ancient history you will find that spirit obsession and possession have always been known. The Indians recognized spirit obsession; they also attributed epilepsy to spirit interference and drove the spirits out by repeatedly immersing the patient in the cold water of rivers or lakes.

"Many think people are obsessed only when they are 'crazy.' All are influenced more or less; they receive mental suggestions and act on them. Everyone has this experience at times; this is spirit influence."

"Help the unfortunate ones in the asylums to understand they are obsessed by earthbound spirits. Advanced spirits can then reach the interfering entities, who are also to be pitied. Help them both."

"There is a great gap between spirits of the higher understanding and the earthbound spirits. It is difficult for intelligent spirits to contact the ignorant ones; you on earth can reach them more easily because earthbound spirits can see only the gross material and are unable to see us although we can see them. They do not know we are there because they are attached to the material world and can see only by coming in contact with mortals."

"Spread the truth regarding obsession; those who scoff do so because of their own ignorance. The time has now come for an awakening. Spiritual Science Universities are needed to teach the philosophy of life. Here the younger generation would be taught to know themselves, to know who they are, where they come from and, most important of all, where they are going. To such places could come those who are in trouble; they could open their hearts to some one who understands and who will help them to understand themselves."

"If such institutions for unfortunate ones could be established there would not be so many suicides, for those in trouble could then talk things over with some one who is interested in them; they would find comfort and cheer and be helped to a much happier condition and to an understanding of the higher things of life."

The entire subject of spirit influence will indisputably prove to be one of the foremost problems for scientific research, as it involves economics, the science of life and the relationship between the two worlds, without which there can never be a reasonable comprehension of an intelligible meaning of existence.

The Creator has established definite problems and has given us intelligence to unravel them for ourselves, this effort being a requisite for an appreciation and comprehension of their meaning. Were it not so, and were everything plainly evident and easily understood, life would lose its necessary incentive for search, the effort whereby understanding is unfolded. Only understanding attained through one's own effort has value, as it illumines the soul in its quest for the hidden meaning of existence.

CHAPTER VII

Dogma Spiritualized

THE existence of a Supreme Being is often denied by infidels and atheists as a result of conclusions drawn from the contradictions of the Bible and the cruelties ascribed to the God of Christian orthodoxy.

It should be self-evident to the real Bible student that the God of the dogmatist is represented as cruel, tyrannical and contradictory, credited with deeds from which a conscientious mortal, had he the power of such a God, would shrink.

Christian orthodoxy, as propounded in the Bible, declares that before the creation of the manifest universe God was All-in-All, omnipresent, omnipotent and omniscient, implying everywhere present, possessed of all powers and being all wise, with full knowledge of the past, present and future.

Yet, according to the biblical story, after angels had been created by God one of them grew disobedient and "fell," becoming the father of all evil, designated by many terms— Lucifer, The Deceiver, Satan—so powerful a being that even the elect often fall through his snares.

Is it not evident that a God having the triune principles of omnipresence, omnipotence and omniscience, being perfect and All-in-All, nothing else existent, could create only beings that possessed the qualities inherent in the Creator?

These qualities being perfect, nothing else existing, how could an angel of his creation fall, a fall implying becoming inferior? How could that which is perfect, nothing else existent, create from that same substance something inferior?

If the universe consisted of absolutely but one substance, how could anything formed from that substance contain qualities other than those existent in the original substance? To change the nature of that product something must of necessity be added; there being nothing from which to acquire additional qualities, how could the nature of the substance be changed?

Furthermore, this omniscient God, being all-wise, must have known that one of his angels would "fall," and become his own rival and antagonist, for, according to this biblical story, God was the originator of Satan, whom creedalists believe to be the source of all temptation and evil.

Would any reasonable person, possessing the power to create, knowingly and willfully originate such a situation as is attributed to an all-wise God?

We are told in Genesis that when Adam and Eve were driven out of the Garden of Eden, owing to their disobedience, they, and mankind ever after, were doomed by a loving God to an existence of endless toil and suffering.

God, being all-wise, must have been fully aware that Adam and Eve would be tempted and beguiled by his arch-enemy, the Devil, his own creature, in the form of a serpent. This omniscient God must also have known that his own handiwork, Adam and Eve, were lacking in certain qualities and would therefore be unable to resist temptation. Yet this Creator cruelly placed temptation before his own children.

Again, in this story, the Supreme Being is credited with an act of cruelty which a mortal, if endowed with the qualities of the creator, would not commit. What intelligent parents, possessing a garden infested with serpents, would encourage their children to play in this garden, knowing the children would be bitten by the serpents?

Many devout Christians and creedalists believe implicitly that "fallen angels" became devils, the rulers of the invisible world about mankind, and that it is the temptings of these devils which cause the evils of the world. Likewise, they fully believe that the deception of Adam and Eve by the Evil One, and the consequent breaking of God's command in the Garden of Eden, brought about the sorrows and sufferings of mankind and accept as evidence the misery, sickness, poverty, injustice, crime, tragedy, catastrophes and deaths everywhere prevalent.

On the other hand, they hold that God is omnipresent, omnipotent, omniscient and is Love and Wisdom.

These viewpoints are self-evidently contradictory, unreasonable and entirely at variance with each other since they maintain that God, although omnipresent, omnipotent and omniscient, failed entirely to foresee that certain of his creatures would fall and cause such a disturbance in his creation, this orthodox Christian interpretation obviously implying that the Ruler of the Universe is both ignorant and tyrannical.

Adam and Eve were preordained to fructify and multiply their own kind. The parents were the creation of a perfect God, yet the first natural-born, Cain, became a murderer. Did this all-wise theological God foresee such a misfortune, or was it a part of his plan?

Another part of the biblical story tells us that God later became displeased with his handiwork and regretted that he had created man. In an effort to eradicate his mistakes a flood was decided upon which was to drown all mankind; however, a few were spared with the hope that, following the lessons learned, they would bring forth a better race. But this also proved a failure.

We are told in the Bible that God is the Father of all and that all are children of God, yet this same God instructed the chosen people of Israel, as they entered various countries of the Promised Land, to kill all inhabitants, men, women and children.

A man would indeed be a human monster who would instruct one group of people to kill another group, men, women and innocent children, and take possession of their land, yet a supposedly loving God gave this instruction to the Israelites in order that they might gain possession of the Land of Canaan. (Exodus 23.31. Deuteronomy 7:1, 2, 10, 21. I Samuel 15:3.)

"Hereby ye shall know that the living God is among you, and that he will without fail drive out from before you the Canaanites, and the Hittites, and the Hivites, and the Perizzites, and the Girgashites, and the Amorites, and the Jebusites." (Joshua 3:10.)

How reconcile this with the admonition: "Thou shalt love they neighbor as thyself?" (James 2:8.)

The Israelites were also instructed by God not to eat the

144

meat of an animal that had died from natural causes, but that they might give it to a stranger within their gates. (Deuteronomy 14:21.) Would not the strangers also be children of God?

"Whoso hath the world's goods, and beholdeth his brother in need, and shutteth up his compassion from him, how doth the love of God abide in him? My little children, let us love in word, neither with the tongue; but in deed and truth." (I John 3:17, 18.)

"Inasmuch as yet have done it unto one of the least of these my brethren, ye have done it unto me." (Matthew 25:40.)

According to the Book of Job, God was conversing with Satan, praising the faithfulness of his servant Job. Satan asserted that Job feared the Lord merely because he had been blessed and said: "Put forth thine hand now and touch all he hath and he will curse thee to thy face." Seemingly doubting this statement, "the Lord said unto Satan, Behold, all that he hath is in thy power." (Job 1:6-12.)

We know to what degree of misery and distress Satan brought Job. Did God lack foresight and fail to realize what would happen? Why did not God, being all-powerful, annihilate his adversary on this occasion?

When God's creation, mankind, had fallen from the way of rectitude and all efforts at restoration had failed, a new plan was adopted to correct all previous errors.

Through a supposed miracle, a special Son of God, immaculately conceived, was born of a virgin and preordained to be sacrificed as a vicarious atonement for the sins of the people. Christians today are taught that only by believing this story can mankind be "saved from hell."

If God, the Creator of all, is everywhere present, all knowing, all powerful and All-in-All ("hell" must be included in the All-in-All), there being no place where God is not, mankind consequently is always in the midst of God and his creation, and is a part of God's nature, hence what is there to be saved from?

Therefore, the theory of such a salvation scheme is illogical; formulated by dogmatism, this fallacious idea has been the cause of great misery and suffering to countless, owing to the fear of a supposed "hell."

In bygone days, when the doctrine of "hell-fire" was particularly emphasized, many children were terrified by this teaching for fear that after death they might be condemned to this fiery furnace.

At a school which Mrs. Wickland attended when seven years of age the teacher elucidated the horrors of hell, saying: "You know how painful it is when you burn only one finger; you can then imagine how much worse one would suffer when he is immersed in the fires of hell. There you will burn forever and forever, and the flames can never be extinguished!"

This description caused Mrs. Wickland to become so distraught that she could not eat or sleep and she prayed God to permit her to die at once, since she feared that if she grew up and made sinful mistakes she would, after death, find herself in that terrible, everlasting fire.

Unable to longer endure this mental torment, she consulted her father as to his belief regarding hell. Her father, being liberal-minded, replied that hell is only a figure of speech, and said: "The doctrine of hell-fire was invented in past ages when people were in a crude stage of development and civilization and needed some effective means to bring them into paths of rectitude."

"Hell is a mental state," he explained; "if you do wrong to yourself or others your conscience will torment you in proportion to your misdeeds, and that is hell enough!"

"By realizing your mistakes, improving your actions and living according to the dictates of conscience, this mental hell will be changed to a condition of peace and happiness."

Accepting her father's explanation as reasonable, the fear of hell was dissipated and Mrs. Wickland was troubled no more.

Many persons have gone insane or been driven to suicide because of this pernicious "hell" doctrine. Such teachings have forced untold numbers from any recognition of a Supreme Being to the conclusion that death ends all, a belief which would make the existence of mankind only a mockery, conclusions which are entirely false and illogical to reasoning minds.

At the Council of Nice, 325 A. D., the Roman Emperor Constantine issued the declaration that Jesus was the Son of God, and very God. Yet, if Jesus was very God, Mary, being the mother of Jesus, would then appear to have anteceded God.

Jesus, at least the physical man, is declared to have come from the House of David, on the strength of Joseph being a descendant of the House of David. (Luke 1:27, 32. Matthew 1:1, 16.) How could this lineage apply to Jesus, since Joseph was not his father?

The story of Jesus and Satan on the high mountain declares that for forty days Satan tempted Jesus to worship him, promising all the glories of the world as a reward. (Luke 4:2, 5, 6, 7.) If Jesus was the Son of God and very God, as declared by Constantine, was it not strange that his own creature, Satan, should have such power over God himself?

Jesus' own statements, "Thou shalt worship the Lord thy God, and him only shalt thou serve" (Luke 4:8), "The Father that dwelleth in me, he doeth the works" (John 14:10), "I do nothing of myself, but as the Father taught me, I speak these things, and he that sent me is with me" (John 8:28, 29), indicate that Jesus did not consider himself God, evidencing that only through theology was Jesus made a God. Again, when Jesus was called "Good Master" he answered: "Why callest thou me good? None is good, save one, even God." (Mark 10:17, 18.)

Many biblical contradictions present themselves to the unbiased student. In Isaiah 9:6 is asserted: "His name shall be called, Wonderful, Counsellor, Mighty God, Everlasting Father, Prince of Peace," but Matthew 10:34 states, "Think not that I came to send peace on the earth; I came not to send peace, but a sword."

In I John 4:16 we read: "God is love; and he that dwelleth in love dwelleth in God." Yet this same God of love is quoted as saying, "I the Lord thy God am a jealous God, visiting the iniquity of the fathers upon the children unto the third and fourth generation of them that hate me." (Exodus 20:5.)

147

On the other hand, many definite statements regarding love are made. "Love therefore is the fulfilment of the law." (Romans 13:10.) "Honour thy father and thy mother; that thy days may be long upon the land which the Lord thy God giveth thee." (Exodus 20:12.) "Bear ye one another's burdens." (Galatians 6:2.)

But still Christ declares, "If any man cometh unto me, and hateth not his own father, and mother, and wife, and children and brethren, and sisters, yea, and his own life also, he cannot be my disciple." (Luke 14:26.)

Opposing this, I John 3:15 states: "Whosoever hateth his brother is a murderer," and in John 13:34, 35, the commandment is given, "Love one another; even as I have loved you . . . love one another. By this shall all men know that ye are my disciples, if ye have love one to another."

Such contradictory teachings may be acceptable to mere believers but they fail to satisfy the minds of those who seek a comprehensible reason for existence and earth's experiences. The orthodox conception of a Supreme Ruler is contrary to the innate human sense of right and justice and is opposed to the dictates of conscience. Can atheists and infidels be censured for rejecting such a God, or for holding an attitude of skepticism toward such illogical doctrines?

Christian orthodoxy accepts the Jewish calendar as the biblical authority for creation; at the last celebration of Rosh Hashana the Jews commemorated the 5694th anniversary of the creation of the world. Yet geologists of today, according to their findings, recognize the earth as being hundreds of millions of years old and that mankind has existed at least 50,000 years and perhaps even 500,000 years.

The theory of annihilation of certain souls, which is held by many, is not reasonable nor is it a credit to a Creator. Not even a human being, if endowed with the creative power of an all-knowing God and having foresight, would create a being merely that it should become exterminated. We cannot conceive of an imperfect Creator, and an all-wise Creator would prohibit such a possibility as the annihilation of his creatures.

God, the Creator, is Good, Beauty, Happiness and all Virtue, as revealed in his creation, and his creatures must have the same qualities. If a soul fully understood its innate higher origin and that it is a part of God and knew of the wonders to be attained through a normal, rational life and would then wilfully act contrary to the higher plan and pursue a life of wickedness, fully aware that certain extinction would follow such a life, then under such circumstances annihilation would be a logical conclusion. But the majority of souls in human existence are like children in kindergarten, they are merely conscious and have no conception of the ultimate of life.

Of writers and illuminati who have delved into the plan and activities of the universe, few, if any, we believe, were so highly endowed as Emanuel Swedenborg. His writings describe conditions in the higher spheres and what constitutes hells, and his works are of utmost importance as these elucidations make many of life's mystifying problems simple and understandable. However, we cannot agree with his conclusions that some souls may become extinguished or annihilated if they have wilfully lived selfish and evil existences.

We are to accept Swedenborg, the Bible or any writings and teachings only so far as they are logical. Truth, to have value, must be self-evident and not dependent upon mere belief. Swedenborg lived in an age when he could not come out freely and boldly with the entire truth; because of the power of the church and the ignorance of the people his teachings would have been rejected altogether had they been too radical a contradiction of the Bible. Therefore the Spirit World allowed Swedenborg to teach part truths. It is also possible that some of his guiding Spirit Forces may have had limitations of understanding, while Swedenborg himself may also have had his own preconceived ideas regarding the evils in the world.

Undoubtedly, life is for ultimate happiness, not destruction, and a future must await the developed soul, a living ecstacy far beyond our present conception. As yet we cannot comprehend what is to be in the fullness of time. "For now we see through a glass darkly; but then face to face." (I Corinthians 13:12.)

Different individuals travel different roads, but all lead to the end of the Mortal Trail, with release from the path-

149

way of ignorance and entrance into the noble Pathway of Spirit, the beauty of which is sensed most fully in proportion to the wrongs and sufferings the soul has endured in the travails of the mortal journey.

THE CHEMISTRY OF CHARACTER

Elizabeth Doten

John, and Peter, and Robert, and Paul,
God in His wisdom created them all.
   John was a statesman, and Peter a slave;
   Robert a preacher; and Paul was a knave.
Evil or good as the case might be,
White or colored, or bond, or free—
   John, and Peter, and Robert, and Paul,
   God in His wisdom created them all.

Out of earth's elements, mingled with flame,
Out of life's compounds of glory and shame
   Fashioned and shaped by no will of their own
   And helplessly into life's history thrown;
Born by the law that compels men to be,
Born to conditions they could not foresee;
   John, and Peter, and Robert, and Paul,
   God in His wisdom created them all.

John was the head and heart of his State,
Was trusted and honored; was noble and great.
   Peter was made 'neath life's burdens to groan,
   And never once dreamed that his soul was his own.
Robert, great glory and honor received
For zealously preaching what no one believed;
   While Paul of the pleasures of sin took his fill,
   And gave up his life to the service of ill.

It chanced that these men in their passing away
From earth and its conflicts, all died the same day.
   John was mourned thro' the length and the breadth
     of the land;
   Peter fell 'neath the lash in a merciless hand;

150

Robert died with the praise of the Lord on his tongue;
While Paul was convicted of murder and hung.
　　John, and Peter, and Robert, and Paul;
　　The purpose of life was fulfilled in them all.

Men said of the Statesman: "How noble and brave!"
But of Peter: "Alas! he was only a Slave."
　　Of Robert: " 'Tis well with his soul—it is well;"
　　While Peter they consigned to the torments of Hell.
Born by one law through all Nature the same,
What made them differ, and who was to blame?
　　John, and Peter, and Robert, and Paul,
　　God in His wisdom created them all.

Out in that region of infinite light,
Where the soul of the black man is pure as the white,
　　Out where the spirit, through sorrow made wise,
　　No longer resorts to deception and lies,
Out where the flesh can no longer control
The freedom and faith of the God-given soul,
　　Who shall determine what change may befall
　　John, and Peter, and Robert, and Paul?

John may in wisdom and goodness increase;
Peter rejoice in an infinite peace;
　　Robert may learn that the truths of the Lord
　　Are more in the spirit and less in the Word;
And Paul may be blest with a holier birth
Than the passions of men had allowed him on earth.
　　John, and Peter, and Robert, and Paul,
　　God in His wisdom created them all.

Dogmatic Christianity accepts a doctrine built upon a belief in supposed historical characters and personalities, in what are presumed to be external revelations, in a story of fallen humanity and a Redeemer who was killed for the sins of mankind.

Evident as are the biblical inconsistencies, obviously manipulated through the years by designing, ambitious leaders, the earnest investigator and Bible student will find that many of the seemingly illogical stories are but wonderful allegories. Once the inner meaning of certain of these narratives is understood, they will be found to present demonstrable hypotheses based upon eternal laws of life. "For the letter killeth, but the spirit giveth life." (II Corinthians 3:6.)

As the trinity principle is predominant in the natural world so also are the leading religions founded on the principle of Trinity, that is, an outer manifestation and an inner causative factor resulting in a third revelation—matter, spirit and life.

In the natural world we can realize concrete evidence but in matters pertaining to religion, dealing as it does with invisible factors, allegories, parables and symbolism are resorted to in order to convey spiritual truths.

While the Bible contains much that is plainly legendary and inapplicable to the present age, it is like a mine of precious stones—much dross and worthless material must be eliminated in the search for the gems.

So in the study of the Bible we need not quarrel as to who wrote this and that; it is sufficient that we seek out the gems of thought which are of value and are applicable and helpful in the interpretation of the enigma of existence. Truth is what we are seeking, regardless of who has uttered it.

One who is interested in chemistry seeks dependable formulas regardless of who has written the text-book. So also the seeker after truth needs dependable, self-evident guiding formulas which will be applicable in the interpretation of the Why of Existence, or the meaning of life, and helpful in unfolding understanding.

As chemical formulas are various so also are the precepts of life various in order that the mental horizon may be broadened. The precepts of greatest value in the Bible pertain to methods of obtaining the desired understanding and mental perception of life's meaning, much as the formulas of greatest value in text-books on scientific subjects are those which point out what is to be done to obtain certain definite results.

In Genesis we read that God created Adam, the first man, from the dust of the ground, endowed him with the breath of life, then made a woman, Eve, from one of his ribs. This pair was established in the Garden of Eden, a paradise, in the midst of which grew the tree of the knowledge of good and evil. Of this fruit Adam and Eve were forbidden to eat lest they surely die.

But the serpent, the Tempter or Evil One, beguiled Eve, saying, "God doth know that in the day ye eat thereof, then your eyes shall be opened, and ye shall be as God, knowing good and evil." (Genesis 3:5.) Adam and Eve ate of the forbidden fruit and the Lord banished them from the Garden of Eden, placing at the East a Cherubim with flaming sword, which turned every way.

From a literal or historical standpoint this story means little, but from an inner sense, interpreted allegorically, it contains important significance, indicative of nature's primary school.

To illustrate, every infant born into this life is a little Adam, in a paradisical state of innocence and ignorance. "Adam" means "earthy"; physically, an infant's body is composed of earthly substances. The infant is oblivious of its very existence, the Unconscious Stage of Infancy, but is in reality a bundle of potential possibilities which are unfolded by means of the five special sense organs, or avenues, sight, hearing, taste, smell and touch, whereby the ego contacts external things.

Of these avenues, sight is the most prominent. The infant opens his eyes and becomes attracted to physical things when Desire, or Eve, becomes manifest. Seduced by the temptings of objective things (figuratively, the Serpent, or Tempter), Desire (Eve) reaches out for the objective and touches, say, a hot object, which causes pain to Adam, the ego.

Such reaching out and receiving painful experiences result in the attainment of a degree of knowledge, as well as in a gradual exclusion from the paradisical state of innocence and ignorance. Through the inter-action of experience and knowledge (eating of the tree of knowledge of right and wrong) reason is gradually evolved, resulting in understanding.

The sun rising in the east gives light, hence East is used symbolically to represent the Light of Understanding, ultimating in Wisdom. The Angel at the East of the Garden symbolizes Wisdom, the Sword, Knowledge; the edges of the Sword, the Sense of Right and Wrong.

Wisdom, realizing the seductive temptings of the evanescent and temporary phases of physical existence, figuratively swings the Sword of Knowledge in various directions, lopping off follies and illusive promptings which would keep the spirit in bondage.

The statement of the Serpent, or Tempter, can thus be understood as being allegorically correct, that eating of the fruit of the tree of knowledge of good and evil will ultimately unfold wisdom. This is Nature's Primary School.

"And the Lord God said, Behold, the man is become as one of us, to know good and evil." (Genesis 3:22.) "The first man Adam became a living soul. The last Adam became a life-giving spirit." (I Corinthians 15:45.)

The first offspring of Adam and Eve, Cain, became the murderer of his brother Abel. This story, in a literal sense, would again indicate lack of forethought on the part of the Creator in that the very first offspring of his created beings became a murderer.

Symbolically, Cain and Abel illustrate two characteristic phases of mind—Cain, Intellect, and Abel, Intuition. The Bible relates that Cain was a tiller of the ground and Abel a keeper of sheep. (Genesis 4:2.) Esoterically, Cain, the tiller of the ground, represents the cold, material intellect, external-mindedness, as we find it in every-day life, following only after the physical side of existence. Abel, keeper of sheep and lambs, the latter typifying innocence and purity, represents the inner intuitive or spiritual urge in man's nature, which, figuratively, is killed by the cold intellect.

The similarity between the teachings of the Bible and the facts revealed by Psychic Research, namely, that service is the keynote to progression and soul advancement, proves that selfishness and self-aggrandizement for one's own sake exclusively are in direct opposition to nature's divine purpose, in that they stifle the dictates of the inner voice, or conscience, shutting out the divine love element innate in every soul by making Mammon the all of life.

"By love serve one another" (Galatians 5:13) is not an

154

idle injunction, for in proportion as service is rendered is self-importance gradually eliminated. "He that is greatest among you shall be your servant" (Matthew 23:11) is counsel which if followed unfolds a "newness of spirit" and a realization that "none of us liveth to himself" (Romans 14:7), that God is no respecter of persons and that in a higher sense we are really our brothers' keepers.

It must be borne in mind that many of our fellow-travelers are handicapped in the struggle of life, often falling by the roadside, and that it behooves the stronger ones, who are more favorably situated, mentally and otherwise, to realize their duty toward their weaker brothers.

"Thou shalt love the Lord thy God with all thy heart, and with all thy soul, and with all thy mind . . . and thy neighbor as thyself" (Matthew 22:37, 39) is illustrated in the allegory of the Good Samaritan. (Luke 10:30-37.)

The soul grows so involved in materiality that it becomes calloused and unconscious of the diviner principles and the real purpose of our earth life, which, when untrammeled, is intended for the cultivation within ourselves of a sense of soul ideals. The souls involved in materiality enclose themselves in a shell of self-sufficiency and are wrapped up in their own thought life.

When such individuals pass to the invisible side of life they receive a rude awakening, similar to the allegory of The Five Foolish Virgins (Matthew 25:1-13) who found themselves without oil in their lamps, meaning that their special five sense organs, avenues of the soul to the external, had not been used for observation and attainment of knowledge of nature's wondrous plan, which, when properly followed, will enrich the soul with understanding and wisdom —the "oil in the lamp."

Having lived only for self and material attractions, these individuals, when they enter the new life lacking wisdom and understanding, find themselves in "outer darkness." (Matthew 8:12.) Such self-seeking souls were characterized by Jesus as having eyes, but seeing not, having ears, yet hearing not, being spiritually blind and deaf. (Mark 8:18.)

The five wise virgins symbolize those who have used the soul avenues for the purpose for which they were intended.

155

These will not enter the next school of life in a state of darkness but will have the "Light of Life" (John 8:12) to which Jesus referred—a broadened understanding of the divine plan.

Many statements of Jesus are absolutely scientific in that they are verified by psychological research and direct contact with discarnated spirits, intelligent ones as well as those who are entirely oblivious of being so-called dead.

The unchangeable laws of progression are summarized in self-abnegation and service to our fellowmen, be it on the physical plane or in the invisible life.

The pivotal points of especial value in the Bible refer particularly to these requirements, as for instance: "He that loveth not his brother whom he hath seen, cannot love God whom he hath not seen." (I John 4:20.) Again, "Bear ye one another's burdens" (Galatians 6:2), also, "Whosoever shall humble himself shall be exalted." (Matthew 23:12.)

The words of Jesus, "I" (the spirit of understanding) "came not to send peace, but a sword" (Matthew 10:34), are not to be understood as applying to worldly warfare but to the struggle of the individual for mastery over self.

Jesus said: "God is Spirit" (not a spirit[1]) "and he that worships him must worship him in spirit and in truth." (John 4:24.) Paul's words, "My little children, of whom I am again in travail until Christ be formed in you" (Galatians 4:19), clearly refer to the spirit of discernment of truth, acquirement of the spirit of "Christ," the inner mental perception alluded to. "Now hath Christ been raised from the dead, the first fruits of them that are asleep." (I Corinthians 15:20.)

As in the mundane sphere knowledge cannot be bought or given us but must be obtained by each one through his own efforts, so must each individual acquire spiritual discernment for himself; it cannot be attained vicariously.

The temptations credited to a supposed devil—"devil" meaning, "Diabolus, liar, deceiver"—are only the alluring attractions of the bodily senses seeking self-gratification, bidding the struggling soul to worship or follow. These

---

[1]See Margin Revised Version of Bible.

156

insinuatingly attempt to distract the soul from the path of rectitude which moral principles admonish the quickened soul to follow if it would be free in a spiritual sense.

But how often are the promptings of the inner conscience unheeded and stifled; through Desire (Eve) the individual side-steps and gives way to tempting allurements resulting in all manner of misery, in this carrying out the symbol of John the Baptist, the admonishing conscience being slain.

The soul is baptized in the bitter water of experience until finally the folly of its way is recognized and the promptings of conscience are heeded, when "Jesus," the Spirit of Truth, arises.

John the Baptist said of himself: "I am the voice of one crying in the wilderness" (John 1:23); "I indeed baptize you with water" (experience) "unto repentance." (Matthew 3:11.) We are also informed that his raiment was camel's hair, and his food locusts and wild honey. (Matthew 3:4.) The nature of the locust is to jump, symbolizing the tendency to evade the dictates of conscience, thus feeding the conscience with the wild honey of bitter experience.

King Herod typifies Selfishness; Herodias represents Vengeance; the daughter is Vanity. Herodias, Vengeance, is troubled by John the Baptist, Conscience, and when Herod, Selfishness, offers the daughter, Vanity, the choice of anything she wishes, the mother asks her to demand the head of the troublesome John the Baptist, Conscience, and to this King Herod, Selfishness, accedes. (Matthew 14:1-11.)

John the Baptist declared that after him would come one who would baptize with fire (Luke 3:16), typifying the birth of Truth, or Son of Man, a quickened conscience. This stage of consciousness recognizes the higher purpose of existence.

There is no need of quarreling about the personality of Jesus. Many deny his existence; others believe that he is the Son of God, sent into the physical world as a Mediator or Savior.

There have been, and are, many saviors of mankind. Anyone who improves the lives of others by conveying to them principles for better living and conduct is, to that

157

extent, a "savior." The searchers in any field of nature are in a sense "saviors" in that they improve and better the conditions of human existence.

Physical laws all exist previous to their revealment. The laws of music existed prior to man's discovery of these laws, as did the laws governing chemistry, physics, the telegraph, the telephone; sound vibrations existed before the radio revealed them; all these were only discovered, not created, by man.

The laws governing requisite conduct and the Science of Life are innate in Nature's Arcana and whoever reveals these laws is in that proportion a "savior."

The teachings credited to Jesus are given allegorically because a spiritual truth is not a physical thing and hence needs to be demonstrated by comparisons. Herein, however, it is necessary to make a distinction between truth and dogmatic theories.

The "righteousness" of the Bible really means living according to the revealed laws of life and nature. "If a man keep my word, he shall never see death," said Jesus. (John 8:51.) It does not matter who uttered these words of law. The statement reveals a law in nature; Psychic Research today amply proves that there is no death, but a transition of the ego from the physical to the invisible side of life.

The precepts of Jesus and other inspired teachers are wonderful formulas for conduct to anyone who is willing to perceive their meaning in the light of understanding. "The words that I have spoken unto you are spirit, and are life." (John 6:63.) "Heaven and earth shall pass away, but my words shall not pass away." (Matthew 24:35.)

The story of the Crucifixion symbolizes the soul's tribulations, and the Cross, the burdens which man must carry in the material realm.

Jesus, the Son of Man, or Truth, realizes he is figuratively carrying the Cross of Matter in the struggle of material experiences. The final crucifixion is the recognition of the fact that man must overcome matter, that the ultimate requirement is to cease being a blind slave to this material cross.

"The Cross was used by the ancients as a sacred symbol

long before the Christian era and it denoted the attainment of life eternal through crucifixion of the body, or lower nature." ("Mystery of the Ages," Countess of Caithness.)

"Take my yoke upon you, and learn of me; for I am meek and lowly in heart; and ye shall find rest unto your souls. For my yoke is easy, and my burden is light." (Matthew 11:29, 30.)

"The Cross is the true symbol of man, with Infinity all around him and Eternity within, rising from Earth to Heaven." ("Mystery of the Ages.")

"The figure of a cross is in the universe; its four inter-spaces extend to Infinity—North, South, East, and West." (Plato.)

Esoterically the cross upon which the Son of Man is crucified symbolizes the four chief elements of the physical plane — earthy, airy, watery and fiery — representing the cross of matter on which the soul in the physical is crucified by the every-day tribulations; with these the individual struggles until he ceases to be exclusively and unduly subject to the seductive promptings of the physical by attaining understanding of their meaning and mastery over them.

Thus is fulfilled the statement of Paul that "As in Adam" (the earthly things) "all die, so also in Christ" (the At-One-Ment) "shall all be made alive" (I Corinthians 15:22), that is, attain the spirit of God-consciousness.

"Where the Spirit of the Lord is, there is liberty." (II Corinthians 3:17.) "For to this end we labour and strive because we have our hope set on the living God, who is the Saviour of all men." (I Timothy 4:10.)

Ascension, or liberation from the cross, is but the attained cognition of the apparent mystery of the soul's journey. "No cross, no crown."

The cross is often alluded to as the Passion Cross, pictured as red. This is symbolical of a spiritual principle, the redness of blood representing sacrifice, when the conscious mind begins to comprehend the mental side of life and the higher ideals which run counter to self-seeking principles. Therein lies the struggle, until the mind overcomes the undue attractions of the physical for their own sake.

159

Hence the saying of Jesus, "If any man will come after me, let him deny himself, and take up his cross, and follow me." (Matthew 16:24.) Also, "Take my yoke upon you and learn of me ... for my yoke is easy and my burden is light." (Matthew 11:29, 30.) To each and every one this becomes a truism as the mind grows more and more cognizant of the higher ideals of existence.

In other words, we must "overcome the world" (John 16:33), renounce the world in a certain sense, that is, after the physical has played its part through which consciousness has been unfolded, the next essential step in progression follows, the mental school.

This realization—referred to by Paul as a "newness of spirit" (Romans 7:6)—does not imply that the soul or mind must become lax or indifferent to the material; it must realize that while it is in the world yet it is not a part of the world; that as long as the individual is here he must carry on all duties pertaining to this life, meanwhile comprehending that when the physical journey is finished the soul will enter the next school.

This is the crucial point which many of the Bible writers attempted to convey in allegory as well as precept. It must be borne in mind that in most instances the stories of "Christ" in Bible allegories represent the world of the individual, his own struggles and an awakened conception of life.

To hold that "Sin against the Holy Ghost cannot be forgiven," as it implies a sin against God, is self-evidently erroneous, since God, the All-Wise, knows our propensity toward shortcomings and knows, in his wisdom, that ultimately, after sufficient experience, like the Prodigal Son, we will return to the road of rectitude.

"Sin against the Holy Ghost" is sinning against one's better nature. If we act against the dictates of conscience ("the oracle of God"), and live according to our own devices, the mistakes made must be corrected through a changed attitude and living in accordance with the dictum of conscience, otherwise they cannot be "forgiven." Only in this manner can the scales of justice be brought to balance.

To illustrate, Peter steals ten dollars from Paul and asks for forgiveness. Although Paul grants this the matter is not forgotten for the money has not been returned. But if

Peter returns the ten dollars and then asks Paul to forgive him, Paul will forgive and forget the offense.

Theologically, purgatory is defined as "an intermediate state after death where souls are made fit for heaven by expiatory suffering." As commonly taught and understood, purgatory is presumed to be a place of punishment for sins committed against God which require penitence, and forgiveness from God before the soul is permitted to enter heaven.

This doctrine is far from the real truth and is the source of much misery to both spirits and mortals. Many sensitive mortals have imbibed the erroneous belief that God is displeased and angry with them for mistakes they have made, and fear of the horrors of an eternal hell as a consequence of their disobedience is instilled into the erring, who are in dread and uncertainty lest after death they find themselves eternally "lost." This doctrine has driven thousands into cowering misery, insanity and suicide.

Dr. Mandel Sherman, of Chicago, states: "One exceedingly common form of insanity is religious mania." The evidence obtained in our research in abnormal psychology has shown that religiosity is a prominent manifestation in mental aberrations and insanity due to the impingement of fanatical religious spirits.

After transition many are in a twilight state of uncertainty since they have not found Jesus or God to be persons, as they had expected; these oftentimes labor under the mental torment that God has disowned them and that they will be consigned to ultimate hell on the fateful day of resurrection and condemnation.

In our experimental research in abnormal psychology we have contacted many spirits in this situation, their minds so warped by this fallacy that they were literally insane and most difficult to disillusion.

One such spirit, upon controlling Mrs. Wickland during a seance, began to shout loud exhortations.

Spirit   Now, friends, come to me and be saved!
Dr.
Wickland   To what church do you belong?

161

Sp.   The Methodist.

Dr.   You came to the right place.

Sp.   Are you Methodists?

Dr.   We try to be methodical. Where did you come from?

Sp.   I was told to come here to find out that I am dead. (Crying.) I want Jesus! Let us sing, "There is power, power in the Blood."

Dr.   We do not care to sing that. You have not told us your name.

Sp.   Bettie Shoemaker; we lived in Chicago, on Indiana Avenue, near Prairie. Then I lived on Calumet. I was in Kankakee. (An Illinois State Insane Asylum.)

Dr.   How did you happen to go to Kankakee?

Sp.   A fool doctor said I had too much religion. I wanted to preach all the time and save everybody. When you get religion you want everybody to get the same thing. Don't you want to belong to Jesus?

Dr.   Would you want everybody to act as you do?

Sp.   Am I acting foolish?

Dr.   Somewhat.

Sp.   I have not found Jesus yet. I have so much sin.

Dr.   I am afraid you will look a long time before you find him as you expect.

Sp.   I went to Dowie's Church, too. Dowie was wonderful. I am always afraid I might go to hell when I die.

Dr.   Your religion is certainly a sad one. Do you know you are a spirit?

Sp.   No.

Dr.   Were you sick?

Sp.   Yes. I went to Moody's Church and Dowie's Church. Then I was sent to Kankakee and I was there for a long, long time. They also said I had too much religion. The doctor said there was

162

something the matter with my mind. I know there was not; he was wrong.

Dr.   I want you to understand you are a spirit, invisible to us. You have lost your physical body but you yourself are not dead. No one ever "dies."

Sp.   My mother died. I went to her funeral. She's buried in Graceland Cemetery. (Chicago.) Oh, there's my father. (Seeing a spirit.) He went out of the church and after that mother did not care for him. He got crazy on Spiritualism.

Dr.   Does he look "crazy" now?

Sp.   No. Mother told him he would go to hell when he died, because that's where all Spiritualists go.

Dr.   Ask your father how he got out of "hell."

Sp.   Father says, "Heaven and hell are states of mind." Are you sure, Father? He says he told me they would have to put me in Kankakee if I didn't change my views.

He says, "You wanted to save everybody. I tried to teach you the truth and you thought I was crazy. I have brought you here to get understanding. You have been preaching religion since you passed out and we could not reach you. You must get a proper understanding of what life means."

"Now understand, there is no death. Heaven and hell are conditions which you bring with you. Christ was asked where the kingdom of Heaven is and he said, 'Within you.'"

"You would not listen to me; you only believed. No one could reason with you. Now you find yourself in darkness. I am right and you and your mother were wrong. I had to bring you here for enlightenment."

Dr.   So you see, your father was not wrong after all. He used reason; you did not.

Sp.   My mother is here, too, but she is still singing and praying.

Dr.   Perhaps you can awaken her to the truth of understanding.

163

Sp.	Father, are you going to take mother along with you? He says, "Yes." Oh, father, is it really true, as you used to tell us? Can I really believe it?
Dr.	You do not need to believe; get knowledge, and when you have knowledge there is no belief. You should study and understand God in the true sense of life, then you will not need to believe. Prove everything.
Sp.	Father, will you help me? (Crying.) I have cried and prayed because I didn't want to go to hell.
Dr.	You have had "hell." You have conditions as you make them.
Sp.	All these years I have believed in hell and now I find out it is not true. How I have suffered!
Dr.	Are you disappointed?
Sp.	I don't know yet. Why should people be taught that heaven and hell are places?
Dr.	The Bible says, "Add to your faith . . . knowledge" (II Peter 1:5) and "God is love; and he that dwelleth in love dwelleth in God." (I John 4:16.) How can you find such a God on the outside? You must find him within yourself through understanding. Jesus said, "Know the truth and the truth shall make you free." (John 8:32.)
Sp.	Do you believe in Jesus?
Dr.	I believe in his principles.
Sp.	Is he your Savior?
Dr.	The only "savior" you need is understanding.
Sp.	There's power in the Blood!
Dr.	Did it help you? You were placed in an asylum because of the "power in the blood" idea.
Sp.	I cried and prayed all the time.
Dr.	Now you must use reason.
Sp.	Father says, "Come with me, Bettie. Neither you nor your mother used reason." Now my

mother begins to realize her condition. Father says all we did was sing and pray. I would not work; I only went to church. He had to put me away.

(This spirit departed and the spirit father assumed control.)

2nd
Spirit   Now, Bettie, you are free. You and your mother will both realize in time what true religion is. I will take you both to my home in the spirit world and help you to understand.

(To Dr. Wickland.) "Thank you for helping my wife and child. I brought my daughter here. She has obsessed many people and they have been sent to asylums. At last I was able to bring her here; now she will begin to understand the new life."

"I thank you all very much for your help."

"Everyone should have understanding before going to the life beyond; the more you understand about the life hereafter the more rapid your progress. You will realize that death is only a sleep and an awakening to a beautiful condition."

"Without understanding, the transition is bewildering. The Bible says, 'Where your treasure is there will your heart be also.' (Matthew 6:21.) When your only treasure is earthly you will remain on earth when you pass out and will fail to realize the change."

"Have understanding in earth life of the next realm; you can then open the door to your spirit friends and relatives. They are anxious to come but doubt closes the door. Do not doubt your spirit friends. Be open-minded and they will come to you to help and guide you through life."

"Good-night and thank you."

165

Purgatory has a wider application than is held by theologians, for in reality it is not limited to the invisible side but has its beginnings even in this life. All of physical existence, from the cradle to the grave, is, in a sense, purgatorial, a process of purging or eliminating ignorance by acquiring knowledge and understanding.

"Enter ye in by the narrow gate: for wide is the gate, and broad is the way, that leadeth to destruction, and many be they that enter thereby. For narrow is the gate, and straightened the way, that leadeth unto life, and few be they that find it." (Matthew 7:13, 14.)

The broad way carries the soul into a spiritual morass; the narrow gate leads to the road of reason whereon few travel. To the orthodox, "destruction" means "hell"; in reality, following exclusively after material satisfaction leads to the "hell" of disappointment, discontent and sorrow, the "hell" of a disturbed conscience. The "narrow way" represents the pathway of reason whereon the hidden meaning of life is perceived.

Satan, or Lucifer, is an allegorical figure misconstrued by the orthodox interpreter as a personality. In early times principles were personified; thus the term "Satan" was only a figure of speech used to represent a principle in the creative scheme, the delusion of matter or the deception of material existence.

"Evil is the result of limitation and Satan is the Lord of Limit; he is the father of lies because matter is the cause of illusion." ("The Perfect Way," Kingsford-Maitland.)

"Matter opposes spirit" not actively but by causing illusion or deception regarding the meaning of existence. The mind is deceived by objective things and many come to the conclusion that when the physical body dies that is the end of existence. This illusory condition is the Deceiving Principle.

Following after the physical and its illusions causes pain and sorrow because mortal mind is so wedded to the physical that it is oblivious of its transitory nature. Our contact with the physical nature is only transient, and striving to cling to the physical and live for it alone ultimates in disappointment and sorrow.

166

"The things which are seen are temporal; but the things which are not seen are eternal." (2 Corinthians 4:18.) The nature of the outermost sphere is deception through which the soul receives its baptism, eventually perceiving that the physical is only a means to an end, namely, discernment of the spiritual principles. In other words, by "overcoming the world," figuratively speaking, man attains discernment of the higher meaning of existence—that life is eternal.

Edgar Allan Poe wrote:

"God is God from the creation;
　　Truth, truth alone, is man's salvation;
But the God that you now worship
　　Soon shall be your God no more;
For the soul, in its unfolding,
　　Ever-more its thought remolding,
Learns more truly, in its progress,
　　How to live and to adore."

CHAPTER VIII

Pictorial Religion

FROM the standpoint of nature's revelations it should be evident that the natural tendency of mankind, when uncontaminated by false human ideas, is toward beauty, love, wisdom and harmony. It has been said, there is no evil, only thinking makes it appear so. There is a great misconception concerning what is termed "sin," which, in the ordinary sense implies an element of evil.

Selfishness is the root of what seems to be evil, yet in reality the mother of Selfishness is Ignorance, or, in other words, lack of discernment of the design involved in the process of unfolding human intelligence from what may seem a chaotic and meaningless beginning into a realization of the divine plan.

Experience and manifold mistakes are the vivifying processes which arouse the thinking faculty and reasoning, ultimating in a quickened conscience, the "oracle of God." So what seems evil, while non-existent as an element, is really a means for attaining discernment.

The biblical statement that "spiritual things . . . are spiritually discerned" (I Corinthians 2:13, 14) pertains to invisible and intangible principles. Discernment is conveyed to the mind through the five special sense organs, hence through the ages symbols and allegorical pictures have been resorted to by teachers, thinkers and philosophers to facilitate the discernment of otherwise often incomprehensible spiritual truths and principles.

Each of the accompanying pictures is but a different presentation of the one fundamental principle pertaining to the soul's advent from the unconscious state to that of conscious self-realization. Each represents, from a different viewpoint, the same objective, the evolving of the conscious-

THE WILD ROSE

ness from the gross every-day material life into an understanding of the progressive principle in life.

"Understanding is a wellspring of life unto him that hath it." (Proverbs 16:22.) "Happy is the man that findeth wisdom, and the man that getteth understanding." (Proverbs 3:13.)

In the picture, "The Wild Rose" (opposite page 168), the wild rose in its struggle for existence is used symbolically to convey a comparative illustration of the soul's struggles with obstacles. The earth is seen as barren and forbidding; the rose begins with a shoot, develops stem, leaves and thorns alternately and struggles along under unfavorable conditions, culminating in the flower from which emanates the delicate fragrance, the soul or essence of the flower, invisible yet discernible at a distance, giving evidence that it is actual substance.

. The veil, springing from the void and descending to the barren earth, symbolizes the soul's advent into materiality. As a veil conceals, thus is depicted the unconscious condition of the soul upon its entry into this mundane sphere, when comprehension of the meaning of existence is yet in an embryonic state.

The green leaf gives promise of harvest to the sower, hence the leaf is used to represent hope. From infancy on, the individual contacts external problems by means of the five special sense organs and he is constantly instilled with hope of attainment. Disappointments, like thorns, agitate the soul yet quicken its understanding and reasoning faculties.

Gradually the soul realizes the evanescent and elusive nature of material attainments and develops a quickened consciousness of life's higher meaning. Slowly it recognizes itself as consciousness and through contemplation gains understanding of The Mystery—that by contacting the physical through the avenue of the five senses, self-realization is accomplished.

In transcendental language the soul is referred to as virgin, hence the soul is presented in the picture as a female figure. As the butterfly wings represent the emergence of the butterfly into the fullness of development and

169

glory, so likewise the soul emerges from the cruder conditions of life into a fuller expression, ascending through understanding and knowledge obtained from the experience acquired through the five senses.

From involvement in the darkness of materiality the soul evolves into the light of understanding, and the radiating, golden hair represents the soul's liberation from ignorance into effulgent understanding.

The rod, pointing downward, symbolizes the knowledge obtained by use of the five special senses (indicated by the five-pointed star) in Time, represented by the dial.

In the picture (opposite page 170) entitled "Night's Swift Dragons Cut the Clouds Full Fast," Night is to be interpreted as the darkness of ignorance, the Dragons as Time, the two heads as the sense of right and wrong acquired in Time; the wings of the Dragons are typical of the flight of Time.

The central figure represents the Soul in Time; the winged Cherub, the Universal Spirit, which guides the journey of the Soul through Time. The slumbering Infant represents Truth, the Son of Man, which is born through the inter-action of the guidance, promptings and inspiration of the Universal Spirit and the Soul's tribulations and experiences in the external world whereby conscience is quickened.

The veil represents the condition of the Soul which is veiled until the Infant, Truth, Son of Man, is born, when the Veil of Ignorance drops away—"Isis unveiled."

The meditative attitude of the Soul, the central figure, is indicative of the thinking or reasoning processes, through which understanding is acquired.

NIGHT'S SWIFT DRAGONS CUT THE CLOUDS FULL FAST

The picture, "Dawn of the Christian Era" (opposite page 172), is symbolic of the admonition of Jesus to overcome the world, and illustrates, as do the other pictures, a mental process.

In the picture Bethlehem is shown at night time—the night of ignorance. "Bethel" means "House of God" (the soul); "Bethlehem" means "Place of Food." Jesus was born in Bethlehem in a stable and laid in a manger, which may be compared to our physical existence, since physically we are only a higher class of animal creatures.

The stable, a place where animals are kept, figuratively depicts our contacts with each other, whereby experiences of various kinds are received. The manger, a place for food, portrays the feeding of our souls, that is, the mind and soul faculties are slowly evolving, through experience, consciousness and the sense of right and wrong, which will ultimately culminate in the birth of Truth, esoterically, the Son of Man.

Seen at the top of the picture is a globe, which, with its radiations, is commonly designated the Star in the East, but is really a representation of the earth. The four prominent radiations symbolize the four chief elements: air, earth, water and fire; the other radiations, the result of the interchanging combinations of these elements.

The five-pointed star in the center represents our five special sense organs, by means of which, as previously stated, the Soul contacts the physical world and thereby unfolds consciousness.

The female figure symbolizes the Soul which has discerned the mystery of life and the meaning of overcoming the world, indicated by the globe, surmounted by the cross, held in the outstretched hand. The cross represents, as before mentioned, the four chief elements, or the Passion Cross, which is symbolic of the struggles and tribulations of earthly experience.

The expression, "flight of thought," is symbolized by wings, hence the wings in the picture signify thinking and reasoning, which have rewarded the soul with an intelligent understanding of nature's hidden meaning.

Through this clear discernment the Soul has secured its

liberation from slavish ignorance and attained the light of understanding, thereby acquiring the laurel wreath of victory and the olive branch of peace.

LIGHT SHINING OUT OF DARKNESS

WILLIAM COWPER

God moves in a mysterious way,
　　His wonders to perform;
He plants his footsteps in the sea
　　And rides upon the storm.

Deep in unfathomable mines
　　Of never failing skill,
He treasures up his bright designs,
　　And works his sovereign will.

Ye fearful saints fresh courage take,
　　The clouds ye so much dread
Are big with mercy, and shall break
　　In blessings on your head.

Judge not the Lord by feeble sense,
　　But trust him for his grace;
Behind a frowning providence
　　He hides a smiling face.

His purposes will ripen fast
　　Unfolding ev'ry hour;
The bud may have a bitter taste,
　　But sweet will be the flow'r.

Blind unbelief is sure to err,
　　And scan his work in vain;
God is his own interpreter,
　　And he will make it plain.

DAWN OF THE CHRISTIAN ERA

The picture, "Flight into Egypt" (opposite page 174), is but another presentation of the Soul's journey through life, the female figure, or Mary, representing the Soul which, raising the veil reveals the Son of Man, or Truth—realized through experience, typified by Joseph—through which wisdom is instilled.

The donkey, one of the most docile and faithful of animals, is used to portray patience, a highly important quality requisite for the Soul's progression in this mortal existence.

The staff is symbolic of faith, which is the companion of experience, aiding the soul onward to a higher destiny.

The spirits, or angels, hovering over the group illustrate the statement "compassed about with so great a cloud of witnesses." (Hebrews 12:1.) The broken column is symbolic of the transient and temporary nature of all things mortal.

The cherub, guiding the donkey, is symbolic of the ever-present Universal Intelligence, or Over-Soul, which, in infinite wisdom recognizes the necessity of the Soul's transit through the mortal sphere of limitations whereby it ultimately realizes its one-ness with the non-limited Spirit.

The picture, "A little Child shall lead them" (opposite page 175), is another beautiful symbolical illustration of the regenerative principles in the mental laboratory of man. Many Bible quotations confirm the meaning which the picture is intended to convey.

"The spirit of the Lord shall rest upon him, the spirit of wisdom and understanding, the spirit of counsel and might, the spirit of knowledge . . . And the wolf shall dwell with the lamb, and the leopard shall lie down with the kid; and the calf and the young lion and the fatling together; and a little child shall lead them." (Isaiah 11:2, 6.)

In the picture desolation and ruin are seen in the right background, depicting the evanescent and transient nature of empires and nations. On the physical plane all is change.

173

The man in the left background, dejected and forlorn, represents one who, in a sense, has reached the end of the trail of self-seeking, the desert depicting such desolation. How many are in that predicament, without a clear conception of the why of mortal tribulations, the intellect having followed only after the grosser material, while the spiritual remained unperceived.

This dejected state of mind impels thinking which awakens the intuitive faculty; then is borne upon the mind the realization that self-seeking is characteristic of intellectual pursuits.

The various characteristics of mortal pursuits and striving are represented by the animals in the picture. The animal propensities of Cain, cold human intellect, which ordinarily are constantly killing Abel, the intuitive faculty, have been subdued and overcome, and harmony prevails.

The signs of the Zodiac are pictured as animals representing characteristics expressed in the mental life of mankind. The nature of the Ram is to butt, hence the first sign of the Zodiac, Aries, or the Ram, is used to symbolize the headstrong and self-willed traits of man when dominated by cold intellect and selfishness.

In the left foreground of the picture a ram's skull indicates that the cold intellect has given place to intuition or spiritual perception; selfish will is dead and new life, or a newness of spirit, like the flowers, springs forth.

The ram's skull signifies the overcoming of selfishness; the fierce selfish trend pertaining to the intellect, represented by the animals, has been subdued.

The angel hovering over the man symbolizes the awakening intuition, or conscience, inspiring man to realize that his pursuit in life has been only along lines of cold intellect and self-seeking, while the inner promptings, urging recognition of a broader purpose of existence, have been ignored. In the regenerative process of reasoning the Soul perceives that self-seeking has ended in bitter disappointment and that a newness of spirit through understanding is necessary.

This soul process does not imply the need of religious emotionalism but the simple discernment of these truths and the adjustment of one's life accordingly.

174

FLIGHT INTO EGYPT

A LITTLE CHILD SHALL LEAD THEM

The Angel of Inspiration points upward, away from objective delusions, to a discernment of the higher meaning of life, hitherto dormant.

After overcoming self, man must replace cold intellect with a child-like spirit. The nature of a child is simple; it has no preconceived notions or opinions and intuitively asks for knowledge. Hence the Child in the picture symbolizes the new attitude required for perception of the meaning of the higher purpose of existence.

"Except . . . ye become as little children . . . ye shall in no wise enter into the kingdom of heaven." (Matthew 18:3.)

"Whosoever shall not receive the kingdom of God as a little child, he shall in no wise enter therein." (Mark 10:15.)

"Whosoever therefore shall humble himself as this little child, the same is the greatest in the kingdom of heaven." (Matthew 18:4.)

The Child symbolizes the spirit of Love, Purity and Understanding, while Spiritual Serenity is indicated by the Branch of Peace held in the hand of the child, for when spiritual illumination enlightens the stony pathway of physical existence the Soul awakens to Harmony and Peace.

175

CHAPTER IX

Is There a God?

"S THERE a God? What shall I believe or not believe? How may I understand the meaning of existence?" These are paramount questions in the minds of many who feel intuitively that there must be a comprehensible interpretation of the enigma of life.

The Atheist denies there is an intelligent, causative factor in nature and life. His reasons for denial of an intelligent Cause in the manifest universe and its activities are largely based upon the apparent contradictions found in the story of a theological God and observance of the upheavals in the world and the many wrongs so manifest on every hand in mundane life.

Ruins of bygone ages prove to him that numberless races aspired and struggled to attain permanency, yet perished, leaving only ruins as mute evidence that decadence is the end. He is therefore convinced from superficial reasoning that there cannot be a guiding Intelligence and that nature and life are the result of mere chance. To him the Ship of the Universe is rudderless, without compass, chart or Captain, subject to the caprices and storms of blind force.

Agnosticism holds the theory that God is unknown and unknowable, that "first truths, substance, cause, especially the human soul and a First Cause, can neither be proved nor disproved, and must remain unknown and unknowable."

The average Agnostic believes that nothing pertaining to creation and life is knowable, and, accepting the foregoing theories dogmatically, avoids reasoning out problems for himself, meanwhile refusing to accept the evidence obtained by research of others in Nature's Arcana, which clearly indicates that much is knowable relating to the purpose of the phenomena of nature and life. In other words, "he will not enter himself, nor will he let others enter."

Many physical scientists who repudiate the illogical doctrines of orthodoxy become atheists and formulate the theory that mind and intelligence are only the resultant of the inter-action of cells—when cells cease to act man is no more.

In rejecting the old worn-out theory of orthodoxy, skeptical scientists reject with it an intelligent Designer, thus attempting to "throw away the baby with the bath water." Science is judging by cold intellect (Cain), and is pushing the intuitive faculty (Abel) into the background.

Fatalists of various degrees deny a future existence and are inclined to ignore the promptings of conscience, assuming the attitude that "We live today, tomorrow we die." Hence many live only for physical attractions, oftentimes becoming callous and indifferent to higher ideals of conduct and, for want of better understanding, do not hesitate to stoop to any wrong activity or crime.

When a clergyman, supposed to be especially protected by God, "goes wrong," deserts his wife and family to elope with a sixteen-year-old girl, and his congregation re-establishes him in his pulpit with full honors, ostracizing, however, not only the girl but her family as well, or when a minister of the gospel, as reported recently, murders his wife that he may marry a girl of nineteen, many declare there is no Divine Justice in the universe.

Disasters overtake the just as well as the unjust. Accidents, floods, epidemics or appalling physical cataclysms afflict believers in an all-wise Providence as well as "sinners"; an earthquake may shatter even the very structure wherein a reverent congregation is gathered in religious devotion. Such disasters shake the faith not only of skeptics but of the believers in a loving Father; they become despondent and conclude there is no God or Justice whatever, contending that otherwise such distress would not be permitted.

The trials of mortal existence and the apparent absence of a Guiding Intelligence in life are conducive, in the average mind, to rejection of the possibility of any supreme Being, purpose of life, existence of the soul or a future life after death. This seeming enigma is the source of much misery and sorrow, as well as evil, in the world today.

Dr. Frank N. Freeman, of the University of Chicago, speaking to the Conference on Research in Child Development in Chicago, declared, "There is no such thing as intelligence apart from training."

Dr. A. Douglas Singer, jointly with other authorities who assert that all metaphysical views must be completely surrendered for a more scientific conception of mind and that psychology must be properly placed in the scale of biologic evolution, states, "It does away altogether with any appeal to a separate will or soul."

Herbert Spencer asserted that he had no reason for hope of a continued existence. Many brilliant men of science hold the opinion that the grave ends all human efforts. The eminent Sir Arthur Keith asserted that as the light of a candle is blown out, so is life extinguished when the body dies. Even the brilliant Edison was reported as believing that mind is the result of cell activity and that when this activity ceases there is no longer any mind.[1]

Many persons who are in distress from various causes read such theories given out by those who are considered authorities and, concluding that after all life is only a meaningless phantasm, are encouraged to attempt self-destruction, hoping that this will end everything.

If it were actually a fact that death ends all one would be inclined, in many instances, to say, "So mote it be." But research in normal and abnormal psychology proves facts to the contrary.

The conclusions of these materialists are totally illogical. They reason only from the materialistic sense, or intellect. Again is illustrated the Bible statement (I Cor. 2:14), "The natural man receiveth not the things of the Spirit of God, for they are foolishness unto him; neither can he know

---

[1] However, following Mr. Edison's death the Associated Press reported: "A few days before Mr. Edison passed away he was sitting in his chair apparently enjoying a pleasant dream. Suddenly opening his eyes and gazing upward into space, his face illuminated with a smile, he said: 'It is very beautiful over there.' Had the great inventor climbed the heights which lead into eternity and caught a glimpse beyond the veil which obstructs our earthly vision?"

them because they are spiritually discerned"; such persons judge only from appearances.

Since the physical body ceases to function at death (so-called) it is therefore concluded that the individual also is dead and that is the end of the chapter. Clarence Darrow declared: "I am glad to take refuge in the one consolation that life does not amount to much, and I should worry!" He also says that man is a mere machine, yet he does not explain what operates the machine.

The physical form has its beginning from the union of two infinitesimal cells; through gestation an intricate, complex body is developed, built up by a multitude of different cells; each organ, in order to carry out its specific function, requires a different class of cells. What is it that carries on this building process?

It is unreasonable to suppose that the individual cells could know where to place themselves in the respective organs for which they are intended or that they could construct each organ in the proper place in the body and develop the organ and its function, all to culminate in a harmonious interaction of organs, a completed, wonderful, living, acting structure.

To make this claim is the same as saying that the individual bricks in a building, had they the faculty of cells, would know where to place themselves, thus resulting in a finished structure. We know how illogical that would be. It requires the architect and the artisan to place the material where it belongs. Always there is the material plus Intelligent Guidance.

A scientific journal recently reported the microscopic observations of Dr. Carl Caskey Speidel, University of Virginia anatomist; these findings revealed the growth of nerves in the living body and show that living nerves sprout from the spinal cord, going directly to the muscle or sense organ they are destined to connect with the central nervous system. The magazine commented upon this: "But out of his success there will arise, as is often the case in science, a still more difficult question—How does the nerve know how to travel unerringly to its destination? Thus the door is held open to some uncomprehended commanding purpose,

179

which some will call a manifestation of some sort of god, to rule the course of the growth of living things."

How can a thinking mind escape from the realization that there is a living, organizing Something which carries on the process of body-building, constructs the organs in their respective places, each to carry on a particular function conjointly and harmoniously with every other organ and its function, all resulting in the wonderful human structure?

Foods of various kinds are placed in the stomach, something activates them, subdividing them into combinations to be carried through the circulation, finally to be absorbed by the functioning organ for which they are intended.

What is it that carries on this chemicalizing process? Let the sophist study anatomy, biology, physiology, organic chemistry and related subjects, always with the view in mind of perceiving that there is a Something Plus, which intelligently carries on the life functions. "Know God by inference."

In studying the egg and the chick we find at first no chick in the egg, yet, warm the egg for a sufficient length of time and we marvel at what emerges from the shell, a living creature, we may say, a machine full of mechanical contrivances, in number up to something like twenty-one, all conforming to one definite, combined activity. Again, what operates this internal machine shop? Did the yolk and the white create that chick, or was it organized by an involved Something, plus a directing Mind?

The biologist strives to prove that life originated in the ocean; beginning with the primary cell, life is declared to evolve, stage after stage, from non-vertebrates gradually to vertebrates, until it finally reaches the human stage only, however, to end in—the grave!

Why do not the scientists, eager to uncover the origin of human existence, follow up with similar enthusiasm the question of what becomes of the ego after apparent death?

This is seemingly a conundrum. What is the use of biological research to determine origins, if life ends at the grave? Logically, from that standpoint, individual existence would be a cruel mockery.

180

After all, what does the process of our physical evolution matter, or how we arrived here? We are now here and the question should be, WHY are we here?

Science speculates and endeavors to measure the limits of the universe. "End there is none to the universe of God," said Jean Paul Richter. It should be evident that the present state of the mind of man is too limited to fully comprehend the vastness of the universe and creation.

Science, delving into chemistry and physics, reveals processes of atomic inter-activity and fundamental laws of mechanics in the construction of atoms and their activity in the formation of various physical substances, demonstrating the inter-play of the invisible and objective nature.

To further illustrate the inter-play of visible and invisible, the three phases of material activity are solid, liquid and gaseous. Water is composed of H_2O, that is, two parts of Hydrogen, an explosive, and one part of Oxygen, which supports combustion, or fire, yet these two combine as water and will put out fire.

Water exhibits threefold phenomena: as liquid it evaporates and becomes invisible vapor; through contacting lower temperature it condenses back into liquid; a greater amount of coldness congeals it into a solid, ice. Thus by the inter-action of varying temperatures these changes occur.

Likewise all material things may be reduced from visible to invisible substance. Attach a wire to a carbon element, another wire to a zinc element, place the two in a jar and add water and a little acid. These are all visible elements, yet by connecting to the other ends of the wires an electric light globe you will have light, or attach a motor and you will have power, energy, again revealing the inter-play of visible and invisible nature.

So through all avenues of research in the physical realm marvelous revelations are obtained of an invisible Source. We do not need to "believe" in the next life; we need only use our minds to observe the evidence on every side.

In contemplating the activities of the universe vast wonders are revealed. Dr. Robert A. Millikan sees in the universe God's fingerprints, and in the cosmic ray the operation of a force which continually renews the universe, a force to which he applies the word "Creator."

Dr. Albert Einstein, the noted German scientist and philosopher, propounder of the theory of relativity, according to a magazine article, "confesses to a profound reverence and awe when he contemplates the cosmic mystery. He does not believe that God is man made large, nor does he believe that there is any such thing as sin in the commonly accepted meaning of that word."

"But he has a point of view which he says is common to those who, like he, have attempted to plumb the sources of the universe and have ever been confronted with the secret of its origin. He names it the 'cosmic religious sense,' and it is the natural result of his research."

"Religion, he says, in effect, is the response to man's inherent needs. Among primitive people it developed into the 'religion of fear'—fear of hunger, of wild animals, of illness and death showing itself in deeds and sacrifices intended to secure the protective favor of an anthropomorphic, or manlike divinity."

"Next came the religion which has its source in the social feelings of human beings—in the longing for guidance, love, comfort by a Providence who protects, decides, rewards and punishes. This, he says, is the social or moral idea of God. But all religions, he holds, are mixed forms, though the moral element rules in the higher levels of social life. Common to these types is the anthropomorphic character of the idea of God."

"To these two forms Dr. Einstein adds a third, which exceptionally gifted individuals may attain, though traces of it are found in some who have never made researches in the universe, as the Psalmist David and the Prophets. And it is this that he calls the 'cosmic religious sense.'"

He says, "The religious geniuses of all times have been distinguished by this cosmic religious sense, which recognizes neither dogmas nor God made in man's image."

"For anyone who is pervaded with the sense of causal law in all that happens, who accepts in real earnest the assumption of causality, the idea of a Being who interferes with the sequence of events in the world is absolutely impossible. Neither the religion of fear nor the social-moral religion can have any hold on him."

"A God who rewards and punishes is for him unthinkable, because man acts in accordance with an inner and outer necessity, and would, in the eyes of God, be as little responsible as an inanimate object for the movements which it makes."

"The ethical behavior of man is better based on sympathy, education, and social relationships, and requires no support from religion. Man's plight would, indeed, be sad if he had to be kept in order through fear of punishment and hope of reward after death."

"I assert," he concludes, "that the cosmic religious experience is the strongest and the noblest driving force behind scientific research."

Dr. Constantine Panunzio, of the faculty of the University of California at Los Angeles, "represents a section of scientific thought that regards as futile any discussion of an unprovable hereafter 'where all tears will be wiped away,'" states the introduction to an article reporting an interview with Dr. Panunzio on social psychology and the political, economic and cultural conditions which are the cause of social evils prevalent in modern life. "He would increase the sum of happiness in this life, ameliorate much of its harshness through education rather than faith, and take chances on the life to come—if any."

Dr. Panunzio is quoted as saying: "Today, owing to what I feel to be the passing of the influence of dogmatic religion —the change from an age of faith to an age of facts—I believe scientific fact-finding will impress more persons than religious dogma."

"The idea that there is a cosmic religion above all creeds, with the idea that eternity is an extended here-and-now rather than endless time—or timelessness—after death . . . carries with it the desire to minimize the necessity of suffering and sacrifice . . . and to find prompt, present happiness."

It is necessary that we realize the vastness of the human soul and mentally separate the limited from the unlimited. Through contact with the physical we recognize ourselves as sentient, conscious beings, discern our transient condition and realize the limitation of the earthly. The mind, freed from limitations through analytical thinking, perceives the relationship between the external and internal, the seen and the unseen and ultimately realizes the importance of the earth experience received through the physical form.

The celebrated Smaragdine Tablet of Hermes Trismegistus wonderfully elucidates the nature of God, the origin of the world, creation and divine illumination, the study of which affords a rich mental pabulum, exercising as it does the mental faculties, for it requires thinking and reasoning which, figuratively, liberate the mind and soul from the mere physical.

"It is true without falsehood, certain and absolute. That which is below is as that which is above, and that which is above is as that which is below, to accomplish the miracles of one thing, and as all things were from one, by the mediation of one, so all born things were from that one thing's adaptation."

"Separate the earth from the fire, the subtle from the gross very carefully and with ingenuity. It ascends from the earth into Heaven, then again descends into the earth and receives the force of above and below."

"Thus shalt thou have the glory of the entire world; then shall every darkness fly before thee."

"Below" is the shadow side of the Creator wherein mankind finds expression in nature, a necessary condition. "Below" is the seen, the external, the mortal phase of existence, the temporary.

"Above" refers to the unseen, the internal, the immortal phase of existence, the eternal.

God is both spirit and substance expressed in the external, at once both Creator and Creation.

In the dialog between Hermes and Intelligence these characters should not be understood as personalities but as principles, Hermes representing the Spirit of Understanding, or the Desire to Know, and Intelligence representing Wisdom.

184

The dialog follows in part:

Hermes to Intelligence:

"The opinions upon the universe and upon God are numerous and different, and I know not the truth. Enlighten me, O Master, for I can but believe thy revelation!"

Intelligence to Hermes:

"Learn, my son, what God and the Universe is—God, Eternity, the World, Time, and Generation. God causes Eternity, Eternity causes the World, the World causes Time, Time causes Generation. Good, Beauty, Happiness and Wisdom are the essence of God."

"The essence of Eternity is Identity, that of the World is Order, that of Time is change, that of Generation is Life and Death."

"The energies of God are intelligence and the soul, those of eternity are permanence and immortality, those of the world, composition and decomposition, those of time are increase and decrease, those of generation, quality."

"Eternity is in God, the world is in eternity. Time is in the world, generation is in time. Eternity remains fixed in God, the world moves in eternity, time is accomplished in the world, generation is produced in time. The power of God is eternity, the work of eternity is the world, which has not been created at one time, but which is ever being created by eternity; also will it never perish, for eternity is imperishable, and nothing is lost in the world because the world is enveloped by eternity."

Eternity is that in which manifestation takes place; it is not a thing, empty and vacant; it is formless, endless space, fixedness, permanence, changeless, forever the same.

In the eternal verities certain causes produce certain effects, exact laws of nature and of mind permit exact developments. In nature everything develops according to definite, innate, unwritten laws.

There is dissolution of the physical form yet the soul, or essence, which is invisible, persists after the form is dissolved. Visible things may be transformed into invisible. Life activity in nature causes appearances which again decompose and disappear, recurring again in endless succession.

"The energies of generation are quality," declares Intelligence. There are certain spirit essences in everything—in plants, medicines, foods, animals, human beings—each has its particular and differing characteristic. Yet that characteristic is an invisible principle. This invisible essence is often sensed by sensitives when contacting the external form.

Without "qualities" life would be chaos. As in the arts the much-used "curve of beauty" is necessary to disclose innate form possibilities, so without an objective creation, a physical world, the invisible principles could not become apparent.

The manifest is revealing itself in an eternal void; all things evidence inherent, intelligent Principle, changeless, eternal.

Again quoting from the Smaragdine Tablet:

Hermes:
"And what is the Wisdom of God?"

Intelligence:
"Good, Beauty, Happiness, all Virtue and Eternity. In penetrating matter, eternity gives it immortality and permanence, for its generation depends upon eternity, and eternity depends upon God. Generation and Time are the two different Natures in Heaven. Immovable and incorruptible in Heaven, movable and perishable on earth. The soul of eternity is God, the soul of the world is eternity, the soul of the earth is Heaven."

"God is in intelligence, Intelligence is in the soul, the Soul is in matter, and all throughout Eternity. The Soul fills the universal body that contains all bodies; Intelligence and God fill the soul. Fill the internal and envelope the externals. The soul animates the universe; from without, that great and perfect animal, the world; from within, all living beings. There on high in Heaven she dwells in identity; here below on earth she transforms generations."

"Eternity sustains the world by necessity, by Providence,

186

by nature; the explanation that can be given matters little. God acts in all the universe. This energy is a sovereign power to which nothing human or Divine can be compared. Believe not, Hermes, that nothing below or above is like God; thou wouldst be far from the truth. Nothing resembles to the dissimilar, the soul, the One; and believe not that another shares his power."

"To which other will you attribute life, immortality, changes? What would it do else? God is not idle, otherwise all would be repose, for God fills all. Inertia exists not in the world, nor anywhere, neither in the Creator, nor in the creation—it is an empty word. It is necessary that all things should become forever and everywhere, for the Creator is all, has no particular abode. He creates not one thing or another, but all things. His creative power dwells not in the beings he has created, they remain dependent on Him. Were God to separate himself from his work life would be withdrawn, and all would be at an end; for He is at once the Creator and the Creation."

"All is living, Life is One, and God is Life. Life is the union of Spirit and Soul; Death is the rupture of what was united. Man calls transformation Death, because the material body is decomposed, and life ceases to be visible or apparent; but my dear Hermes, you may understand that the world itself is transformed continually. Each day some part of it disappears without its ever decomposing. These revolutions and these disappearances are the passions (or phases) of the world. Revolution is a return; disappearance is a renewal. The world contains every form, they are not outside of it, it transforms itself in them."

"But if every form is in the world, what must be the form of the Creator? He cannot be without form, and if he had but one form, he would be inferior to the world. What then shall we say of Him that we may not say anything imperfect? For one cannot think of God as incomplete. He has a form which is His own; which does not appear to the eyes of the body, but which is in all bodies. Be not astonished that He has an incorporeal form. So it is with the form of a discourse, or the margin of a manuscript which borders the lines, and is even and equal."

"Reflect upon a word which is bold and true. Just as a

187

man cannot live without life, so God cannot live without doing good. The life and the movement of God is to move and make live. Some words have a particular sense; reflect then upon what I shall tell you."

"All is in God, not as something placed in a place, for the place is corporeal and immovable, and things which are in a place have no movement. God is in the incorporeal, otherwise than in appearance. Understand that He contains all; understand that nothing is so rapid, so vast, so strong, as the incorporeal; it surpasses everything in capacity, in celerity, in power."

"Perceive this in yourself—order your soul to go to India, and it is there, and it is there quicker than your order. Order it to go to the ocean, and it is there at once, not by moving from one place to another, but on the instant. Order it to mount to Heaven, and to do so it requires no wings; nothing will stop it, neither fire nor sun, nor ether, nor whirl-winds, nor the bodies of the stars—it will traverse all and will fly beyond all bodies."

"Do you desire to pass this limit and to contemplate what is outside of the world? If there is anything, you can do so. See what power, what quickness you possess, and think you that what you can do, God cannot? Conceive of God as having in Himself all thoughts, the whole world. If you cannot equal and compare yourself to God, you cannot comprehend Him. Like comprehends like. Enlarge yourself to an immense size; outpass all bodies; traverse all times, become eternity, and you will conceive and understand God. Nothing can prevent you from supposing yourself immortal and all-knowing, Arts, Sciences, the habits of all animals."

"Lift yourself above all heights; descend below all depths, collect in yourself every sensation of all created things, of water, of fire, of the dry and the wet. Suppose that you are everywhere at the same time, on Earth, in the Sea, in Heaven; that you have never been born; that you are still in embryo; that you are young, old, dead, beyond death; comprehend all things at once, time, place, things, quantities, qualities, and you will comprehend God."

"But if you shut up your soul in the body and if you humble yourself and say: 'I understand nothing, I can do

188

nothing; I neither know what I am, nor what I shall be,' what are you in common with God? If you are bad and attached to a body, what can you understand of great and good things?"

"Not to recognize the Divine is the perfection of evil, but to be able to perceive, to desire it, and to hope for it, is the means of reaching it by a direct and easy road. By following it, you will see it everywhere; in the places and in the hour where you least expect it; in wakefulness and in sleep; at sea, in traveling, by night and by day, in speaking and in keeping silence; for there is not anything but what is the image of God."

"God is not invisible; there is nothing more apparent than God. If he has created all things, it is that we may see Him in and through all things. This is the good of God; this is His virtue, to appear in all; nothing is invisible, even amongst the incorporeal."

"Intelligence is seen in thought; God in creation. This is what I had to reveal to you, oh, Trismegistus! Look for it in yourself and you will not lose your way."

It is impossible to think of God as being outside of eternity; eternity is unlimited and God is unlimited. "God is to the soul what the soul is to the body," said Plutarch. While God, time and eternity are incomprehensible to mortal man they have, according to enlightened spirits, a different aspect in the spirit world, and fuller understanding of the original Source is attained in the next life.

CHAPTER X

Christian Science

NATURE'S processes are evolutionary and progressive; our minds, likewise, should be resilient at all times, open to new truths and ready to accept what seems most reasonable. It behooves us to constantly scrutinize various premises of faith instead of adopting fixed, dogmatic mental attitudes as final. Truth, to be of value, must be self-evident.

"Truth" was the subject of a recent Christian Science Lesson-Sermon in which the following excerpt from "Science and Health with Key to the Scriptures," by Mary Baker Eddy, was given:

"Truth has no consciousness of error. Love has no sense of hatred. Life has no partnership with death. Truth, Life and Love are a law of annihilation to everything unlike themselves, because they declare nothing except God."

That the above assertions are absorbed as undeniable truths by Christian Science devotees goes without saying, but after all, are they actually scientific statements, as the Church assumes them to be?

The question arises, if truth has no consciousness of error how is one to know that the implied truth is not in itself an error?

Why is not the soul at its first awakening into consciousness aware of its divine nature, of its oneness with the Source of its being and fully conscious of the state of perfection alluded to in the citation?

If an inexperienced human entity were born into this perfect state, now only vaguely sensed, would it not be unable to fathom the meaning of such a condition? Hence the need of the mortal.

Since God is all-in-all why are we in this transient plane of travail? Is not the attainment of truth the very keynote of the purpose of our physical mortal journey of the spirit?

Why do Christian Scientists talk about error when they do not recognize the existence of such? If "hatred" is non-existent, why use the expression? If there is no "death," why use the term?

If "Truth, Life and Love are a law of annihilation to everything unlike themselves" and "error, hatred and death" do not exist, what is there to annihilate?

To affirm "God is good; God is love; all will be provided," does not obviate physical necessities and will not fill an empty stomach. We must apply ourselves to fulfilling physical needs for which the Creator has provided means of sustenance.

Even Christian Scientists pass through the genetic state of what they term "error" and occupy a physical form, which is only "error," they depend upon air, food, clothing and money—all "errors"—and remain in these physical errors until the objective form (error) is disposed of in the grave or goes up in smoke, steam and ashes in the crematory —mortal errors.

Seriously, why the need of closing our eyes to the facts of life? We are born into a vehicle or house—the transient, mortal form—having five windows (sight, hearing, taste, smell and touch) through which the occupant, or indwelling spirit, contacts the external expression of nature.

When first entering the physical, the indwelling spirit is unconscious of itself, but through the means of the "windows" the spirit reaches out and thereby enters the rough school of mortal existence.[1] Slowly the inherent qualities of consciousness, intelligence and the faculty of reasoning are unfolded and gradually Truth is discerned and Love is developed.

Paul's definition of Love (I Corinthians 13:4-6) is clearly elucidated by Henry Drummond:

" 'Love suffereth long'................................Patience.
'And is kind'................................Kindness.
'Love envieth not'................................Generosity.

[1] See "Adam and Eve," Chapter VII, "Dogma Spiritualized," Page 153.

'Love vaunteth not itself,
　　is not puffed up'.................................Humility.
'Doth not behave itself unseemly'.............Courtesy.
'Seeketh not her own'.............................Unselfishness.
'Is not easily provoked'.........................Good Temper.
'Thinketh no evil'...................................Guilelessness.
'Rejoiceth not in iniquity,
　　but rejoiceth in the truth'.................Sincerity."

Let us analyze what these Ingredients of Love—Patience, Kindness, Generosity, Humility, Courtesy, Unselfishness, Good Temper, Guilelessness and Sincerity—represent; let us make a practice of emulating them in every-day life. It will soon be discovered that this is no easy task but requires time, perseverance and constant self-examination to make each a living reality in our daily life.

Through experience in this school of right and wrong is unfolded the analytical principle—Wisdom, which discerns the meaning of the Divine Comedy, namely, the necessity of the journey through the transient mortal, a mere Passing-Through State.

The spirit having entered the Visible unconsciously, re-enters the Invisible consciously, stepping out of the physical through the Gateway of Transition ("Death" being only a releasing of the indwelling Intelligence from the physical tabernacle) into a Higher School of Attainment.

Christian Science teaches the Allness of God, Spirit, and the consequent unreality or nothingness of matter. In "Science and Health with Key to the Scriptures," Mrs. Eddy says: "There is no life, truth, intelligence, nor substance in matter. All is infinite Mind and its infinite manifestation, for God is All-in-All."

In this advanced stage of scientific research such statements are meaningless affirmations, a mere play of words. Who knows the ultimate reality of matter? Just as no one can define the nature of life, so no one knows the kinship of life and matter.

After all, what is matter? To say that objective forms and all manifestations that reach our senses are not real facts and not substantial, as the senses perceive these facts, is neither logic nor science.

That many fail to use reason but accept fiction for fact was illustrated by a woman, a Christian Scientist, who claimed that the latest discovery was that the brain is not necessary and related the story of a man who was undergoing a brain operation at a hospital in New York.

The physician had temporarily removed the brain when a fire broke out, the patient ran away and the brain was placed in alcohol. Some years later the doctor met this patient on the street and said to him, "You had better come back to the hospital to get your brain." The man replied, "I don't need any brain now; I am working for the Government!"

"But that is only a story," the woman was told.

"Oh, no," she said, "this actually happened and it proves that we do not need any brain; it is only imagination."

If it were a fact that objective forms are only an illusion of mind, how explain that physical, tangible objects, such as a tree,[1] or a house, appear alike to all minds? If they are only illusions, why should all these minds have the same illusions?

What, after all, is the physical plane, with its untold avenues for research, but a vast laboratory? What intelligence or understanding was there in the cave-man state? Although brute force prevailed, the understanding faculty was latent and gradually, through the necessity for self-preservation, crude implements were made, both for self-protection and for obtaining food.

Through the ages, little by little, new discoveries were made. From stage to stage, through evolutionary processes, mind expanded and discovered more and more truths in this laboratory of matter until the highly developed civilization of the present was developed.

In observing the various discoveries which have made life more endurable and more intelligible we see that each discovery has played its part in broadening the mind. Let us imagine that all modern improvements were swept away,

---

[1] See "Non-reality of a tree," Chapter XII, "Dangers of Occult Practices," Page 230.

that we were back in the cave life, and assume the point that all objective things were delusions and deceptions—what would become of humanity and all the present advantages of civilization which material discoveries have made possible? Why not be reasonable and recognize facts as they are?

A Christian Science lecturer, in illustrating the infinite beneficence of Love, uses the following simile: "Did anyone ever hear of a conflict arising because of the use of the multiplication table? Why not? Because one can use it or a thousand can use it, and still it is available to all."

Originally the law of multiplication, as a principle in nature, was unknown to primitive man until mental evolutionary processes evolved the thinking mind of the mathematician which discovered the underlying principles and transposed them into objectivity by means of a text-book which is available to all.

Herein we see the need of objective manifestation through which invisible principles are worked out in classified objective form, and of actual visible symbols and characters whereby others may learn the meaning of the invisible principle.

The same holds true of all of nature's activities. The objective is a vehicle through which nature's higher principles are revealed from stage to stage and made understandable. "The things which are seen are temporal; but the things which are not seen are eternal." (II Corinthians 4:18.)

If there were no substance or matter could anyone imagine a child being born into this life and being perceived by the parents? If there were no physical material form how would they know there was a child? Suppose it were possible that a spirit, an emanation from God, could be born, come into this conscious existence, without a physical form, would the parents know it was there? Would they be conscious of its existence at all, or would the child itself be conscious of its own existence?

Is it not evident that the material form of the child is a necessity, both for the parents' appreciation of the presence of the indwelling consciousness and because that indwelling consciousness needs the material form and faculties in order

194

that through experience it may ultimately discern its real self as intelligent consciousness, an intangible being with unlimited faculties for expanding in understanding.

In the wonderful laboratory of the physical are all manner of possibilities for object lessons which broaden the intellect. As the ox-cart was superseded by the horse and buggy, and the latter by the automobile, so, from crude beginnings, step by step, through persistent experimentation and determination to discover nature's hidden secrets, the innate laws of nature were revealed.

Were not these laws pre-existent to their discovery? Were they not intended to be discovered by mind in order that mind might be educated?

In analyzing matter we find the law of relativity, or changeability, of material substance. The form is real in its present state, yet the substance from which it is formed is subject to changes in appearance and manifestation.[1]

While it is true that the substance of matter is not what it appears to be, the law of relativity must be recognized. For instance, wood is real as wood, water is real as water, but if we ask, "What is wood?" the answer is, chiefly carbon, which manifests both visibly and invisibly; or we ask, "What is water?" and the answer is, the combination of two invisible gases.

Science today knows that all visible things can be transposed into invisibility, into atoms and electrons. In other words, there is a constant play between the visible and the invisible, and through this material play mind is exercised and unfolded.

Who can say what matter really is? A wound is inflicted upon the body and it heals; through cell activity new tissue is formed, dead cells are discarded and wonderful repairs are made—who knows by what process?

Christian Science claims to be of scriptural origin and accepts without reservation all of the teachings and works of Jesus Christ. "And Jesus went about . . . healing all manner of sickness and all manner of disease among the people . . . And they brought unto him all sick people that

[1]See "Inter-play of visible and invisible nature," Chapter IX, "Is there a God?" Page 181.

were taken with divers diseases and torments, and those which were possessed with devils, and those which were lunatic, and those that had the palsy, and he healed them" (Matthew 4:23, 24), was quoted in a Christian Science Lesson-Sermon. If there were no body, and there were no disease, what was it that Jesus healed?

In another Lesson-Sermon on "Love" presented in all branches of The Mother Church, the following scriptural verse was quoted: "When the even was come, they brought unto him (Jesus) many that were possessed with devils; and he cast out the spirits with his word, and healed all that were sick." (Matthew 8:16.)

Yet Christian Scientists hold that there is nothing in common between Christian Science and spirit phenomena, and they have no interest in intercourse with discarnate spirits.

Casting out of "unclean spirits" was a particular part of the instructions which Jesus gave to his disciples. Not only was this a common practice of Jesus himself but this ability was required as proof of discipleship.

"And he (Jesus) called the twelve together, and gave them power and authority over all devils, and to cure diseases." (Luke 9:1.) "And the seventy returned with joy, saying, Lord, even the devils are subject unto us in thy name." (Luke 10:17.)

If spirit obsession was a thoroughly recognized condition demonstrated by Jesus, why do Christian Scientists, as well as other Christian bodies, deny or disregard so important a factor? Jesus said: "Neither will they be persuaded, though one rose from the dead." (Luke 16:31.)

Interference by discarnated spirit entities was a recognized fact in the time of Christ; such conditions have always existed and exist today, a statement easily verified by research in normal as well as abnormal psychology.[1]

That Mrs. Eddy herself was interfered with by discarnated spirits is clearly discernible if the facts of her early years of invalidism and later sufferings are studied by earnest researchers in the abnormal phase of psychology.

---

[1]See "Thirty Years Among the Dead," Carl A. Wickland, M.D.; "The Demonism of the Ages and Spirit Obsession," J. M. Peebles, M.D.; "Demon Possession and Allied Themes," Rev. John L. Nevius.

The records of Mrs. Eddy's early years, of her tantrums and abnormal actions, clearly indicate that she was a natural psychic sensitive, for these tantrums and "spells" were undoubtedly due to the impingement of discarnated entities.

Georgine Milmine writes in "Life of Mary Baker Eddy and History of Christian Science": "Mary Baker was extremely nervous and hysterical, and, as child and woman, subject to certain violent seizures. These 'fits' frequently came on without the slightest warning. At times the attack resembled a convulsion. Mary pitched headlong on the floor, and rolled and kicked, writhing and screaming in apparent agony. Again she dropped limp and lay motionless. At other times, like a cataleptic, she lay rigid, almost in a state of suspended animation."

"As a precautionary measure the family gave in to all the girl's whims. Outside the Baker home, Mary's spells did not inspire the same sympathy. The uncharitable called them 'tantrums.' They even said that Mary took advantage of them to enforce her own way. Mary repeatedly used her nerves, they noted, against her father. Nervous as she was, she found the quiet, blue-law Sunday especially irksome. Sunday, it happened, was the great day for these fits." . . .

"Mrs. Glover's (Mrs. Eddy's) hysterical spells became more violent as she grew older. For months at a time she lived in an almost continuous state of collapse. She was given to long and lonely wanderings, especially at night. During her many illnesses her family would leave her in bed, apparently helpless, and returning a moment later find that she had disappeared. One manifestation of her pathological condition was a mania for being rocked and swung." . . .

"Mrs. Glover (Mrs. Eddy) now dabbled in mesmerism on her own account. She started as an amateur clairvoyant; the superstitious country folk frequently sought her advice. Occasionally, in the course of a social call, she would go into a trance. She closed her eyes, sank backwards, apparently lost consciousness, and, while in this state, described scenes and events. A mesmerist of some local fame used her to trace lost or stolen articles. Like the Fox sisters, she heard rappings at night." . . .

"At the home of Mrs. Sarah G. Crosby, of Albion, Maine, Mrs. Patterson (Mary B. Eddy) spent several months in 1864 where she acted as medium in their spiritualistic seances . . . Several times in the course of this visit Mrs. Patterson went into trances . . . talking in a sepulchral, mannish voice. The voice said that 'he' was Albert Baker, Mrs. Patterson's brother. . . . After leaving Albion, Mrs. Patterson continued to receive messages from Albert." . . .

"Yet Mrs. Eddy herself was not always well, was not always happy. She used first to account for this seeming inconsistency by explaining that she bore in her person the ills from which she released others." . . .

"In 1863 Mrs. Eddy wrote Dr. Quimby that while treating her nephew, to rid him of the habit of smoking, she herself felt a desire to smoke . . ."

"Mrs. Eddy told her students that she had a congenital susceptibility to assume the mental and physical ills of others."

In the biography, "Mrs. Eddy," Edwin Franden Dakin states: "When Mr. Eddy first died . . . Mrs. Eddy was in a nervous and exhausted condition, and there were many nights when Mr. Buswell was called upon to treat her for the same hysterical attacks with which all of her students who were near her for any length of time had to deal. Whatever the horrors of the frantic night, Mrs. Eddy usually managed to gather herself together during the day."

"In her worst moments (Mrs. Mary Baker Eddy) secluded herself in her room . . . and when she again came down the stairs . . . none knew about those terrible moments she had spent in the fights against herself and her physical torture . . . When in the middle of the night the alarm was called and the students gathered at her bedside to see a Mrs. Eddy who was utterly unknown, who writhed and twisted like a tortured victim of the Inquisition, it was not difficult for them to believe that in this state she was indeed possessed."

When religious bodies will seriously recognize the importance of the works of Jesus as they relate to the casting out of "unclean spirits" they will realize that the same natural laws prevail today as in ancient times.

By setting aside bias and skeptical attitudes and giving

intelligent attention to research in normal and abnormal psychology, it will be discovered that many of the reported instantaneous cures of invalidism and mental aberrations are chiefly due to the dislodgment of ignorant or mischievous earthbound spirits from the sufferer.

When any group of students assumes to be scientific one expects their tenets to be consistent and logical, which is not the case with our friends, the Christian Scientists, when, among other assertions, they repeatedly proclaim that there is no death (obviously an affirmation), yet, paradoxically, refuse to acknowledge or include in their doctrine the verifiable evidence, easily obtained through Psychic Research, of the survival of the ego, and of communication between the two worlds as a scientific reality.

Christian Science asserts there is no spirit communication and yet teaches there is no death. How can Christian Scientists know there is no death without evidence from those who have passed through the gateway of death, who alone can verify continued existence?

Why should the Christian Science Church search heaven and earth for all evidence that Mrs. Eddy at one time practiced mediumship, in order that they may destroy the same?

The fact that Mrs. Eddy was a medium has been abundantly proven and there are still persons living who affirm that they not only witnessed, but also assisted in, Mrs. Eddy's psychic work as a medium. Among our correspondents is a man who attended Mrs. Eddy's mediumistic work for the period of some three years. Many others have informed us that they had personally known Mrs. Eddy as a medium. We ourselves have seen a clipping from a Boston paper wherein Mrs. Eddy advertised herself as a medium, giving readings at fifty cents a sitting.

How did Mrs. Eddy obtain her assurance that there is no death but by contact with the invisible world through her own mediumship? Discarnated spirits spoke through her as they do through other trance mediums, making the declaration that there is no death, and by proving their identity gave evidence that there is no death of personality.

The assertion that there is no matter could also easily have emanated from discarnated spirits who were impressing Mrs. Eddy. Since spirits exist in an inner or higher state of vibration they are in position from their vantage ground to know that the physical substances, as we recognize them in form and solidarity, are, on our objective plane, in reality due to the combination of invisible substances or elements.

To be a psychic sensitive, or what is usually termed mediumistic, is in no sense a discredit to anyone but rather a very important and desirable faculty, offering as it does the only definite knowledge of a continued existence.

Had Mrs. Eddy been courageous enough to include in her Science the knowledge she had of spirit communication she would then indeed have had a verifiable science and the usefulness of the Christian Science Church would have been increased manifold. (So likewise would all other denominations or religious bodies enhance their usefulness by adding the verifiable knowledge of survival to their teachings.)

The spirit of Mary Baker Eddy recently spoke as follows through Mrs. Wickland:

"I have come back to say that on earth I hid the real truth; I gave out just a little of it and some which I gave out was not the truth at all. I said there is no such thing as matter—that is not true. We DO have matter."

"I should have taught my people to overcome trouble and fear by using the will, but not that sickness is only imagination. When there is a disease we must use some of the wonders of nature that God has provided for the use of humanity."

"When people do not get the proper elements in food which the system needs, they should use what God has provided for that purpose and not deny their sickness. God furnished these things for us to use. Everything in nature is for the use of mankind."

"Do not deny and condemn as I did. I was self-centered and at one time I hypnotized myself into the belief that I would not die; I thought I could keep my spirit in my physical body forever. I thought I had the will to conquer and when I found I did not it was a great disappointment."

"When I awoke from the sleep of death I was very weak and had no power to progress until I learned to become humble and serve. In the last days of my life I was waited upon and regarded as a little God; I am sorry to say that my people worship me even more than God, our Maker. All that I had to conquer; my lesson was a very bitter one. I had my pride to conquer."

"Now I have to serve and teach my followers to serve, when they come to this side. I am humble now and strive to help the unfortunate spirits who are earthbound and suffering."

"You will hear of me through other mediums,[1] and you will know I have been there to help waken somebody and so do all I can to help myself."

"If any of you can say just a little word to any of my followers regarding spirit existence, please do so. It might not do much good now; they might not receive it at the time but they will later. When the sleep of death comes, the words you have spoken will be a little light to them and they will follow it and learn the way to progress to the higher life."

"Say a word here and there about the higher life in the spirit world and that there is no death; give them a few thoughts of the real truth."

"Many of my followers will know that these statements really came from me; they will know it intuitively. Those who do not recognize it will do so later; they may deny it now but they will realize it is the truth when they come to the spirit side of life."

"There is no death for the spirit, but there is disintegration and change for matter, and when the body can no longer function, then what?"

"Many of my people will not believe I have said this because I did not teach it while here. I taught that there is no matter; that was a great mistake. I should have taught liberation of the mind. Spirit, or mind, cannot manifest without matter; I did not know that when I taught my theories on earth."

"I should have explained that there is a physical body but we can live above the conditions of fear and gloom."

---

[1] Reports of such communications through other psychics come to us from various sources, all coinciding with Mrs. Eddy's statements given through Mrs. Wickland.

"There is no sickness in the mind" (per se), "but of course there is physical sickness; that is where many misunderstand."

"As I told you once before,[1] I had a vision and saw a hospital in the spirit world and the method of treating patients. Many spirits retain their thoughts of a diseased body; they have not overcome their mental habits and think they are still sick. They are there taught that they have discarded their physical bodies and how to overcome old habits of thinking."

"Christian Scientists accomplish wonderful things because they make many forget themselves. When they have learned the lesson of concentration a great number overcome the conditions about them and are cured; otherwise my people could not go on. There is much that is true in Christian Science and my people do many wonderful things."

"Some persons have imaginary sickness; fear brings sickness. Mind can poison the system and can cure it by the proper thinking. Learn right thinking; learn to think of health, strength and power. Learn to concentrate and you will have power over your body. Concentration has a great power."

"If you will read my early history you will see that I gave readings in Boston, but I wanted a church of my own; I concentrated and I accomplished this."

"I wish I had retained my mediumship; I would be far happier in the spirit world. I have to struggle with my followers who come here; when I teach them the truth they say, 'You are not Mrs. Eddy because that is not what she taught on earth.' I have to try to wake them up and find a home for them where they can be enlightened as to their true condition."

"When I talk to them they do not recognize me because my thoughts have changed. I learned my mistakes a long time ago. There is truth in all things but we must not add falsehood to the truth. I did, because I wanted to have a religion of my own."

"I felt that if it were known I was a psychic and that I received my inspirations from the spirit side of life, I would

[1]See spirit communication from Mrs. Eddy in our book, "Thirty Years Among the Dead," Chapter 14, "Christian Science."

not have as many followers. Now I surely wish that I did not have so many."

"I wish they would change their way of thinking but I am sorry to say many will not; they cling together. On earth they are taught they must read and think about my books, and in that lies their strength; this belief is so set in their minds that when they come to the other side of life and I try to get them to change their minds, they will not believe me."

"It is hard to undo my work. I told my people they should read nothing but my books and follow only my teachings and that they should read my books over and over. Christian Scientists still teach that and remain in a mental circle, hypnotizing themselves with their concentration, and when they pass to the spirit side of life they still remain in that circle of thought—in what they call 'the understanding.' "

"But how much do they understand of the real life? When my followers come to the spirit world and I endeavor to teach them regarding spirit life and spirit return, many refuse to listen. I have a great deal to contend with. I should have given out this truth on earth; now I have to do all I can to help my people progress when they come here, and to give them understanding."

"But they have their own gatherings just as they had on earth and remain together; they do not advance because they are hypnotized in my former theories and cannot get away from them. They all join together—'Within, within, within'—and are not aware of anything outside themselves."

"The love they should give out to help others is not developed; I killed that. I taught that you must be firm and overcome self; you must be master of self. But I killed the better love for mankind, the better nature."

This has been proven to us many times. Individuals who had been our friends for years, upon becoming Christian Scientists invariably explained that the friendship must be discontinued, stating, "You are broadminded and will readily realize that we cannot continue our friendship any longer, as that would cause cross currents."

Such ideas are contrary to the teachings of Jesus who stressed particularly that we should love one another. The keynote of his message was the inculcating of love among mortals—and surely friendship is an element in love and above theories and creeds.

(On the other hand, many Christian Scientists, as well as followers of other doctrines, not satisfied with the narrow interpretation of the Science of Life, attend our research work desirous of adding more knowledge to their faith.)

Mrs. Eddy said in conclusion: "I let intellect be the ruling power over my people; I killed sympathy. Oh, if only I could make them understand that Life is made up of sympathy and love for others!"

"Some day they will be more liberal and will work along a different channel. The truth of spirit life should be taught and understood. The spirit world is the Real World!"

A. Hervey-Bathurst, C.S.B., of London, England, a member of The Mother Church, The First Church of Christ, Scientist, in Boston, Mass., quoted from the first chapter of Genesis, verse 26, "Let us make man in our image, after our likeness," adding, "But one might ask, what makes it possible for men to have a true concept of God? The answer to this question is—the fact that man really is spiritual—the image and likeness of God. On page 465 of 'Science and Health,' Mrs. Eddy gives us the following definition of God: 'God is incorporeal, divine, supreme, infinite Mind, Spirit, Soul, Principle, Life, Truth, Love.'"

"This God is the only creator and He created all that was made, as the Bible states. Must it not follow then that, since God's creation is the only creation and it is good, we have a very erroneous concept of that creation, including man, so long as we believe that the creation of God includes evil, sickness, destruction, fear, vice or death? Can man, the image and likeness or reflection of God, be subject to what God does not include? The answer is emphatically—No."

The above delineation of the nature and qualities of the Architect of the Universe is beautifully stated and analytical minds can come to no other conclusion than that the essence of the Creator is incorporeal and everywhere present. But this lecturer makes no distinction between the spiritual or soul factors which are beyond death and the mortal, physical aspect.

204

How can sickness or disease be denied? Physiologically considered our bodies are made up of simple chemical elements. Biologically or metabolically analyzing our bodily functions, metabolism consists of two processes—anabolism, "the process by which matter is transformed into the tissues of a living organism," and catabolism, "the process by which protoplasm within a cell or organism is broken down into less complex, waste substances." When these activities are in perfect balance there is ease; when there is imbalance there is dis-ease.

How many individuals maintain the balance which nature provides? This law is constantly sinned against by improper diet and faulty respiration (which latter means insufficient oxygen for oxidation in the metabolic process; few persons know why they breathe or how to breathe). Anxieties, fears, vices and all manner of destructive habits and erroneous thinking dominate the majority of mankind, interfering with the normal nervous activity, which again reacts unfavorably upon the life processes.

What are the above conditions but, in a sense, "evil" and destructive? As for "death," nothing is more evident since all organized life ceases to be apparent with the dissolution of the physical form. But there is no death of the spirit.

Why close the eyes of the mind to the necessary and yet transient phase of the physical side of our nature which is so necessary for the expression and unfoldment of the ego?

Did not God create the earth, the firmament, our physical tabernacles and objective phenomena—all real, though transient—for a very definite purpose? As in vegetation a living force struggles with adverse conditions yet produces wonderful growth (physical development) ultimating in flowers, with their invisible aroma, fruit which will sustain physical life, and seeds for procreation, so also in human life the living entities clothe themselves in physical bodies which have organs and functions necessary for acquiring experience in this material school.

In the struggle with nature's obstacles under adverse conditions, the soul attains consciousness of itself and a perception of its independence of the physical, of the dual principle of mind and body.

205

Those who deny the existence of objective phenomena and so-called "evils" fail to make a distinction between objective phenomena and the inner spiritual life principle and activities. We have herein two phases, the invisible nature of God and man on one hand, and on the other, the objective universe of manifestation.

God's many-sided qualities are admittedly all invisible; likewise are the soul and the mental qualities of man, who is the image or reflection of the Creator, invisible. Who has seen Harmony, Love, Thoughts or Emotions?

Since the Creator endowed our souls with his own qualities why are we not directly conscious of our oneness with our Source until after we have been born into the physical form? The Creator in his wisdom saw the need for his creatures passing through a mortal objective experience such as can only be obtained in the physical objective manifestation.

The soul, born into the physical form, is left to its own resources with what is presumed to be free will; tribulations, sorrows and griefs in this transitory existence cause pain, pain causes thinking, and thought plus difficulties compels questioning regarding life's purpose. Thus ultimately we reach conscious discernment of our oneness with the Source of our being — revealed Intelligence, Love, Harmony.

God did not create "evil." Man, self-seeking, blind in the beginning to his true nature, stumbles about seeking happiness, which can never be fully attained while he is sojourning in this transient physical, discovering himself, until so-called "death" is experienced. But this is merely the freeing of the spirit from the bonds of material attractions and illusions and man is destined ultimately to progress from sphere to sphere, recognizing with greater fullness his oneness with the All.

206

CHAPTER XI

Reincarnation and Theosophy

LONG years of contact with the Invisible World and the lessons obtained from dwellers in that school of life cause the doctrine of reincarnation to lose its plausibility. Any foundation for belief in this theory receives a better interpretation when we understand the influence and thought waves emanating from discarnate spirits which act upon a sensitive brain much as sound waves are conveyed through the radio, a fact equally demonstrated through Psychic Research, especially the abnormal phase.

The theory of reincarnation can undoubtedly be traced to early stages of mankind when departed spirits took possession of the bodies of sensitive individuals and lived and acted through them, thus seemingly indicating reincarnation. But in reality this was only spirit obsession or possession.

Swedenborg states in "Heaven and its Wonders and Hell": "There is such conjunction between the spiritual world and the natural world in man that the two are seemingly one . . . (It is) provided that there should be angels and spirits with each individual." . . .

"With every individual there are good spirits and evil spirits . . . by the two he is kept in equilibrium, and being in equilibrium he is in freedom." . . .

"Good and evil are two opposites . . . Unless man were between these two he could have no thought nor any will, still less any freedom or any choice, for all these man has by virtue of the equilibrium between good and evil." . . .

"Every man in respect to his spirit, even while he is living in the body, is in some society with spirits although he does not know it." . . .

"If a spirit were to speak from his own memory with a man, the man would not know otherwise than that the thoughts then in his mind were his own, although they were the spirit's thoughts. This would be like the recollection of something which the man had never heard or seen."

"This is the source of the belief held by some of the ancients that after some thousands of years they were to return into their former life, or had returned. This they concluded because at times there came to them a sort of recollection of things they had never seen or heard. This came from an influx from the memory of spirits into their ideas of thought."

Such occurrences are not limited to primitive races but obtain today in the possession by selfish or ignorant spirits of sensitive persons whose identity becomes entirely changed by these various forms of encroachment; but today this is designated as mental aberration or insanity.

The supposed "memories" of past lives of those who believe in reincarnation are far better accounted for by the presence of invisible intelligences whose memories of their own mortal careers are conveyed through thought waves to the reincarnationists who have become sensitized to such impressions by their meditations and negativism.

Mischievous entities who enjoy playing pranks can also impress upon sensitive minds all sorts of false "memories" which please the victim's vanity.

A woman who was a Theosophist stated to us, as proof of reincarnation, that whenever she read ancient history she invariably remembered the events about which she was reading, not realizing that interfering spirits were producing those mental pictures.

Is it not curious that the "memories" of past lives which "recur" to these believers in the theory of reincarnation are essentially concerned with wonderful careers of greatness in the past, they usually recalling themselves only as Kings, Cleopatras, Apostles, Great Patriarchs, etc.?

Annie Besant believed herself to be the reincarnation of Hypatia and Giordano Bruno, and a report from England states there are at least fifty presumed Cleopatras in that country today. Individuals holding such beliefs are not real analysts but mere sentimentalists; they mistake the impressions of discarnated spirits for memories of their own past lives.

A case may be quoted which shows to what unfortunate entanglements the reincarnation doctrine may lead. A gentleman, a student of New Thought, Christian Science and Theosophy, became infatuated with the theory of reincarnation and, developing what he supposed was the faculty of recalling past lives, discovered (?) that his wife had been his mother in a former incarnation. Upon making this "discovery" he decided he must leave his loyal, intelligent wife and family of grown children; he obtained a divorce and the home was broken up.

He then became enamored of another woman, a divorcee; believing themselves to be soul-mates, the two left for another part of the country to live on "higher planes." But this blissful existence did not last long; owing to his negative state, the gentleman became entirely possessed by foreign entities and lost his mental balance, whereupon his "soul-mate" promptly deserted him and had him sent back to his family.

As various means resorted to in an endeavor to reestablish the mental equilibrium of the gentleman were of no avail, members of his family, who understood obsession, urged us to take charge of him. He proved to be a very unruly patient, although his actions changed from time to time as various entities were removed from him by static electrical treatments and hydro-therapy.

During the period of several months no less than eleven spirits were dislodged from the patient and allowed to temporarily control Mrs. Wickland. Each entity manifested a distinct personality and characteristics similar to those which previously had been enacted through the patient—one grimaced, another made unusual noises, another had caused the patient to refuse to eat, some spoke in a foreign language, and one gave his name as "The Great I Am." The latter claimed to be a "Super-Master of Metaphysics" and said, "I have the Secret Doctrine of Life; I can perform black magic and I know everything."

After the gentleman was freed from all these entities

209

he gradually regained his mental poise and during the past ten years has been engaged in his former occupation.

If reincarnation had been a fact through the ages should we not find evidence of it in a goodly portion of superior human beings who had advanced to a high degree of knowledge and development? But there is no evidence of such supermen; only a general average is noticeable among mankind.

Were the theory true that re-birth is required for attaining perfection, should there not be more evidence of perfected souls among us than is discernible—aside from the number of self-hypnotized individuals who imagine themselves to have attained that goal?

As the above was being written, a spirit visitor, Madam Katherine Tingley, who had in earth life been a staunch advocate of reincarnation, unexpectedly controlled Mrs. Wickland and expressed her present views on the subject of reincarnation and the new life.

"I came here today because your writing about reincarnation made an opportunity. Why should reincarnation be taught? I see now that the theory of reincarnation is only a hindrance to progression. I am Tingley."

"When I passed out I had knowledge of the change and had understanding. But passing out is not a pleasant experience for everyone. It is pleasant for those who understand, but very different for those who cling to earthly things."

"For many, when they waken, there is a wall, a gray, cloudy condition, a neutral state where the soul remains until it realizes the change it has made and where it is."

"The physical body is an overcoat for the spirit body; all through earth life you are building the spirit body; when you pass from the physical you throw off the overcoat. The spiritual body is only a form for the soul to manifest through—the Theosophists would say 'an astral shell.' "

"When realization of the change from the physical takes place (this may occur soon after transition or after an extended period, according to the light or strong attachment of the spirit to physical habits and ideas) the soul still holds the old ideas which it had in the physical existence."

"Spirit bodies can be of very coarse material or they can

210

be of very fine vibration. Those with coarse vibrations and strong physical attractions may sometimes be seen, as in haunted houses."

"When one who has learned to build the spiritual body through understanding passes from the physical, the spiritual body has light and strength, and when the awakening comes such a soul progresses."

"Pure Theosophy, the pure Hindu philosophy, does not teach reincarnation. It teaches we are one with the Maker and we must develop in ourselves an understanding of the higher life."

"Theosophists sit and meditate but they only enter a coma state; they live in a negative condition. They meditate and want to be spiritual; they desire to become 'Masters.' "

"To sit in the silence and meditate is dangerous; you really contact the neutral gray sphere. You become negative and lose the world; your spirit tries to enter what the Theosophists call the 'Astral World.' "

"In this state you see nothing, you know nothing, since that is the condition of the next sphere, which is also a place of rest."

"But as long as you have your physical body, the soul is not yet ready to go into this negative state. Other souls who have passed out of the physical and do not yet understand themselves may then step in. Some are trying to 'reincarnate,' and with this thought they float around. These are the ones Theosophists call 'astral shells.' They do not want to progress in their spiritual bodies, so they drift about, not really as developed spirits but in a negative condition."

"This gray sphere, the 'astral plane,' is real, but spirits do not progress there. There are many kinds of spirits in the gray, neutral condition; it is a laboratory and spirits there have not yet strength or power."

"The first stage in this sphere is a gray, negative state, the second stage is one in which you waken to a realization of a change and must decide about development."

"The first and second states are conditions in which old ideas are thrown off. If you are ignorant you think only of your earthly home and go back to be near earth life."

211

"If you understand, you progress. In this state the sun of understanding is rising. It is like the light of dawn, like the peace and harmony of a beautiful morn; it is a wonderful awakening. You will then seek God within."

"The third state is one of homes and home life. Every soul wants a home, companionship and harmony. This is the waiting place where you may wait until your friends and relatives come. You may then progress or you may remain there, for it is very beautiful, with music, art and harmony. Or, if you feel you have left something undone on earth you can make it your work to carry out some mission. There is no development until selfishness is overcome."

"Why should we, after passing through the first two stages of the gray sphere, go back to earth when we can develop into the bliss where all are as one? Some say 'lost in God'; yes, that is true, but it is not loss of the individual. I cannot describe how harmonious is the state of this third sphere, where all can be if they wish."

"I have told all this only to show the folly of trying to reincarnate when the law of the ego is always to go forward and upward through many stages of development and progress in the higher realms."

In our book, "Thirty Years Among the Dead," mention is made of an entity who had in earth life imbibed the notion of reincarnation and after discarding the physical body had attempted to reincarnate and became enmeshed in the aura of a young boy of five, causing the latter to act as an adult, entirely foreign to his normal self. A spirit entity was attracted from the boy, after which he fully regained his mental poise.

The spirit, when controlling Mrs. Wickland, explained that he had been homely and pock-marked and that people had shunned him, which grieved him. Having heard something about the theory of reincarnation he determined to reincarnate for the purpose of obtaining more attractive

212

features to obviate being shunned and thus had unwittingly obsessed the boy.

Seven years after the publication of our book we received a letter which read in part as follows: "I have just read 'Thirty Years Among the Dead.' On Page 333, opening your chapter, 'Theosophy,' you describe the case of one Charlie Herrman, who lived all his life near Raymond, Illinois. He died in middle age, about twenty-five or thirty years ago. He was never spoken of by any other name than 'Charlie,' and he and his parents used the double 'r' in spelling 'Herrman,' though my father's folks simplified the spelling thus: 'Herman.' He, Charlie, had smallpox which left his eyesight greatly impaired and his face full of pock marks . . . Most Sincerely Yours, (Signed) ———— Herman."

During our years of Psychic Research we have contacted many discarnated spirits of various conditions who said they had been seeking for a chance to reincarnate but with the only result of becoming lodged in the aura of some person sensitive to spirit encroachment, thereby causing great distress to the victim of such obsession.[1]

Often such entities inspire bizarre notions and hallucinations in the victim's mind, yet the individual may be unaware that a spirit is causing the delusions and the entity may be unaware of being a spirit or of interfering with anyone, and both may be skeptical regarding spirit influence.

Instead of being helpful, the doctrine of reincarnation is very pernicious, since earthly-minded individuals with strong attractions to the physical world, may learn of the theory of rebirth and fix firmly in their minds the determination to reincarnate again, hoping to obtain a better opportunity to carry out their earthly propensities. We have contacted many such spirits who were firm believers in reincarnation yet were unaware of being so-called dead; often in their ignorance they claimed to be wonderful "Mas-

[1] See case of the crawling man, Chapter XII, "Dangers of Occult Practices." Page 241.

ters," and yet they were only earthbound spirits. A great deal of reasoning was required to disillusion them, cause them to realize their situation and open their mental eyes to the road of spiritual progression.

Several children with mental aberrations, who came under our care, proved to be influenced by spirits who had attempted to reincarnate and found themselves enmeshed in the auras of the children, thus interfering with the children's normal physical and mental development as well as hindering their own spiritual progression.

We had been treating a young boy who was subject to attacks of petit mal, and a number of spirits had been removed from him. During a subsequent treatment, while his mother, Mrs. J., was present, Mrs. Wickland also was in the office and the spirit of an intelligent former reincarnationist was dislodged from the boy and allowed to control Mrs. Wickland.

Dr. Wickland	How do you do, and who are you?
Spirit	A man, of course. How could I be anything else? I am born again. I was a Theosophist and was going to reincarnate but when I tried to reincarnate there were about a dozen ahead of me. (Other spirits obsessing patient.)
	And I don't like it—all of us crowded into one little body. I was a man, a student studying Theosophy, and I died, but I have not yet reached what I am going to become.
Mrs. J.	How did you find my son?
Sp.	Through you. I found you first. I thought you were quite a nice lady and I saw that if I could get into your family I could have a good home and a quiet, easy life.
	But circumstances prevented my reincarnating and I only got into a boy. I know better now and I understand that reincarnation is all buncombe. I knew where I was all the time.
Dr.	What is your name?

214

Sp.   My name is Ralph James and I was a lecturer in London. (The patient's family had lived in England.)

Dr.   Who was the ruler at that time?

Sp.   King Edward. I wish that I could go out and shout to the world how many children are sent to the idiot asylums by spirits of Theosophists who have hovered around mothers trying to reincarnate through a young baby.

"When one gets into a child and cannot get out it is a great mistake. Sometimes there are two, three or more minds interfering with one child, the child is declared insane and they all go to the asylum and remain with the child until it dies."

"Once in a while an obsessing spirit can get away but only by holding continuously the thought of leaving. This is very difficult."

"Sometimes I was able to slip away but came back again. I have been watching the whole proposition here (removal of obsessing spirits, one by one, from the patient) and watched for my time to get out."

"I have observed obsession here and the treatments given, the effect of electricity on the vital organs, the magnetic current being cut and the wonderful results accomplished by means of this psychic. (Mrs. Wickland.)"

"Why people cannot master themselves in the earth life I cannot understand. They should study nature instead of growing so negative from following various fads, such as eating only vegetables. They should understand that everything depends upon everything else, from microbes on up."

"Many Theosophists travel around in the astral world in a blind condition but hold the thought of finding a place to reincarnate. Many want to become leaders and have their own religion."

215

Dr.   How old are you?

Sp.   "I cannot tell exactly. I think I was about forty-five years old. You can count the interval, as King Edward came to the throne in 1901."

"I knew all about my own death. After I left my physical body, I wanted to travel with people, so I went to India and elsewhere, following others."

"If you are conscious of passing out, it is a wonderful study to observe where you are going. Very few travel on, however. Generally they prefer to remain in their own homes."

"Especially is that so of England. There departed spirits remain for centuries, abiding in old castles and haunted houses, fighting among themselves."

"Those in the physical life cannot remain long in such places so in time all of these old castles will be torn down, because people cannot live comfortably in haunted houses, and the owners cannot afford to keep up these places. If only people would understand this influence."

"Some day I will come to you again and tell you all about my experiences. I am not a bad spirit, merely a foolish one."

"I visited mediums; some considered themselves controlled by Cleopatra and some by St. John, but these were only obsessing spirits pretending to be great personages."

"It is going to take time to break up false beliefs, but there will be a new religion and it will be a sensible one."

"I must go now. Thank you for freeing me."

I am fully persuaded that some day it will be found not only that ignorant, designing spirits are often serious contributing factors in the case of the imbecile, idiot and moron, but also that the reincarnation doctrine has, in many cases, played a role in the unfortunate situation.

The spirit of Madam Blavatsky, speaking through Mrs. Wickland, said of the theory of reincarnation: "I see now that my teachings caused many to become psychic sensitives and that the theory of reincarnation causes much obsession. I also taught that one should be a vegetarian, but the majority live under too great a nervous tension for this and become too sensitive."

"I have found that 'reincarnation' is possible only through obsession, and I have also found, to my great sorrow, that many of my followers become obsessed."

"It is dangerous to teach the theory of reincarnation because many selfish people, who come to the other side of life, look for what they consider the right place to reincarnate but they do not understand obsession and therefore disturb and obsess children. That is one reason there are so many idiot children in the asylums."

"I was a psychic when in earth life and I knew spirits could come back and control mortals. I realize now that if I had taught the philosophy of Theosophy and the truth of spirit return it would have been much better."

"We cannot progress to the higher life of understanding with a falsehood on our minds; an understanding of the truth is necessary."

World travelers, missionaries, authors and lecturers alike bear testimony that in India, where belief in reincarnation is general, cases of obsession and possession are exceedingly prevalent.

Rev. John L. Nevius, for forty years a missionary to the Chinese, in his book, "Demon Possession and Allied Themes," quotes from an article by the Rev. Robert C. Cardwell, well known English missionary in India: "Do there exist in the present day such instances of demoniacal possession as those which elicited the marvelous intervention of Christ? If the case nowadays of the demonolators of Southern India differs from that of the Hebrews, who in the time of Christ were possessed with devils, will anyone point out to me the exact bound and limit of the difference?"

"The question I raise is surely one which Christians of

all creeds may fairly and calmly consider and argue. Is there such a thing as 'demoniacal possession' in the present day, amongst barbarous and uncivilized tribes? And if it does exist, does it materially differ from the kindred afflictions which the Great Physician, in His infinite mercy, deigned to cure, whilst He walked as man amongst men?"

Dr. J. M. Peebles devoted sixty years to the study of Psychic Research and the Science of Religion; he was a prolific writer and made five journeys around the world to obtain data pertaining to these problems.

The interference of discarnated spirits in human affairs was particularly brought to his attention and he wrote a large volume on this subject entitled, "The Demonism of the Ages, Spirit Obsessions," in which he states, "The belief is universal among the various races and tribes of India that spirits, good and bad, especially the latter, have access to, and the power to influence, mortals. Among the hill-tribes, demoniacal obsession has become a sort of religion."

Jeddu Krishnamurti, Hindu philosopher and lecturer, in an address on the need of individual freedom of thought, declared that the theory of reincarnation is a theory of the lazy, and urged liberation from all dogma.

Reincarnation is also a convenient excuse for selfishness since those with wealth and those born in more favorable circumstances may credit their own position to many incarnations and attainment through rebirths and assume they are now enjoying their just dues because of their "good Karma"; while the lowly and unfortunate ones who, because they were born in unfavorable conditions and raised in squalor and poverty, have been deprived of the better opportunities of life, are regarded as supposed victims of their own "bad Karma."

To hold that the inequalities and miseries in this world are due to wrong acts, or acts of omission and commission in former lives which have established an unbalance necessitating reincarnation in order to work out the supposed "Karmic Law of Justice," merely condones the selfishness so prevalent in the world and the self-aggrandizement of the few which deprives the many of proper opportunity to realize the purpose of existence.

Selfishness and ignorance have blinded humanity to the purpose of the Creator; the idea that self-preservation is the first law in nature has prevailed from the dawn of existence to the present time. This has been the source of much evil and wrong all through the ages, as well as the cause of untold oppression by the worldly mighty and of untold misery to the less fortunate, who have been held down by unreasonable creeds, cults and dogmas, and deprived of all opportunity to gain any intelligent understanding of the meaning of their existence.

The theory of reincarnation subverts the natural spiritual progression; too much stress and importance is placed upon this brief mortal life. The teaching of the reincarnationists that we must return again and again to earth life to become perfected is equivalent to saying that, after one has passed through kindergarten, grade schools and university, he must return to kindergarten over and over again to learn everything that is to be learned pertaining to life.

What is mortal life but a kindergarten? Too little is credited to the vaster opportunities of the next school in the spiritual realm, the verity of which has been so abundantly demonstrated and which may be easily verified by the unprejudiced student through intelligent Psychic Research.

The entire scheme of reincarnation is a limited idea, one that fails to recognize this is a formative plane and that there are many planes and schools on the Invisible Side which offer far greater opportunities for the higher soul culture than does this mortal plane. There is no need of returning to the mundane when we can progress from sphere to sphere, or school to school, and thus ultimately realize the "God within."

To live morally and uprightly, to learn in this life what we are living for, and to realize there are future opportunities, is undoubtedly the cardinal object of our human existence.

The spirit of Rudolph Valentino, communicating through Mrs. Wickland, spoke at length of the reincarnation theory and of conditions as they actually are in the spirit world.

Spirit   This is the first time I have talked through this instrument. Each instrument or medium is different from another and we must learn the law of controlling mediums and how to pass from the spirit world to this world. We go to many circles, from one to another. This is the first opportunity I have had to come into this circle.

Ques.   May we ask who you are?

Sp.   I am Rudolph Valentino.

Ques.   You were interested in psychic matters when you were on earth, were you not?

Sp.   Yes.

Ques.   And you have communicated often since passing over?

Sp.   Yes, through a most excellent instrument, a trance medium who is very easily controlled.

Ques.   Do you still believe in reincarnation?

Sp.   "I have found matters to be very different in that respect from what I thought. Reincarnation, as it is generally understood, is not necessary. A spirit that realizes his condition and understands progression is not interested in reincarnation; to reincarnate in a physical body on this earth again would be very foolish."

"But very few spirits seek for the spirit world when they pass out. Some spirits who have gone beyond the veil of death are in the dark, some are in semi-darkness, some are in twilight, some in the light."

"The ones who have found the light are those who understand, who have knowledge of life in spirit; these would never think of coming back to earth again in a physical body."

"They come back as spirits, to be invisible teachers, to guide and help humanity. This might be called a 'reincarnation of the soul,' but without physical birth; it is only a temporary measure. It is not reincarnation in the flesh, but in spirit, to help and serve. They can

220

come back to their dear ones and help them in many ways when they know the laws."

"But many spirits are ignorant of their true situation and very few seek for the spirit world when they pass out. Ignorance is darkness and they have to be awakened to see the light."

"Intelligent spirits enlighten and teach these ignorant ones, often taking them to earth to contact material things; in this way many souls are brought to earth to acquire earth experience with the help of enlightened spirits. Through matter they awaken and see and learn through different experiences."

"We may say this is reincarnating to earth life in soul, but not in a physical body. They are brought to earth as spirits to correct their mistakes. In that way they can be of help to those they have wronged by serving, protecting and guarding them. That is their mission."

"They must do good for any wrong committed; they cannot progress until they have served in one way or another the ones they have injured. No matter how small the misdeed, the wrong must be replaced by good."

"That is justice; the scales of justice must balance. After spirits have done their duty they are taken to other spheres to learn lessons which lead to progression."

"Is this not much better than to reincarnate as a child? A spirit who believed in reincarnation on earth wakens from the sleep into which he has hypnotized himself and thinks it is time for him to reincarnate. He hopes to come in contact with the birth of some child; sometimes he succeeds in doing this—but what has actually happened?"

"He has possessed that child and that is a sin. These facts should be taught during earth life; people will then understand and be so much happier."

"People should be taught that if they do harm to their fellowmen they cannot be forgiven until they have served the ones they have harmed or have helped others."

"A spirit who on earth has lived only for self must learn to serve and to overcome self. It is a very hard matter to conquer self but one who has not learned the lesson of self-sacrifice cannot be happy in the spirit world."

"How could one be happy in the spirit world if he had a jealous, selfish mind? He could not, because he would see others there in a happy condition, all light and beauty, yet he would be different. His selfish thoughts and jealousy would disturb the minds of those in their happy state and that would not be 'heaven.'"

"But when he has learned to overcome selfishness, jealousy and envy, and has learned to sacrifice self, then he is ready to take a step forward. He will be in a much happier frame of mind and will then be in a position to enter the home in the spirit world which he has prepared for himself while on earth."

"Some may ask, Would that be 'Heaven'? To some, yes, but to those who have not learned harmony it would be 'hell.' On earth those who understand music enjoy symphonies and the classics, but if those who do not understand music should go where the most wonderful music is being played, they would be miserable because they are not attuned to higher music or harmony. They would enjoy jazz, or something like it."

"Some think that all are mingled together in the spirit world; no, each goes where he belongs and only as far as he has progressed while on earth."

"The spirit of one who on earth had lived for higher science and to investigate nature could not, when he passed to the spirit side of life, be happy for very long in any other line of thought."

222

"One who had been inclined to higher soul music would go to the sphere of music; another whose main interests had been electricity would follow that line."

"But first all must learn the lesson of overcoming selfishness; they must study, not for glory or fame, but from the heart. Then, when self has been overcome, they go to the life where they belong."

"Happiness awaits all finally because they go where their hearts desire. But they must first overcome self and learn to help others who do not have as much understanding as they."

"We all have dear ones on earth of whom we think; we try to help these, but, at the same time, when we progress and have light and knowledge, material things no longer hold us. We want to cast off matter, especially the physical body and its attractions. That is why spirits who understand life in the spirit world are not interested in the theory of reincarnation; they know the law of progression."

"What that beautiful understanding of soul life is, cannot be described to anyone; each must attain it for himself."

In "Illuminated Brahminism," a communication transmitted by the spirit Ranga Hilyod, the ancient Indian teacher called the Great Brahma, an explanation is given of the original Brahminical doctrines and "the perversion of a great truth into a malign superstition . . . which has become a source of the most pestilent spiritual mischief."

"There is one effect of the doctrine of reincarnation of the souls of the dead that is felt with direful power in the spiritual world of India. Myriads who have left the physical life hover over the mortals of that country seeking for opportunities to become re-embodied, in order that they may realize the promised relief from their imperfect development in the former earth life. They are earth-bound to a degree that infects the mental atmosphere of its people with almost hopeless despair, for however intense may be their desire, they are never able to obtain the fancied reincarnation."

"Could India emancipate herself from the tyranny of the idea of reincarnation, she would rise in the scale of spiritual enlightenment far higher than she rose in the age of the Vedas or when Capilya or Gautama led her hosts toward the heavenly paradise. She must do this or she must remain the prey to vile superstitions, and her moral nature be degraded by the mental influx of myriad hosts who strive in vain to realize the truth of the dogma."

"I taught that one God alone was Supreme, and the true object of adoration and praise. I taught that from this Being proceeded all that had life and existence in the world of spirit or mortal being. I taught that to this Being all who passed from physical life would return, but I never taught that returning to the presence spiritual of the great Om would result in the annihilation of the individual or his inability to return to earth as a spirit."

"I did teach that all spirits could return to earth to manifest, and influence mortals, and I also taught that such a return would be determined by the mental bias of the individual."

"There were those who could not understand how a spirit could come to earth without being re-embodied in physical life . . . To suppose that in the statements which I left on record as to the nature of the soul there is or ever was any basis for the present theory of transmigration, is to pervert a great truth until it has become a most grievous error. I taught that the pathway of the race was upward, not downward, and that the world of spirit held in itself the power to emancipate all souls from the thralldom of spiritual slavery."

"Whenever any great soul arises upon earth, manifesting the attributes of wisdom and love, such a soul does not lose its power of expression upon earth, for there will ever be correlative spirits born there through which the higher developed mind in spirit can give expression to its own existence . . . As individuals they can only return through the power of the spiritual transfer of thought, which enables them to register upon the mentality of mortals the wisdom that pertains to the world of developed mind."

"The law of spiritual unfoldment is this, that the better the conditions the wiser and purer the life; and while it may be necessary for the spiritual entity to lay its foundation in planetary life, the sooner it can escape from bad conditions there the more likely it will be to have a beautiful development. It may have to stay in the mortal environment for a season to perfect the form powers, but when that is once accomplished no necessity exists for further imprisonment upon earth, for all that earth can teach is what pertains to the physical senses rather than to the spiritual life, and to condemn a spirit to return to it after once having had its nature developed in that direction would be to degrade rather than exalt the soul, nor could anything be gained by it." ...

"By the law of spiritual evolution, the spirit once having had its formative stages in earthly or planetary life has no more necessity for returning to that condition than the developed bird has to reenter the shell of the embryonic period."

"The law does not call for the return to the environment of earth after its escape from the atmosphere of earthly thoughts, nor does it ever need to express itself again in the realm of earthly embodiment. Its pathway to Nirvana is away from earth, and happy the soul who is freed from the idea of ever having to tread the path through mortal life again."

The communication, "Illuminated Buddhism," purported to have been psychically received from the spirit, Siddartha, Sakya Muni, presents the following views of reincarnation:

"When the error went forth from what was considered competent authority, through the Brahmin priesthood, that metempsychosis was the destiny of the spirit, the mentality of India was so poisoned by it that for centuries there was no improvement or desire for relief except in annihilation." ...

"The myriad victims (of this error) have been seeking the relief from consequences that result from the notations of the natural law of spirit unfoldment and have crowded back to the earth, seeking in vain to become reincarnated

225

over and over again, hoping against hope for generations
. . . By inductive transfer of thought (these spirits) have
infected the mental world of the mortals of India with a
hopeless despair . . . and the nation has sunk under the
burden of this weight of ignorance."

"The only incarnation that will give relief is the embodiment of spiritual light upon a basis of scientific demonstra-
tion, and the only metempsychosis that will avail its people
is the lifting of the soul from the belief or desire of any
further experience in the world of physical life to the infinite
unfoldment that awaits the spirit in the worlds immortal. It
is there that the true metempsychosis is to be experienced."

"Developed spirits who have attained the states of freedom from desire and the disposition of benevolence do not
wish to ever return to the atmosphere of earth, but on the
part of those who are ignorant devotees of transmigration
there is a great tendency to cling to earth . . . The hope of
reincarnation is entirely vain and serves no good purpose,
but retards the spirit from going forward in the spheres of
unfolding thought. When the spirit is freed from its earthly
form it should be able to go onward in the spheres of eternal
unfoldment."

We need to realize that this mundane existence is but a
primary school for the unfoldment of consciousness and
other innate mental faculties and that at "death" the spirit,
freed from physical cares and hindrances, enters the next
school where greater opportunities are available for progressive attainment and understanding of God's Plan.

If mankind will set aside prejudice and, in place of the
dogmatic cults and isms which, aside from any moral precepts they may contain, are in so many instances only opiates
to the soul, open-mindedly co-operate with the Intelligences
from the next school of life, who are ever eager to convey
the assurance that they are not "dead," it will revolutionize
the world's conception of the Creator and the creation of
which we are a part and afford an intelligent understanding
of the meaning of life, the lack of which is keeping the world
in doubt and despair.

When this inter-communication is fully established then,
and then only, will humanity begin to discern the fundamental wrongs of the prevailing system of economics which

have hitherto not been fully comprehended. It will reveal
that the education and enlightenment of the soul, as it
passes through this mundane sphere, is a primary object and
that experiences pertaining to the physical life are only a
means for that accomplishment.

> "Lo, the Sculptor sees form in a block of marble,
>   Visioning a figure of beauty and grace,
> Hews from that form its cumbersome wrapping,
>   Endows it with Life, inspiring the Race
> Of all ages, to shed its clumsy trapping
>   Of ignorance, to seek inward for a trace
> Of Beauty, and hew from the Soul its wrapping,
>   The layers of selfishness, that hide the Face
> Of the Spiritual nature the Soul is housing."
>
>   (H. R. B.)

The advancement of science and research and the inventions for human betterment are gradually bringing about
the dawn of a new era and, in spite of opposition, are replacing dogmas and useless creeds with enlightenment and
knowledge.

In lieu of accepting dogmas, reincarnation theories or
other beliefs let humanity waken to the fact that the teachings of the Nazarene have a scientific background, that all
mankind is bound together and no man can live unto himself
alone. Everyone born into this life should have the fullest
opportunity for soul culture.

Change the economic system; let ideal educational opportunities be provided and each individual, from early infancy,
have the proper surroundings where the best possible physical and mental environment are afforded; let the latent finer
sensibilities be evolved through loving kindness and quickened through object lessons—music, arts, sciences and the
beautiful in nature.

If such ideal conditions could obtain through a few generations the average of human intelligence would be so far
advanced that dogmas and creeds, as well as the idea of
reincarnation, would be as obsolete as the gods of mythology.
Onward and upward is the trend of evolution—from the
darkness of ignorance to the light of understanding. This is
clearly Nature's Plan.

227

CHAPTER XII

Dangers of Occult Practices

ABSURD as it would be for a butterfly, had it reasoning powers when freed from its chrysalis and finding itself in a new and more perfect state of existence, to fail to recognize the importance of the humble pathway it has traveled to attain the new condition, so also admittedly absurd are the assertions of those who, assuming they have attained "Reality" or "Oneness with the Universal Spirit," declare the physical universe and earth life to be of no importance.

These persons are like the youths who go through school and college, then assume an air of superior knowledge and attainment; they become ashamed of their parents and ignore them; oftentimes neglecting those who perhaps have struggled greatly to give them the opportunities of education.

Such reasoning is merely superficial sophistry, and fails to recognize that the materiality into which the spirit is born is the school in which the mind first gropes in ignorance but, by means of the five senses and through many experiences and travail in the physical conditions, which are transient to the spirit but necessary factors for the unfoldment of consciousness and discernment of the spiritual self apart from the material, at last slowly and intelligently recognizes its goal.

This goal is a realization of oneness with Reality and that, while the elements of spirit are not of mortal mold, but invisible and intangible, it is necessary for the spirit to pass through the state of the transient physical before it gradually emerges into realization of the spiritual.

How could the spirit find itself except through experience in the physical universe? Consistency is indeed a jewel. Why stultify Reason, which is the hand-maid of Intelligence?

Why not take in the whole gamut of Life's Play, recognizing therein the wise forethought of the Over-Ruling Principle, or Governing Intelligence of the Universe, which foresaw that were the ego, or spirit, to be originally born into a state of perfection it would be unconscious of its heavenly or perfect estate, having had no other experience.

Hence the Creator in his wisdom brought about an external plane, or school of limitations, wherein the embryonic spirit is born and is allowed to follow its own devices for a time. Through contacting the illusive appearances, pain, disappointment and disillusionment all contribute to unfold the thinking faculty and a discernment of the right and wrong principles.

This discernment in turn will gradually culminate in wisdom which admonishes the spirit that all material things are only a means to an end. "As the moon has phases, although what they indicate are not real, so the different phenomena from birth to death belong to the body and not to the soul."

Through the material the unconscious spirit, as it enters the mortal, ultimately becomes cognizant that the spirit, while in the physical, is yet not of the physical, but conscious recognition of itself as Intelligence is arrived at through the physical, and thus is each individual destined to slowly acquire a realization of oneness with the Source of its being. "The fear of the Lord" (conscience) "is the beginning of wisdom." (Psalms 111:10.)

The Prodigal Son allegorically represents this process of the soul becoming involved in transient phenomena and following its own devices until it realizes that something is lacking. Through intelligence and reason it senses an indefinable urge to return to the Father—the Great Source—and is then better able to appreciate the Divine Plan.

When the infant in the mortal school arrives at a suitable age he enters the kindergarten, then through the successive stages of primary school, high school and university unfolds the intellect and broadens his views of various problems, usually concerning matters belonging to the physical.

Would the graduate, his consciousness having expanded and outgrown the lower grades, be justified in denying, for

229

those coming after, the necessity for the grades through which he has acquired his advanced mental state?

Mental Scientists, in their eagerness to attain the "Real," strive to repudiate even the faculty of mind through the very use of which they are gradually stepping out of the difficult school of experience and beginning to partly awaken to the fact that the spirit is the real individuality, and yet in their blindness they attempt to relegate that wonderful faculty of mind to the limbo of myth.

Some schools go to the extreme of asserting that our mortal mind, consciousness, perceives only a notion of a tree, that there is in reality no tree at all but only a false image created by the mind. This idea is carried to the extent of declaring that even if the tree were to fall and kill an individual it would still be only the notion of a tree, his own belief, that killed the man.[1]

Others teach that the mortal mind is an unreality and that the natural things, as the ordinary mortal discerns them, have no existence in reality.

Eliminate the mind from an individual and what have we left? An idiot, an imbecile or what not. These enthusiasts seem to forget, or fail to comprehend, that that which they call the "mortal mind" is a part of the ego, that faculty which goes out to explore and receives knowledge, the activity of which is a matter of directivity.

As the mind may at one moment go out through the physical sense organs into external observations and activities in the school of life, so it may also withdraw, retreat from the objective into the inner sense and meditate upon problems pertaining to the spiritual. Yet it is the same mind; its action is only a matter of changed directivity.

No experience can be bought nor can the experience of one be transferred to another, yet many apparently fail to comprehend that others following them in the pathway of life require the same schooling they have received, similar lessons and experiences, in order to reach the same understanding as those who have attained realization, for they teach that material things are only mental illusions to be ignored as having no existence or reality, and that spirit is

---

[1]See "Business Man of Syria," Stocking—Totheroh, Pages 30, 31.

all. Thereby they strive to force ignorant and inexperienced minds to comprehend that which really belongs to a higher degree of mental unfoldment.

It is as if they were to say that the school in which they had received instruction is not to be entered by others; that while the kindergarten and other grades of school had been useful to them they are not necessary for others who are beginning their education.

Is it not evident that kindergarten and early training are necessary for all as a preliminary to the upper grades? Just so has nature provided what may be termed the A-B-C School of Life for all. As the various grades of school, from kindergarten to the university, are all essential factors in cultivating and enlightening the mind regarding the more material phase of existence, so likewise is the mental school of experience, relating to the intellectual and spiritual phase of our being, obviously a necessity.

These truths should be inculcated from earliest infancy all through life. Hence a part of the curriculum in all schools, jointly with training concerning the physical aspect of existence, should be devoted to this latter phase, not taught as a dogma for any pretended salvation but to lead the individual out of ignorance into a concept of the motive of life higher than merely the material.

Self-analysis will slowly evolve the realization that while we are exercising the faculties of thinking which belong to the mind, the mind is manifesting through the body, yet it is not of the body. The body is an instrument for the soul as the piano is an instrument for harmony and music. As the piano is not the music so is the body not the soul. "Form is an external expression of internal attributes." (Hartmann.)

If we analyze ourselves, the various organs or the brain, in no part of the physical organism can the abode of consciousness be found in objective form. Compared with the physical there is nothing objective about consciousness; it is intangible and formless, its perception is limited or unlimited according to its non-use or its use. "It is the mind that is really alive and sees things yet it hardly sees anything without preliminary instruction." (Charcot.) It may be semi-dormant or it may encompass, in the spirit of understanding, figuratively speaking, the entire universe.

Cicero said in "Contempt of Death," "The soul is pure, perfect; it can escape easily through the air and break through it; it is swiftest, that it in reality sees and hears although eyes and ears are its windows ... The proper habitation of the soul is pure ether and not the body; it is self-moved, eternal ... I would swear that the soul ... is divine."

As knowledge of science, such as higher mathematics, biology, chemistry, astronomy, the many marvels of physics, etc., cannot be inherited but must be mastered and perceived by each individual, so an understanding of spiritual things must be acquired by each individual through his own faculties of discernment.

It is a common mistake of many of the present-day teachers of the new interpretations of life relating to the mind and spirit, to hold that since God, the Divine Principle, is Love, Truth and Wisdom, we may, by emulating him, meditating and attempting to realize our one-ness with him, attain a realization of wisdom, perfection and bliss.

It is obvious that such extreme ideas pervert the facts and are misleading in that they attempt to establish a short cut from a state of ignorance to a condition of perfection. This, however, is as impossible as it would be to teach a child in kindergarten the university curriculum. Such an effort would be futile and would necessarily result in failure, since the intelligence of a child has not as yet unfolded its faculties sufficiently to comprehend higher learning.

As it is impossible for the perception of a child to grasp advanced university subjects so likewise is it impossible for the undeveloped mind to intelligently perceive in fullness the nature of the Divine Principle, although mere emotions are often mistaken for understanding, which is only attained through experience and reason.

Therefore it behooves us to recognize first principles and appreciate the wisdom of the Divine Mind in ordering matters so that wisdom cannot be implanted but must be attained, step by step, through experience.

One of the aims in establishing the Constitution of the United States was to "secure the blessings of liberty to ourselves." Yet one of the consequences of this liberty has been the growth of so vast a number of conflicting schools of thought that the resultant confusion has become detrimental.

A little knowledge is indeed a dangerous thing. So many are at the present time carried off their feet by the various schools which presume to teach their devotees how to "live on a higher plane," or "attain mastery by overcoming" and subduing the natural physical requirements.

Mystic practices are advocated which keep the system in a nervous tension and thereby interfere with the natural functions of the mind and body. Meditation is advised, dark circles are attended for "development," sitting in the silence is practiced, and diet is restricted according to dietary fads which often exclude food elements necessary for the well-being of the body.

The purpose of such devotees is to liberate themselves from the supposed contaminating physical elements in certain foods, to spiritualize themselves by abstaining from the grosser things belonging to the physical plane and asserted mischievous mortal-mindedness and thereby presumably to realize the "I AM" within.

While these practices are carried on with the best of intentions they are too often fraught with baneful and distressing consequences, being founded, as they generally are, on mere sentiment, instead of reason and understanding of nature's wonderful plan, and frequently result in all manner of mental aberrations, delusions and insanity. "The Kingdom of God is not meat and drink." (Romans 14:17.)

The tendency of such practices is to produce negativism, a condition of self-hypnosis and an undue sensitiveness to influences from outside sources. The devotees may receive "inspirations," and even hear voices which are presumed to originate from Christ or God, but being ignorant of psychic laws and facts they may not realize that these are usually only deceptions instigated by ignorant or mischievous discarnated entities who parade as "Masters," Christ or God himself in order to attract attention.

Without reason or judgment the victims blindly follow the dictates of these voices and false inspirers which often lead them into the most absurd notions and practices in the belief that they are carrying out the mandates of "Great Masters," or "The Lord," but which only too frequently result in suicide, crime and insanity.

233

That these conditions prevail is not mere theory but revealed facts which our many years of research in normal and abnormal psychology have abundantly verified.

The Unity School of Christianity publishes the following statement: "Evil spirits do not have any power in Truth, because they do not exist in Truth at all . . . All obsessions, dual personalities, and all mental aberrations of that character, are the result of personal error thoughts crystallizing around the will of the man. This crystallization must be broken up by a focalized thought energy of greater power, such as is found in the Christ I AM . . . Affirm your unity with the Christ I AM; then silently, or audibly if you are so moved, speak the word of rebuke directly to the false personality."

If "evil spirits do not exist" and are only "personal error thoughts," what was it that Jesus commanded to "come out" of the "man with an unclean spirit" and "enter into the swine" causing the latter to "run down a steep place into the sea"? (Mark 5:2-13.)

If obsession were only a "crystallized error thought" how account for the fact that such an "error" has more than once been transferred from a suffering devotee of Unity to a psychic sensitive, whereupon this "error" has proven to be a discarnated human entity, often entirely ignorant of being such, whose identity has been verified?

In our research work we have frequently contacted followers of Unity, Rosicrucianism, Theosophy and kindred movements who, by following the advocated practices of "silent affirmations," "affirming unity with the Christ I AM," "meditating," etc., had become highly sensitized and thus subject to interference by ignorant or cunning spirits. These spirits were often eager to play any part to please the devotees causing the latter to believe they had attained the "Great I AM," "the Christ within" state, or had contacted a "Master," when in reality they were only receptive to spirits who were dominating them.

A teacher of a "Higher Philosophy" movement closely allied with Unity became very sensitive to spirit impressions and, while at first believing these to be revelations from the "highest sources," finally was so tormented by spirits that

she was unable to find relief from the intense pains which
caused continual suffering, especially on the right side of
the head. She came to us for help and after several static
treatments a spirit was removed who later controlled Mrs.
Wickland and claimed to be a "Teacher of the Highest," a
"Prophet of the Purple Order" and even "Allah" himself!

When the spirit assumed control of the psychic he leaned
forward, hand on right side of head, moaning as if in pain.

Spirit	My head!
Dr. Wickland	What is the matter with your head?
Sp.	I am very sick.
Dr.	You must forget your old habits. You evidently carried the idea of former sickness in your mind. You are no longer sick.
Sp.	I am sick and I want to lie down. I am a wonderful student. I belong to the Highest.
Dr.	How high are you?
Sp.	You should understand the higher things. You should not associate with anyone who does not understand.
Dr.	How else can we learn?
Sp.	You must have your own little group because the outside world is so ignorant. Few understand the higher life.
Dr.	Who are you?
Sp.	I am a Prophet! I do not have anything to do with earthly things; they belong to the mortal mind.
Dr.	What is your philosophy?
Sp.	You would not understand. What is the use of throwing pearls before swine? (Placing hands in an attitude of prayer.)
Dr.	To what order do you belong?
Sp.	To the Order of the Sacred Flame. I am on the Rainbow Path of the Soul. I belong to the Purple Order. (The patient usually wore purple.)
Dr.	Is that higher than the White Brotherhood?

Sp.   Yes, the Purple Order is the highest.

Dr.   You must have been with a lady who was here today.

Sp.   That dear, little loving girl! She is my soul-mate.

Dr.   Is that so? Does she know it?

Sp.   I do not know, but some day she will. I have recently had a terrible experience. When you want to climb to the Highest of the Holies you have to sacrifice; you have to go through fire. I had that today.

Dr.   The one you call your soul-mate had that "fire." (Static electricity.)

Sp.   My soul-mate did not like it. The fire was like lightning.

Dr.   If you are so great why didn't you dodge that fire?

Sp.   That belongs to the physical.

Dr.   The lady had that "fire" because you bothered her head too much. She complained of pains on the right side of her head. You are only a fake prophet.

Sp.   You do not know anything about it. (Making strange gestures.)

Dr.   What is this mystic rite?

Sp.   I say to you, "Get out of here!"

Dr.   Who are you?

Sp.   I am Allah!

Dr.   How long have you been dead?

Sp.   I will not talk to you any more. I am going to a higher and more glorious life. You want to know who I am? I am like the sun's rays!

Dr.   Yes, we can all see through you. You only brought trouble to that lady.

Sp.   She is a teacher of the highest order. You should be glad she comes here. She will soon be such that no earthly man or woman can talk to her.

Dr.   How do you explain the fact that she comes here to get rid of these things that bother her head?

236

	She suffers so much that she does not know what to do.
Sp.	She is very high.
Dr.	You impress her with that idea. Are you not ashamed to torment that poor woman?
Sp.	I belong to the Holy Order.
Dr.	You say you are a man?
Sp.	Of course I am a man.
Dr.	Then how do you happen to be wearing a dress? (Referring to Mrs. Wickland's dress.)
Sp.	I do not like this dress.
Dr.	(Holding mirror before spirit.) Do you recognize that face?
Sp.	That is not my face.
Dr.	The lips move when you speak.
Sp.	You can't fool me. I am a man of the Highest Degree.
Dr.	What benefit do you derive from bothering that lady?
Sp.	(With upturned face.) Jehovah, Jehovah, Jehovah! I do not know where I am but I have never been in such a low region. You have no understanding.
Dr.	We try to apply common sense to all our viewpoints.
Sp.	I am a Teacher and I am teaching in the Holy of Holies.
Dr.	What is your name?
Sp.	Samoyah.
Dr.	Don't you realize we can see through all this pretense? Why not listen to reason?
Sp.	I would not care to listen.
Dr.	You know you are nothing but a fraud. You are now talking through a woman's body. We do not see you, we only hear you talk.
Sp.	I do not like to be killed by such fire as I had.

237

Dr.   That was an electrical treatment, but I did not give that treatment to you; I gave it to the lady to help her get rid of you. She comes here of her own free will. She has tried everything imaginable to free herself from the condition that troubles her. We "fired" you out. Do you realize you have lost your physical body, or do you think you are in the physical?

Sp.   No.

Dr.   Are you in the physical or spirit world?

Sp.   I am in the Understanding. I come to the physical to teach the poor people. That lady gives lessons; she is a marvelous healer. She can heal everyone who is sick.

Dr.   What business is that of yours?

Sp.   I am her helper.

Dr.   That lady has gone to many healers to rid herself of her tormentors. She wants relief. That is why she is coming here. How can you explain that?

Sp.   I was taken away and sent to a prison.

Dr.   Intelligent spirits took you away from her and now you have been brought here that we may cause you to realize your true condition. You are so-called dead and have lost your physical body.

Sp.   (Loftily.) I am a Teacher.

Dr.   You are self-hypnotized by foolish ideas. You know in your heart that you are a pretender.

Sp.   I have studied a great deal. I will have nothing to do with you.

Dr.   Intelligent spirits brought you here to make you understand your folly. You are an earthbound spirit and have been troubling that lady. We are trying to bring you to a realization of your condition.

Sp.   (Angrily.) I will not have anything to do with you—no, I will not!

238

As the spirit could not be brought to an understanding he was taken away by advanced spirits. In later letters from the patient she stated that she was relieved from her former suffering.

A prominent leader of the Unity movement consulted us about his son, a young man who had become so erratic and unruly that he had been placed in a sanitarium where it had been necessary to use forcible measures of restraint.

We concentrated for the patient, knowing that our Co-Workers, the Mercy Band of Spirit Forces, would do whatever was possible to relieve the young man. Shortly thereafter our Invisible Helpers dislodged from the patient a stubborn, boastful spirit who, speaking through Mrs. Wickland, loudly asserted that he was a "Teacher of Unity and Higher Philosophy" and as such should not have been disturbed.

Spirit — I do not like being brought here. I am a Holy Man. I belong to Unity. I am a Teacher.

Dr. Wickland — What do you teach?

Sp. — What you do not know. I am teaching higher and purer philosophy. I travel in the astral. You only travel in the sphere of ignorance.

Dr. — How long have you been dead?

Sp. — I am not dead. I have a fine, beautiful, high mind.

Dr. — You have all the earmarks of a faking spirit.

Sp. — You must be made pure and good.

Dr. — From where did you come?

Sp. — I have been doing a great deal for Unity by talking. I am a holy Unity man. Unity is doing wonderful work.

Dr. — What were your latest experiences?

239

Sp.   They put me away temporarily. (Referring to patient having been placed in sanitarium.)

Dr.   How could they do that to such a wonderful man as you say you are?

Sp.   I got in with people who have malicious animal magnetism. I fought because they restrained me. I thought I would scare them. They put me in a straight-jacket.

Dr.   That was a strange situation.

Sp.   Once I thought I had power over matter.

Dr.   Have you found you were mistaken?

Sp.   Matter is only thoughts.

Dr.   Then the straight-jacket must have existed only in your state of mind.

Sp.   You must get understanding.

Dr.   We understand that you are dead, and are a pretending spirit.

Sp.   (Indignantly.) Why, I am wonderful!

Dr.   You are so wonderful you cannot even control yourself.

Sp.   I wish you could see how wonderful I am!

Dr.   You have been controlling a young man and disturbing him so that he had to be sent to a sanitarium.

Sp.   His father is one of the finest teachers. We all have beautiful conditions.

Dr.   Have they been beautiful lately?

Sp.   No, we could not get through the evil thoughts. I was sent to a sanitarium.

Dr.   A young man was sent to a sanitarium because you, as a selfish, earthbound spirit, were controlling him. He wore a straight-jacket. You made him act as if he were insane.

Sp.   How dare you talk to me like that? I am out in the astral!

Dr.   Do you know that you have severed the connection with your physical body?

Sp.   I am in the astral!

Dr.   Be honest with yourself.

As the spirit would not listen to reason he was taken away by the intelligent spirits. Later the mother of the young man informed us that her son was again well and normal and had returned home.

An elderly man, who had followed occult studies for many years and was a firm believer in reincarnation, had become subject to strange seizures during which he was unable to walk upright but crawled about on the floor. When he was brought to us and assisted from the automobile he immediately dropped to his hands and knees and crawled swiftly into the reception room.

After being seated, he conversed with more than ordinary intelligence but declared he had reincarnated many times, always to be bothered by spirits, and when questioned as to his extraordinary method of locomotion, invariably replied, "That is a secret." However, following a static electrical treatment he walked in normal manner and unaided from the room, having been freed from an obsessing spirit who had prompted his unusual behavior.

At a subsequent seance Mrs. Wickland became controlled by this spirit who at once attempted to crawl about the room but was restrained and placed in a chair.

Dr.
Wickland What is the matter? Can't you walk upright?

Spirit   I am a Great Teacher!

Ques.   No one ever heard of a teacher crawling on his hands and feet.

Sp.   You do not understand. That is part of a religious ceremony. You do not understand the higher philosophy of life.

Ques.   Will you expound that philosophy to us?

241

Sp.	When you have gone to a higher state you have to crawl like a dog. I have been to earth a thousand times.
Ques.	It does not seem that you have made much progress if you have to come back as a dog.
Sp.	That has to be understood. I am the Light and the Way!
Ques.	And still you walk like a dog?
Sp.	I did that many years ago.
Dr.	We have a patient who walks on his hands and feet; he says he understands the mystic, and the reason spirits bother him is a secret which others do not know.
Sp.	Very few do. You have to come into that state like I did. You will all crawl as I do, and if you have done some wrong during your life you will get down on your hands and feet when you want to walk.
	I am coming back to teach and preach to the people who are ignorant and do not understand life. They must learn the laws that govern the mysteries of this earth.
Dr.	If everyone crawled on his hands and feet, what would be the result?
Sp.	That all belongs to the wonderful mystery of life. I am a philosopher. You cannot mention the name of a Teacher because it is a secret. I am whatever you think. I am a Master and have advanced to the Highest of the High.
Dr.	You are not fooling anybody but yourself.
Sp.	I will have to pray for you and then teach you the mystery of life.
Ques.	Will we have to crawl on our hands and knees?
Sp.	You will have to be lower than a dog. A dog is faithful and we have to learn the faithfulness of a dog. I am a wonderful Master! I have reincarnated on earth time after time, a thousand times, to teach ignorant people that they know nothing about the whole mystery of life.

Dr.	You are "dead" and do not know it.
Sp.	Dead?
Dr.	So-called dead. How did you get away from the man who crawls around?
Sp.	I got some kind of a shock and could not stand it. (Static electrical treatment given patient.)
Dr.	That was static electricity. As a "master" you should have been able to withstand that.
Sp.	I came too close to matter; I felt that terrible shock. I will tell you, you will have to go through a great deal for giving a Master that shock. You will go down like Lucifer for that! The time will come when you will crawl like an insect.
	None of you know the secret of life. I have to teach people to know the faithfulness of a dog. I have reincarnated many, many times to show people how ignorant they are. They do not understand and they will not.
Dr.	When you say you have reincarnated many times, no doubt you mean you have obsessed many persons and made them insane. That has been your reincarnation. Because of you, many have been sent to the asylum.
Sp.	I will tell you, if they have it is their own fault. They should have developed a higher understanding of God.
Dr.	You interfered with their mental action and they were sent to the asylum because they did not act in a natural manner. You controlled the man who was here the other day.
Sp.	He is happy to crawl because he is going through his incarnation.
Dr.	How could he be happy having some one like you attached to him?
Sp.	(Angrily.) How dare you? You will be still lower than an insect!
Dr.	You only pretend to be a "master."
Sp.	(Bombastically.) I am One of the Mightiest.

243

Dr.	What is your name?
Sp.	That is a secret. My name you do not need to know. I am far above names.
Dr.	We call you a fraud and a prevaricator.
Sp.	I will tell you, you will go down and be a pig!
Dr.	You are so-called dead and do not know it.
Sp.	You will have to reincarnate ten thousand times before you can understand the secret of our doctrine.
Dr.	How do you happen to be here in a woman's body and wearing a dress? Look at this hand (lifting hand of psychic) ; it does not belong to you.
Sp.	I do not argue with anyone.
Dr.	(Holding up mirror.) Do you recognize that face? Does it look like that of a "master"?
Sp.	I have reincarnated a thousand times and I suppose I am now a woman. I reincarnated as a dog, and now I am a woman.
Dr.	Wake up to the facts.
Sp.	I am awake, and I am as smart as you think you are.
Dr.	Why can't you be honest with yourself?
Sp.	I am.
Dr.	You are nothing but a fraud.
Sp.	You don't know me. My name is not given to those who do not understand the law.
Dr.	Did you have a family?
Sp.	No, I never married. I was a Master, and I gave myself up to wonderful things.
Dr.	Where was this?
Sp.	I was a Master in Calcutta.
Dr.	Where do you think you are now?
Sp.	I am here, I suppose, because during my life I did things I should not have done. But it makes no difference. I am a Master, and I have to go through all manner of experiences so I will know the Law of Nature.

244

Dr.   How did you travel?

Sp.   By mind. After you have learned to control matter you can go through matter and that is what all should do. The spell was broken when I had that electricity on my back. It was terrible!

Dr.   It dislodged you from that man. Are you not ashamed to make a man act as he did?

Sp.   I have done nothing. I am next to Jesus Christ. I am above him. I have reincarnated many times but he has not. He has yet to come back.

Dr.   You have been obsessing people and making them become demented. The gentleman who came to my office the other day came in on his hands and feet.

Sp.   He can walk but I will not allow him to do so. He has to learn the lesson of faithfulness to me. I want him to be a dog and learn to serve me. That is the real reason I made him crawl.

Dr.   Why should he serve you? Did you crawl for somebody?

Sp.   I used to fly. (Travel as a spirit.) I have learned to overcome matter. I am next to God! Don't you give any more of those electric sparks to that man.

Dr.   They freed him of you.

Sp.   (Threateningly.) I will make you as little as a small grasshopper!

Dr.   You are only an ignorant spirit.

Sp.   I have studied philosophy.

Dr.   Your mind became twisted. You do not even know you have lost your physical body.

Sp.   I have not lost my physical body; I have controlled matter. But I tell you I do not want any more of that electricity. Why should you punish me like that?

Dr.   To bring you to your senses and make you leave that man alone.

Sp.   He is a student and I am his Teacher.

Dr.   He is sixty-seven years old. Why do you make him walk as he does?

Sp.   He has to learn to be humble. I want him to crucify matter and be like a dog—to crawl.

Dr.   That is not natural.

Sp.   There are many who have reincarnated a thousand times or more.

Dr.   By becoming obsessing spirits like yourself. Be honest and face facts. Be sensible and sincere.

Sp.   (Cringing from a sight invisible to mortal eyes.) Oh—Oh! (Covering face with hands.) See them! I don't want to have anything to do with that crowd. (Spirits accusing him of having misled them.)

Dr.   Listen to what those people have to say.

Sp.   (Overwhelmed.) I know—I know. I know you, and you, and you!

Dr.   Face your mistakes.

Sp.   No, no, I cannot!

Dr.   You cannot be a coward. You will have to correct your mistakes. What did you do that you should fear these people?

Sp.   So many of them—they shout at me, "You have ruined our lives!"

Dr.   Why did you do that?

Sp.   Because I wanted to be a great Teacher.

Dr.   You have played the part of the blind leading the blind. You do not even understand yourself. How could you teach others?

Sp.   (To invisibles.) I see now what I have not seen before. I held classes and collected a great deal of money by fooling poor, deluded victims. Some of them would crawl up trees. I finally ran away from it all.

(Distressed.) Do not come here! I cannot stand it! Look at all those people! They are all accusing me. I cannot endure this. (Writhing in mental agony.)

246

Dr.   Listen to intelligent spirits who will help you and teach you how to overcome your mistakes.

Sp.   Why did you wake me up?

Dr.   To bring you to a realization of the truth.

Sp.   I wish I could hide myself from all these accusers.

Dr.   Intelligent spirit friends will help you and teach you.

Sp.   I was very selfish. (Seeing an invisible.) That poor woman! I took all the money she had and the last I heard of her was that she had been put in an asylum. I told her I must have all her money if she wanted to be a Master. Oh—I can't stand it any longer!

Dr.   Conscience is a terrible accuser.

Sp.   Look at that poor crippled man! I took all his money and told him I would cure him. Take them all away; I can't stand any more!

    (Seeing another spirit.) Mother, mother! Please do not come here!

Dr.   She does not accuse you; she comes to help you.

Sp.   I condemned her because she would not listen to me. I took all her money and left her. Oh, mother!

    She says, "John, John!"

    Oh, mother, can you ever forgive me?

    She says that gradually I shall have to help those whom I have harmed. (Abjectly.) Mother, I feel I am nothing—nothing! She says I have obsessed one person after another. Oh, see what I have done! Mother, I will leave reincarnation alone after this.

Dr.   Evidently when you left your body you did not know anything about it.

Sp.   In a way I was buried alive. I was a demonstrator and allowed myself to be buried alive many times, but one time I did not come back to physical life. They buried my physical body but I was still alive (a spirit) and went from one

	place to another. After that, I became a "Master"—a pretender. That was in Calcutta, India. From there I went to New York.
Dr.	How long ago was that?
Sp.	About 1882.
Dr.	That is a long time ago.
Sp.	I told you I have reincarnated many, many times.
Dr.	You have been obsessing and controlling people; you unbalanced them.
Sp.	I have been with that man (patient) a very long time.
Dr.	He is sixty-seven years old and has been bothered nearly all his life.
Sp.	I have been with him many years. Once in a while I left him to go to some one else. I liked to reincarnate.
Dr.	That was only obsession.
Sp.	Mother, take me away; I am so tired. I have no power any more.
Dr.	Be brave and acquire understanding, then you can help those you have harmed. Intelligent spirits will aid you.
Sp.	I am going. Good-bye.

Such practices as meditation and striving to attain the "Christ Spirit" or "Mastership" are largely a condition of self-hypnosis; this too frequently brings about a negative dream state conducive to interference by discarnated spirits which not only leads to most unfortunate results but also stunts the faculties for thinking and reasoning with which the mind is imbued.

Reason, the guide on the pathway of life, is ignored and no analysis is made of the true principle of the Divine; such enthusiasts are merely followers of blind faith.

248

"Know then that salvation is not attained by uttering mantrams, nor by the burning of incense, or observing thousands of fasts. Until the incarnated soul knows that he is divine he cannot attain salvation." (Mahanirvana Tantra.)

We should have more than only faith in the Divine or a mere belief in immortality; we should analyze ourselves, our faculties and our relationship to the Great Purpose of Life and thus attune ourselves and sensitize our minds, not by "sitting in the silence" and dreaming, nor by "meditating" and making unnecessary self-denials, but by thinking and by research in nature; thus we can gradually discern in and through all things a design, which implies a Designer. "Nature is the only book that teems with meaning on every page," said Goethe.

To realize Nature's Purpose does not mean the false conception which many entertain of "attaining spirituality," "realizing the I AM within," "attaining unity with the Christ I AM," etc. The ocean of life, in which we live and move and have our being, is Intelligence, all wonderfully, beautifully and clearly manifested in the physical nature.

By comprehending that the thinking faculty, the self-conscious "Something" within us, is the real mind, or ego, that the physical body is only the outer tabernacle through which we develop expression, we gradually unfold mental discernment. "Mind is the Man"; "I think, therefore I am"; "I am a spirit here and hereafter."

The real life is the mind or soul life, not dependent upon cold creed, but to be realized in one's own inner self, this realization culminating in an understanding of ourselves as an integral part of the Great Creative Scheme. When we can catch the vibrations radiating from the minds of those advanced Intelligences in the spirit world who constantly send out their thoughts to benefit humanity, our perspective of life will be broadened and our souls will then become illumined.

But we must not fail to remember the admonition, "Believe not every spirit, but try the spirits whether they are of God: because many false prophets are gone out into the world." (I John 4:1.)

249

CHAPTER XIII

The Great Designer

N ORDER to appreciate and understand the purpose of life it is important to reason from a premise. We are here, conscious, sentient beings with mental faculties unlimited in possibilities if we but choose to make use of the same.

Regarding the importance or non-importance of our existence in the scheme of things, for the sake of analysis let us imagine a person waking one morning to find no human being in existence excepting himself. He would, however, observe that nature's activities had not changed but, regardless of the absence of humanity, were continuing as usual, indicating the non-importance of mankind in the activities of nature.

Yet we are here. It should be obvious that our existence must imply some ultimate purpose. By what method are we to ascertain our part in this plan?

Is it not evident that the faculties with which we are endowed, intelligence and the ability to reason, are the working tools we possess for research in nature's laboratory? Therein we can obtain self-evident realization that intelligent design is indicated on every hand, and through common sense and experience we know that where there is design there must be a Designer.

By analogy we perceive that the result of human ideations is represented when we see an intricate machine or a magnificent structure, for everything has its origin in imagination and ideation, which are intangible factors. "Life is thought. Causation itself is intelligence." ("Spirit Life in Higher Realms.")

All objective constructions have their origin in the mind. The towering building originates in ideation. The architect, in addition to planning the form of the structure, must be familiar with all details, such as quality of materials used, and the weakness as well as potential strength of all the parts; he must calculate the ultimate weight of the proposed structure and the requirements of a foundation to support it.

The electric light, the telephone, the radio, inventions from the small to the great, as well as all sciences, have been revealed through the wondrous faculty of mind.

"The created universe is not God, but is from God." (Swedenborg.) Analysis of nature in its intricate manifestations is a necessity in order to comprehend an intelligent, causative factor which, through formative activity, brings creation into the objective and manifest.

The theory of evolution postulates that all life and organisms originate from a single cell which by cell division slowly evolves various biological forms, culminating in the human organism. From the materialistic standpoint this hypothesis would imply that that which seems to be inferior, the cell, is capable of becoming the superior, man.

We may be justified in postulating that there is a Principle, a Divine Plan, involved in the cell, the Principle of Becoming, of ultimately culminating in human consciousness, manifest in intelligence and the finer spiritual qualities.

It is evident that as there is a physical evolution so also is there conjointly a mental evolution, both phases indicating an intelligent, directing Principle. As bricks cannot in themselves construct a house, a guiding intelligence and trained hand being required, it should be evident that in all animal and plant life the individual cells, or congregation of cells, cannot of their own initiative know where to place themselves in forming the structure, but must be subject to a directing Principle implanted by the Architect of the Universe.

"In the spiritual world are the causes of all things; in the natural world are the effects of all things." (Swedenborg.) "As above so below." There may be clearly discerned in nature's activities an evident, inner, intangible propelling force, seemingly ruled by definite laws, suggesting an intelligent guidance.

Huxley, observing transformations of living matter, says, "One is almost possessed of the notion that with better vision one might see the hidden artist with his plan before him, striving with skilful manipulation to perfect his work."

The protoplasm of each variety of plant life must contain certain proportions of elements for the reproduction of its peculiar kind. What is it that governs this selection of elements?

Through the microscope we analyze a seed, say, a peach stone. Within a hard shell is held the seed; the contents of the seed reveal nothing of its potential ability to evolve a tree and ultimate fruit. Yet, placed in the proper soil the seed opens and a sprout springs forth which culminates in a tree, flowers and finally fruit. In the fruit is formed another vitalized seed for reproduction of its kind.

To further consider this activity, some innate power in the seed must of necessity possess the faculty of carrying on intricate chemicalizing processes. Innumerable elements are segregated in definite proportions from the soil and the air in the production of protoplasm. Therein are the various cells necessary for building up the structure of the tree, some for the bark, some for the woody fibre, some for the chlorophyll in the leaves, which produces a green appearance, the color most soothing to the eye.

How do these various cells find their proper places in the structure? Again, would it be reasonable to say that each individual cell knows just where to go to find its proper location?

Should it not be self-evident that there is an intelligent power engineering the process of development, carrying out a principle, designing the structure and symmetry of trunk, branches and leaves?

The aroma of the flower is discernible at a distance evidencing the same to be substance, although unseen, still further showing the handiwork of invisible, intelligent Activity.

Our solar system is composed of the sun and some nine planets, each planet maintaining its respective orbit around the sun. The planets are situated at varying distances from the sun; Mercury, the nearest, being approximately 36,000,-000 miles away; Neptune, 2,795,000,000, and the newly discovered planet, Pluto, being 4,620,240,000 miles away. What holds the planets in their courses?

Our little globe, the earth, travels through space at approximately eighteen and a half miles a second around the sun, about thirty-five times faster than the speed of a swift bullet, yet with such marvelous regularity and precision that an astronomer can calculate years ahead the earth's position at a given time.

The earth tilts from north to south and reverses this motion every six months, in December and June, producing the seasons, alternately giving the northern and southern hemispheres the needed seasons for productivity.

The moon, in its journey around the earth every twenty-eight days, not only reflects light but causes, in conjunction with the sun, the invisible pull which results in the ebb and flow of the waters. Science proves that the tides, influenced by the sun and moon, have, in their ebb and flow a purpose, that of washing the shores of continents, of carrying accumulated impurities from the shores out to sea for purification, the incoming flow returning purified waters. Does not that imply design?

Vapor is extracted from the seas by the energy of the sun and is conveyed by the sustaining atmosphere over vast areas. Reaching colder air-strata the vapor condenses into drops which, overcoming the atmospheric resistance, are precipitated as rain. Does that not suggest design?

What regulates these invisible activities? Science answers that it is natural law. Reason suggests that where there is law there must be a Law-Giver.

How evidently is this manifested in the human structure with its infinite ramifications of organs and functions. Chemical analysis shows that the human body contains some sixteen material elements—carbon, phosphorous, iron, lime, sulphur, magnesium, soda, potassium, hydrogen, oxygen, nitrogen, etc.—chemical elements all fundamentally necessary for the construction of the physical body. These elements are transformed into sensitized living tissues. What is it that activates this transformation but that same mysterious innate Law?

Innumerable varieties of cells fill different functions in

the construction of various parts of the body, some forming the bony structures, the muscular system, ligaments and tendons, some the circulatory system of the blood, as the heart, lungs, the arterial, venous and lymphatic systems, others the liver, spleen, pancreas, kidneys and alimentary systems.

The intricacies of the brain and the nervous apparatus —motor, sensory and sympathetic—are the avenues through which the vital functions, both voluntary and involuntary, are carried on.

Observing the harmonious conjoint action of parts and organs of the human body, how can we avoid or exclude an active, intelligent, vitalizing Force which permeates the whole organism?

"The blooming of the flower is energy, the increase of fruit is energy, the growth of the body is energy; yet in all these there is no violence. The efficacy is not destructive, but vital; without it, the whole frame must fall at once into corruption; with it, instead of corruption, we have life." (Anon.)

The various cells are so definite and true to their kind in the genetic processes, in the multiplication of organs in one body, that science can tell exactly what kind of cells occur in similar organs in other bodies.

It might seem reasonable to expect that since certain cells produce a certain type of mind in one body, similar cells would duplicate a similar mind in another body. But evidence proves that as there are no two physiognomies alike, so are there no two minds alike; all differ as to personality, individuality, character and behavior.

Furthermore, the entire mental life attitude of man changes with each period of development—infancy, childhood, adolescence, the active age of maturity—undergoing, as fruit in its growth, processes of unfoldment from stage to stage, evolving the involved qualities of becoming, the plan of Nature.

There is a marked similarity between the human brain and a radio apparatus, both being receiving centers. The multitude was more or less unaware that the millions of sounds given off in the world set up sound waves which traveled in all directions; these waves were unnoticed and unperceived by the majority until the radio apparatus revealed their existence and transformed them into audibility.

These audible sounds enter the auditory apparatus, the ear, invisibly and are carried from there to the brain. However, as the radio apparatus merely conveys sound but does not understand what is passing through it, so is the ear only an organ for conveying impressions to the brain. Likewise each of the other four sense organs is only an apparatus for receiving the various vibrations of sight, smell, taste and touch.

The eye does not understand what it sees, being only a window, or a camera obscura, which receives the vibrations of reflected objects. The vibrations of odors reach the olfactory apparatus, those of taste reach the gustatory apparatus of the tongue, and the vibrations of touch or feeling are distributed over the entire human body. All these vibrations reach the brain, the receiving center, but the brain, like the radio, does not understand what it receives or the meaning of the vibrations.

Only the perceptive mind is able to interpret the various radiations and to understand the meaning of them. "I respect my soul though I cannot see it," said Socrates. Plato declared, "Man is nothing else but soul."

It should be obvious that "Mind is the man" and that the body and brain are only vehicles through which the mind functions. Were it not so, and were mind to become extinct at cessation of cell activity, since mind is the highest expression in manifest nature, what would be the object or use of life at all? It would negate an intelligent purpose of existence. "But there is a spirit in man, and the breath of the Almighty giveth them understanding." (Job 32:8.)

Emma Hardinge Britten, in "Art Magic," wrote: "Can the answer to the mystery of being ever be rendered? If so, it must come from the realm of knowledge, the esoteric innermost. The physical universe . . . and the human race are the expression of a Spiritual ideal . . . Matter created nothing. It is only the mold which Spirit uses to externalize its ideas for the sake of external uses."

"The Solar Universe, of which the earth is a part, con-

255

sists of Matter, Force, and Spirit. Matter is an aggregation of minute, indestructible atoms" (now further subdivided by science), "existing in the four states known as solid, fluid, gaseous, and ethereal . . . The general attributes which distinguish matter in the three first conditions are indestructibility, extension, divisibility, impenetrability, and inertia . . . Ether is matter in so rare and sublimated a condition, that its divisibility into particles is no longer possible to man in his present stage of scientific attainment."

"Force is the life principle of being . . . it permeates, vitalizes and moves matter. It is motion per se . . . Its attributes are . . . Attraction and Repulsion . . . It is Electricity in the air; magnetism in the earth; galvanism between different metallic particles . . . Life in plants, animals and men, the aural, astral, or magnetic body of spirits."

"Spirit is the one primordial, uncreated, eternal infinite Alpha and Omega of Being . . . Its one sole attribute . . . Will . . . is itself the cause of all effects."

"In Matter, Force, and Spirit is the grand Trinity of Being, which constitutes the solar universe and its inhabitants."

"We have authority for supposing that the astral and all other universes included in the illimitable fields of being may have proceeded from and include the same primordial Trinity of elements, and that Spirit, Force, and Matter form that stupendous Ego, the totality of which, to finite beings, is vaguely called God, the separated units of which include Astral and Solar Systems, Suns, Satellites, Worlds, Spirits, Men, animate and inanimate Things, and Atoms."

"The Solar System of which our earth is a part, moves around the physical sun as a centre of light, heat, and attraction. By well defined astronomical laws we know that this Solar System forms only a part of a larger and far grander aggregation of starry worlds, called the Astral System."

"The exact centre of this system is not arrived at, yet all the observations of astronomy point to such a pivotal centre, and the known laws of Science determine that in the visible universe all motions proceed in and are sustained by the dual modes of centrifugal and centripetal force."

"Physical Science and spiritual revelation supplementing each other, assure us there is one grand central Sun of being . . . That central Sun is God. This perfection of being exists in the form of a globe, the only point of union being mathematics and geometry, and occupies the centre, the only position whereby revolving universes can live, move, and have their being, and life be born, sustained, and renewed.

"God is the dispenser of heat and light, the two elements in being which account for generation and revelation, love and wisdom, life and sense. This Spiritual Sun throws off from the centre the elements of new-created worlds by centrifugal force, and draws them back and keeps them in determinate orbits by centripetal force. Its nature is Spirit; its attribute, Will; its manifestations, Love, Wisdom, and Power. This is God."

"The early conceptions of the Hindoos . . . cherished ideas so exalted of the First Great Cause, that they ventured not to embody their thought of Him in any form, symbol, or even to assign to Him a name. The Supreme Being was with them, the Unknowable, and only became typified as Brahm, which interpreted, signifies The Void, the Silent Region which cannot be pierced, the unfathomable which cannot be . . . understood." . . .

"The sages of India taught that there were three subordinate emanations from the First Great Cause, who embodied the Grand Trinity of his Deific attributes. This primordial Trinity consisted of Brahma, the Creator; Vishnu, the Preserver; and Siva, the Destroyer and Reproducer."

"Each of these Deific emanations was so intimately connected in the Hindoo mind with the attributes of heat and light, that the earliest Hindoostanee worship may with truth be assumed to have laid the foundation of that stupendous system known in later ages as the astronomical religion." . . .

"The Vedic hymns are nearly all invocations to the Solar and Astral Sources of light and heat; the Vedic philosophy, speculating on the origin of Being, ever re-affirming the influence of Solar and Astral agency in creation." . . .

257

"In the Egyptian and Persian Theogony, the direct acknowledgment of one Supreme Being corresponding to the Sun and its attributes, is as marked as in the Aryan and Indian records. The elaborate woof of Grecian and Roman Mythology partakes of the same golden threads of belief."

"In the medieval, and still later ages, we find the most illuminated of the mystics either re-affirming the ancient beliefs of India and Egypt in the Great Central Sun, or claiming to receive confirmation of this truth from spiritual inspiration, direct revelations, or intercourse with superior orders of being. Cornelius Agrippa, Paracelsus, Jacob Boehme, and Swedenborg taught this idea of Deity with more or less distinctness."

Teachings of certain spirits on this subject are quoted from "Hardinge's Twenty Years' History of Modern American Spiritualism":

"There is a grand central territory in the universe known to exist by all spirits, and in all worlds . . . Its position as a vast central point is defined from the fact that from thence and to thence, seem to trend all the illimitable lines of attraction, gravitation, and force, which connect terrestrial bodies, and link together firmaments teeming with lives and systems . . . Sometimes it is called 'the Celestial Realm,' 'the Central Sun,' 'Heaven,' 'God,' 'The Infinite Realm,' 'The Eternal Life.' "

"Through the ecstatic Bruno was declared, 'There is in the heaven of heavens but one Sun, which is the Spiritual Sun, the form in which God appears. Our terrestrial sun is but the reflection of the rays dispersed from the Great Central Spiritual Sun, which is God.' "

Swedenborg wrote in "Divine Providence": "What the Infinite and Eternal is, the finite cannot comprehend; and yet it can comprehend it because there are abstract ideas by means of which the existence of things can be seen, if not the nature of them. Such ideas are possible respecting the Infinite, God."

"God is called the Infinite because He is infinite . . . Nothing whatever is lacking, and from this He has infinite perfection . . . Man, because his ideas are natural, is unable

258

by any refinement or approximation to come into a perception of the infinite things in God; and an angel, while he is able, because he is in spiritual ideas, to rise by refinement and approximation, above the degree of man, is still unable to attain to that perception."

In "Divine Love and Wisdom" Swedenborg states: "The Divine, that is God, is not in space, although omnipresent and with every man in the world, and with every angel in heaven . . . (this) cannot be comprehended by a merely natural idea, but it can by a spiritual idea." . . .

"Spiritual idea derives nothing from space, but it derives its all from state . . . love, life, wisdom, affections, and joys therefrom; in general, of Good and of Truth."

"Without a knowledge and some perception that the Divine is everywhere and yet . . . is not in space . . . nothing can be understood about the Divine Life, which is Love and Wisdom, and hence little, if anything, about Divine Providence, omnipresence, omniscience, omnipotence, infinity, and eternity . . . They cannot be comprehended by any natural idea, but only by a spiritual idea . . . Reception of love and wisdom causes affinity with the Lord."

"In the spiritual world the Divine Love of the Lord appears as a sun, and from it proceed the spiritual heat and the spiritual light from which the angels derive love and wisdom."

"The universal of all things . . . is Love and Wisdom . . . These are the two essentials of all things of man's life; everything of that life, civil, moral, and spiritual, hinges upon these two, and apart from these two is nothing . . . The Divine Essence itself is Love and Wisdom."

"Everything that proceeds from love is called good, and everything that proceeds from wisdom is called truth. It is because the Divine Essence itself is Love and Wisdom, that the universe and all things in it, alive and not alive, have unceasing existence from heat and light; for heat corresponds to love, and light corresponds to wisdom; and therefore spiritual heat is love and spiritual light is wisdom."

Without the sun's effulgent rays life on the physical plane could not exist or be revealed. The sun's warmth is the maternal principle through which life is revealed; the

259

sun's light is the sustainer of life. Hence the sun is often referred to as the externalized expression of the Divine Mind, as Love and Wisdom—Love, warmth, the maternal, and Wisdom, light, the intellectual.

Franz Hartmann writes in "The Life and Doctrines of Jacob Boehme": "God is self-existent, self-sufficient, infinite will, having no origin. That Will, by conceiving of its own self, thereby creates a mirror within its own self. The same takes place in the microcosm of man. By conceiving of his own self man creates a mirror in which he "feels" his own self, and thereby he becomes self-conscious and realizes his existence as an individual being."

"We cannot conceive of a man without a body of some kind, nor of a universal God without a universal nature. The very essence which constitutes man is will and intelligence manifesting itself in a human form. God begins to exist as a being only when He is manifesting Himself in nature. From all eternity has God thus been revealing Himself to Himself . . . This eternal mirroring, or God beholding Himself within Himself, may be called divine imagination."

In "Mysterium," Jacob Boehme wrote: "God in His primitive aspect is not to be conceived of as a being, but merely as the power or the intelligence constituting the potentiality for being—as an unfathomable, eternal will, wherein everything is contained, and which, although being itself everything, is nevertheless only one, but desirous of revealing itself and to enter into a state of spiritual being. . . . God is the will of eternal wisdom, and the wisdom eternally generated from Him in His revelation."

It is said that God geometrizes, also that he is both the Creator and the Creation. That this is true is evident if we will only think and observe nature's handiwork. "The soul of Wisdom lies in the acknowledgment and knowledge of the Deity." (Swedenborg.) Activities indicating design and intelligence back of all things offer self-evident proof of a Master Builder, the Architect of the Universe. The study of God is the study of man and nature.

260

CHAPTER XIV

Origin of Religions

FROM the many sources which could be quoted in regard to the origin of religions the following extracts are of special interest.

In "Illuminated Brahminism" the statement is made that the Christians "proclaim to the world that to them alone is given the monopoly of spiritual wisdom and the fullness of Divine revelation, although all the written words of their oracles, that they have preserved in mutilated form, came from India originally." . . .

"The Gods of the Christian world are ideals in material form. The worship of them is only another form of idolatry which has descended to it through a natural evolution of the polytheism of the ancient nations of Greece and Egypt. In their divinely begotten Son of God they preserve the traditions of Egyptian and Grecian mythology as well as the avatarship of India."

Edgar Tozer writes in "The Kalpaka": "To trace the origin of the Biblical Jesus story we must revert to the time of the reign of the Roman Emperor Constantine the Great. In the year 325 A. D., Constantine called together a great council of the wise men of the religionists of Arabia, Italy, Persia, Egypt, Greece, and other surrounding countries. This council consisted of 1,786 learned men, scribes and teachers of religion . . . who brought with them 2,231 books and legendary tales of Gods and Saviors and great men, and records of many doctrinal teachings of the many sects of those times. There existed then sixty-two Gods . . . and about sixty saviors and leaders of religion." . . .

"One God only was to be chosen for the new religion, thus by a ballot of men was the Deity chosen, and 'Kriste' was the designated name, which in the Ahanic language means knowledge."

261

"Similarly by a ballot of men was the name Jesus chosen; the origin of this name was 'Iesu.' This word means 'sexless,' and in choosing it the idea was to typify the pure man as savior. Then later the Phoenician symbol I.H.S. was latinized into 'Jesus.' Thus it was the Council of Nice proclaimed that their new God-representative was to hereafter be known on earth as 'Jesus.'

"The ballot for the heavenly God took seventeen months to finalize and that for the God-son or savior took twelve months." . . .

"The biblical word 'Christ' seems to have originated from Phoenician, Greek, and Egyptian symbols and simply means anointed or illuminated, yet the Council of Nice added this to make it appear that its God-man was deified and that he was above the order of man."

"The composite aspect of the character was introduced thus: several characters of prominence of those days came under review and parts of the lives of Apollonius of Tyana, Jose (or Joshu) the Nazarene, and Jehoshua ben Pandira of Egypt were chosen to compose it." . . .

"Along with alternations and interpolations . . . the Indian God story of the incarnation, birth, life and death of Chrisna . . . was embodied into the Christian gospel . . . Parts of the life of Zoroaster were used also . . ."

"Jesus is likely to continue to be an enigma until the realization of the fact that the character is a composite one."

The late M. Farady presents in "The Origin of Religions, and their influence upon the mental development of the Human Race," the teachings of advanced spirits regarding the confusion of religious ideas prevalent today.

"It is time the world should understand the truth about its religions, and that none can truthfully claim a divine origin, while all demonstrate the evolutionary processes of growth in this as in other phases of mental action."

"All religions were fabrications, to conceal truths given to man by spirits, supplemented by concessions to popular superstitions concerning the astronomical phases of natural phenomena." . . .

"The present religious systems, which have succeeded those of past ages . . . are but modifications of the primitive ideas, caused by the acts of craft; ignorance of the signification of the original terms, and the mental action upon mortals induced by the proximity of all grades of spirits, account for much of the religious chaos now reigning upon earth."

"Myriads of spirits, intense devotees, who on earth were abnormally religious, and whose natures were absorbed in devotion to fanatical religious ideas, are the monomaniacs who often fill people on earth with extravagant fancies concerning God, Jesus, the Virgin, or the Saints in the Calendar, and cause their victims to manifest the strange forms of religious fanaticism. Nearly all revivalists are influenced by this class of spirits, and the superstition and ignorance of their congregations afford congenial soil for the work of their invisible assistants."

"The ideas of men concerning a Supreme Being can be traced back by us (enlightened spirits) to the time when spiritual intercourse was very imperfectly comprehended, although sufficiently powerful to excite the attention of the ancient savage people. They perceived the existence of an external intelligent power, but not being able to get the influence transmitted with such accuracy as to instruct them as to its source, they imagined it to be superior in its nature and worshipped it as divine . . . Primitive spiritual intercourse was mixed with the superstitions originating in the imagination of the savage mind concerning the visible operations of nature." . . .

"The ignorance prevalent among men prevented correct knowledge from being transmitted, and it was only as the evolution of the intellectual powers raised the spiritual nature of man to an intelligent status that the powers of mediumship could be used to give truth concerning the nature of spirit life."

"Meanwhile upon earth had arisen the priestly orders which sought to monopolize the spiritual powers for personal aggrandizement, and then began the warfare between spiritual science and superstition that has ever continued."

"The ignorance upon earth concerning the nature of spiritual life placed great power in the hands of crafty religious leaders, enabling them to largely suppress true ideas which only can be given through mediumship by educated spirits. And even if such ideas were announced the machinery of the civil law, as well as social influence, were directed against the visible representative of those ideas. While this feeling exists among men concerning the truth and sacredness of religious ideas, there can be little mental progress made by those who are subject to their influence."

"The greatest evil which ever befell the civilized portion of the race was the successful attempt of ambitious and selfish men to monopolize the benefits of spiritual knowledge. Denying the true source from which all knowledge of this character is derived they falsely claimed this power of spiritual intercourse to be of a different nature from what it is and peopled the abodes of the invisible world with imaginary beings."

"In this way the actual status became so mystified by their fabulous statements that the world lost its bearings and without reason to guide, accepted by faith monstrous fictions about future life."

"Although in reality the world of spirits differs from the world of mortals so much as to be hardly capable of a truthful delineation in mortal language, yet in principle they are not so different as to be incapable of comprehension by minds rightly educated while in the earthly state. These minds must be free from superstitious regard or even reverence for erroneous ideas as sacred or as worthy of serious consideration. They must not be afraid to separate truth from error by personal experience, and they must be ready to receive and value truth from whatever source it proceeds."

"The only safeguard against the perpetuation of evil conditions upon earth is to BEGIN THE REFORMATION WHILE ON EARTH by teaching and recognizing the claims of scientific truth upon all subjects."

In "Disclosures by the Pagan Priests of Rome," transcribed by the spirit M. Farady and given some years ago through a well known psychic, regarding the connection of organized Christianity with Paganism, the spirit of Publius Agrentius, a Roman Augur in the temple of Jupiter Capitolinus during the reign of Constantine the Great, throws much light upon the transition of the Empire from Paganism to Christianity.

"The spread of Grecian Philosophy had undermined the old faith in the existence of the Gods and the temples were becoming deserted by their former worshipers."

"We were obliged to do something to prevent the entire abandonment of the altars by the wealthy and influential. In casting about for new methods we saw that Philosophy must be copied and religion recognize its ideas if we would retain our power over the people."

"The tendency of Philosophy was to monotheism, and we had to recognize that idea . . . We therefore seized upon the idea of having one God supreme, and in order to compromise with the old ideas we invented the story of his begetting an only Son and located the birth and life of this character in Palestine, where monotheism had long prevailed as the state religion."

"We attributed to this fictitious character all that we had received concerning Apollonius of Tyana and other marvelous wonder workers . . . We used the name Christos to designate the type of character we invented and in attempting to combine the attributes of Jesus with Christos we gave the name which generations have worshiped as we worshiped Jupiter and Hercules."

"The JES (in Greek) was taken from an old altar of the Sun which originally came from Syria, and the Latin terminal US added. By tantology we made the meaning of Jesus the same as Christus or correctly, KRISTOS, the illuminated." . . .

"We purposely changed the names of some of the leading characters in Indian legends of Buddha and added to them the acts of Apollonius and others, as parts of the narrative. We did not commit these changes to writing at first, but secretly taught them through chosen disciples who mingled with the philosophic schools and afterwards took some of the writings of the schools as the basis of the canonical New Testament Scriptures, but changed them from time to time."

"After we had manufactured the character of Jesus we secretly launched it upon the world as a new revelation from the Gods . . . In launching the new religion upon the world we depended upon two motives ever predominant among men."

265

"For the first time we had the wisest maxims of the Philosophers so artfully incorporated into the doctrines that the honest seekers for truth were confounded at such a concentration of virtue in one personality, and for the others we had the assurance that this fictitious character possessed Divine Power which he could delegate to those who accepted him."

"The tale of the miraculous incarnation and birth of Jesus was inserted in the Gospels about the beginning of the fourth century and was the work of Philenus, a scribe, who inserted it in the writings which were based upon the Gospel of Lucian."

"There were no authenticated writings previous to the fourth century, but there were frequent biographies and epistles from the leaders of various sects as early as 120 A. D. These writings were not of any one school but varied much. They were mostly found among the Gnostics who valued them for their secrets."

"It was a matter of policy with us to seemingly oppose, but really favor the new faith, so that by the time the people were ready, the priests were ready also, and the change from the old forms of worship to the new forms was more easily made." . . .

"The religious revolution which was started by us at Rome escaped our control by the avidity with which the masses accepted our ideas as containing the gist of the old ideas."

"The new faith spread rapidly among both classes and we were astonished at the readiness with which people accepted it . . . Under Constantine we made it a success. Our motives were to retain the power which as priests of religion we had held for ages . . . we were in antagonism with Neoplatonism and while we accepted a portion of its teachings we falsified, at will, the rest." . . .

"The scheme was grand for our purpose but the purpose itself was bad . . . We did the world more harm than ages of repentance can repair."

In the same book a spirit communication from Fabricus Paternus, a Roman priest, who helped to found Christianity, gives further elucidation of the motives which prompted the formulation of a new religion: "Can you not see that there is one light (the Sun) which lighteth all who come into the world; that upon every nation it shines . . . and that it is the best symbol for that everlasting truth which enables man to walk strongly and uprightly without stumbling or danger?"

"We knew the secrets of Nature and understood the processes of growth and decay. We saw that the Gods of Rome must, in time, pass away like the Gods of other nations. We sought to preserve the great truths of Nature in myths and allegories and we acted in such a manner as should conserve and control the ideas which should arise in future ages and enable us to maintain a perpetual influence upon the earth."

"We sought for power and we found it in controlling ignorance. We have held this power for ages, unknown and unsuspected by the race of mortals, who have filled our realms with countless myriads of spirits who know not the source of their own ideas. Through them we exert the great influence which causes minds upon earth to obey our wishes."

A fund of information regarding the antiquity of astronomical religion is to be found in the book, "Art Magic," arranged for publication by Emma Hardinge Britten, English lecturer and author. We quote at length:

"The mythical character of the worship of the ancients is stamped with unmistakable fidelity upon every form of modern theology . . . forms which originally contained only the spirit of an impersonated myth. The worshipers of the name of Christ are adoring the Sun-God of the ancients."

"At what period the early man first commenced to worship the starry host of heaven, or in what nation the germ was first planted of that stupendous system which overlaid the earth with temples and survived all the wrecks of chance, change and time, none can say."

"When the mind of man rose out of the lethargy of savagism to the dawn of reason . . . he began to perceive that all the grand machinery of nature was coincident with the apparition and disappearance of the resplendent lights which spangled the canopy of the over-arching heavens. The God whom his earliest perceptions recognized in the majestic sun was unquestionably the source of the climacteric changes . . . None could fail to observe that every change on the face of nature kept step with the succession of certain solar and astral phenomena . . . How many ages it required to outwork a complete theology from the book of nature and the starry heavens, man may never determine." . . .

"The constellated heavens were studied out; charts drawn; numerical Bibles written. The starry legions were divided into geometrical proportions, and their motions calculated with mathematical precision. Even the forward movement of the entire solar system around what Science now asserts to be an undiscovered but inevitable centre had been perceived and the precession of the equinoxes was understood." . . .

"All this realm of power and mystery . . . the ancient mind discovered, by thousands of years of patient and untiring study, to be all in motion—motion of one continuous and correspondential order . . . defined . . . as one grand and interblended universe of Love, Wisdom and Power." . . .

"It is only necessary to consult the diagram of the heavens, as mapped out on any common almanac . . . to perceive that the apparent path of the sun is laid down in an imaginary waving track called the Ecliptic."

"This path (assuming, as did the ancients, that the sun moves around the earth) crosses the equator, or fanciful belt encircling the earth, at two periods of time, which, by the relative positions of the sun towards the earth, divide up the solar year into winter and summer, and place the sun in the aspect of South and North towards the earth."

"The path of the sun on the Ecliptic was defined by ancient astronomers between two lines, parallel to each other, sixteen degrees apart, the sun's march being between them. This space was, and still is, called the Zodiac. The Zodiacal circle was divided into four right angles of ninety degrees each, and the whole into twelve signs, consisting each of thirty degrees."

"These signs were, with the ancients, arbitrary divisions of certain groups of stars called constellations. They were named chiefly in accordance with the climacteric changes transpiring on the earth at the period when the sun was passing through them."

"In January . . . the sun passed through the constellation . . . called, from the seasons of storms and heavy rains that then prevail, Aquarius, the washer, or the Greek, Baptize."

"In February the sun enters the sign of Pisces or the Fishes, a time of famine, dearth, and distress, when the fruits and roots are consumed, and little is left to the primitive man but the spoil of the accumulating waters."

"In March the sun enters Aries the Lamb, significant of the young and tender products of the approaching Spring."

"In April, when the energy of the agricultural season is to be typified, the constellated group through which the sun passes is called the Bull."

"In May, when Summer and Winter are reconciled, and the sweet genial period of flowers and bloom seems to knit up the opposing seasons in fraternal harmony, the constellation then prevailing is called Gemini, or the Twins."

"In June, when the sun appears to undergo a retrograde motion significantly explained in astronomy, the sign in the ascendant is termed Cancer, or the Crab."

"In July the raging heat of the burning Summer suggests for the ascendant sign the significant title of the Lion."

"The Virgin of August, the Scales of September, the Scorpion or Great Dragon of October, the Archer of November, and the Goat of December, are supposed to have somewhat more direct reference to fancied resemblances in the shape of the constellations, than for the physical correspondence between their names and the climacteric conditions of the earth."

"Besides these subdivisions of the Zodiacal path, there were two other methods of marking the astronomical year. The first was the division of the whole twelve months into four seasons, each of which contained ninety degrees, and were symbolized by a special emblem, as—an Ox, a Lion, an Eagle, and a Man.[1]

[1]See Ezekiel 1:10.

"The Ox denoted the agricultural pursuits of the spring, the Lion the fierce heat of the summer, the Eagle was adopted for certain symbolical reasons as a substitute for the Scorpion of Autumn, and the man was still retained as the Winter emblem of Aquarius, or the Water-bearer."

"Added to this quaternial division of the year were the two primal and opposing conditions of Summer and Winter, always held significant by the ancients of good and evil principles."

"The most solemn and important periods of the astronomical year were when the Sun descended from the North at the close of summer to cross the plane of the autumnal equinox, and that when he ascended from the South in the Spring to cross the vernal equinox. The first motion heralded death to the great light-bringer and famine and desolation to the earth; the second inaugurated the rejuvenating power of his triumph and glory in the promise of Spring and the fulfillment of Summer."

"Slight as seems this foundation for a theology, it is on this system only that the superstructure of every theological system of the earth has been upreared." . . .

"Each separate star visible in the heavens had its name and was supposed to exert an influence peculiar to itself for good or evil upon mankind."

"Thus, all the stars . . . near which the sun passed in Summer were deemed to be beneficent and in harmony with the sun, favorable also to the inhabitants of earth, whom they aided in dispensing seed-time and harvest, fruits, flowers and all manner of blessings."

"On the other hand, the stars of Winter were assumed to exert a malignant influence not only on the mighty Sun-God, whom they opposed, but also upon man and his planet, causing storms, tempests, pestilence, and famine. By these malignant astral influences the gracious Sun was shorn of his heat-dispensing powers, and the hours of his illumination upon earth were shortened." . . .

"On the opposing spiritual forces inhabiting the Summer and Winter constellations, was founded the apocalyptic leg-

270

end of 'the war in heaven,'[1] and endless flights of visionary astronomical myths." . . .

"The ancient priests . . . invented thousands and tens of thousands of allegorical fables descriptive of the scenes, incidents and angelic personages of the celestial drama." . . .

"When the sun entered the sign of Aries, or the Lamb, in March, he was assumed to have crossed the vernal equinox and become the *Redeemer* of the world from the sufferings and privations of Winter. Then the earth and its inhabitants rejoiced greatly. The young *Savior* had entered upon his divine mission, *bringing the earth out of darkness into light; miraculously healing the sick, feeding starving multitudes,* and filling the world with blessing."

"This triumphant career culminated in its fullest glory between the months of July and August, which, in the figurative language of the astronomical religion, was sometimes called the *betrothal of the Virgin,* sometimes the *marriage feast of the Lion,* of July, and the *Virgin,* of August. This was the season of the grape harvest, the time when the sun converted, by his radiant heat, the waters which had desolated the earth in Winter into the luscious wine of the vintage. Then it was, as the ancient astronomers proclaimed, that the great miracle of the Solar year was performed, and the Sun manifested forth his most triumphant glory."

"From thence the constellation of the Scales, or Balances, seemed for a time to maintain the celestial hero in a just and even path; his miraculous power and life-giving presence were hailed with feasts and rejoicings, which lasted until the fatal period when the Great Dragon of the Skies, the mighty Scorpio, of October, appeared in the ascendant. Then Sorrow and lamentation possessed the earth. The *Savior of men* must cross the autumnal equinox and from thence descend into the South, the Hades, Acheron, Sheol, Hell, Pit, of many ancient nations."

"To announce the dire calamity at hand, the Dragon, of October, is preceded by a bright and glorious star called in

---

[1] "And there was war in heaven: Michael and his angels going forth to war with the dragon; and the dragon warred and his angels; and they prevailed not, neither was their place found any more in heaven. And the great dragon was cast down." (Revelation 12:7.)

the Spring, Vesper, or the evening star; in autumn, Lucifer, or *'the son of the morning.'* . . .[1] (In the spring it appears high in the heavens . . . the brightest and most beautiful of all the heavenly host . . . the herald of Summer.)" . . .

"Appearing in the boding season of Autumn, low on the edge of the horizon, and shining only in the early dawn, its name is changed with its station—it is now the *fallen angel;* the mighty rebel, who seduced by pride and vaulting ambition, has been dethroned and *cast down to the ominous depths of the lowest hell.* Transformed into Lucifer, 'Son of the Morning,' this star becomes the herald of the darkest ill that can beset the path of the *Celestial Savior.* As it appears in advance of the great constellation of the Dragon, it is assumed to be the rebel Angel that incited 'a third of the host of heaven to disobedience'; hence it is often confounded with the Dragon of which, however, it is only the prototype."

"The constellation of the great Dragon is the most powerful of the entire Zodiac. From its peculiar form, and the immense group of shining stars that extend in the convolutions of its resplendent train, it has been called the Starry Serpent of the Skies. Its attendant luminaries are assumed to be that third of the host of heaven seduced by the rebel angel from their allegiance, and its position as the inaugural constellation of the much-dreaded wintry season impresses upon it the ominous name of Satan, or the adversary."

"Thus, from the position of a group of stars, and their apparition in the season deemed fatal to the prosperity of earth and its inhabitants, has arisen that stupendous myth, that legend of world-wide fear, the supposititious existence of an incarnate spirit of evil, the Satan of the Persians, the Typhon of Egypt, the Pluto of the Greeks, the old Serpent of the Jews, and the most popular of all objects of alternate fear and worship, the Devil of the enlightened Christians."

"Following up the astronomical legend, we find the great Dragon of October waging its annual war against the Sun-God. By the influence of its leader, Lucifer, the celestial

[1] "How art thou fallen from Heaven, O Lucifer, son of the morning! how art thou cut down to the ground, which didst weaken the nations! For thou hast said in thine heart, I will ascend into heaven, I will exalt my throne above the stars of God; I will sit also upon the mount of the congregation, in the sides of the north: I will ascend above the heights of the clouds: I will be like the Most High. Yet thou shalt be brought down to hell, to the sides of the pit." (Isaiah 14:12-15.)

Sun-God has already been put to death in his *crossifiction* of the autumnal equinox; from thence he is cast down into the power of the two evil months—November and December—who are crucified with him on the autumnal equinox." [1]

"It is just at midwinter when Capricorn, the Goat—signifying in ancient mythical language the renewer of life—is in the hands of life—is in the ascendant, that the Sun-God reappears as a *new-born babe*.

"In the fanciful imaginings of the astronomical historians, the cluster of stars which appear in the midwinter sky bear a resemblance to a manger or stable, whilst they discover the reappearance of the Virgin of Summer, with her companion, Bootes, or the constellation called Joseppe, or *Joseph*. For three days at midwinter the feeble radiance of the Sun appears to remain stationary, yet so greatly obscured, that the legend declares he descends to the nethermost parts of the universe and is lost to sight." . . .

"At length, on the 25th day of December he reappears, and amidst the figurative paraphernalia of constellated stars then in the ascendant, he is declared to have been *born in a manger* through the *maternity* of the Zodiacal *Virgin*."

"The women who have wept for Tammuz, the Syrian Sun-God, the mourners who have lamented with Isis for the Egyptian Osiris, the Greeks who have wandered with Ceres in search of the lost Proserpina, the devotees who have wailed for the slain Chrishna, one of the Sun-Gods of the Hindoos, and the Marys who weep at the sepulchre for the Christ of the Jews, all the nations of antiquity throughout the Orient—each of whom, under many names and in many forms, have adored the Sun-God, and believed in his annual birth, life, miracles, death, and resurrection—all have united to celebrate the new birth of their idol on the 25th of December, the period at which the solar orb actually passes through the constellation of the Zodiacal sign Capricorn, or 'the renewer of life.' [2] After the 25th of December the legend again loses sight of its *new-born Savior*."

---

[1] See John 19-18.

[2] December 25th is the astronomical New Year, the earth having reached its northernmost tilt. On that date the earth reverses its motion, tilting southward, giving us longer days. As the sun from day to day reaches a higher elevation, increasing its radiation, nature awakens into renewed activity.

"In all Eastern theogonies Egypt[1] is represented as the land of darkness and the symbol of obscurity. During the prevalence of the two constellations of January and February it is supposed that antagonistic influences threaten the young child's life. The royal power of Winter, with its storms and tempests, is in the ascendant, hence the *world's Redeemer* is in *danger from a mighty king.* To avert the evil the young child is carried by stealth to the land of Egypt; there in concealment he remains until the season of danger is passed, when he recrosses the equator at the vernal equinox, ascending from the southern depth of Egypt into the light and glory of an acknowledged worker of miracles."

"Again the earth rejoices in the presence of the young *Lamb*[2] of Spring who *"taketh away the sins of the world,"* and redeems it from the famine, desolation, and evils of the past Winter. From this time forth the Sun-God proclaims "peace on earth, and good-will to men" and fulfills his promise in miracles of healing, feeding the hungry, clothing the naked and bringing life and plenty to all.'

"The Sun-God is the central figure of . . . this famous myth, and his passage through the constellated stars of the Zodiac, together with the peculiar changes of atmosphere, climate, and natural productions effected on earth by solar and astral configurations, form the connected woof of the celestial drama."

"Next in importance in the mythical history is the impersonation of the Virgin Mother of the Sun-God. This constellated figure is assumed to hold in her hand a sprig, flower or

---

[1] "Egypt is a term denoting the body, which itself is the divinely appointed residence of the soul during its term of probation; it denotes the lessons to be derived from the world and the body, the learning of which is indispensable to the soul's development."—"The Perfect Way," Maitland and Kingsford.

[2] "The figure of a Lamb with a cross resting on its shoulder . . . has nothing whatever to do with the Christian religion; it was designed and employed centuries before the cross became a religious emblem. (The Cross only became an emblem of Christianity when the Emperor Constantine made it so in the fourth century, and it was not included in Clement of Alexandra's Christian symbols.) It is purely an astrological symbol which can be traced back to the early Phoenicians. It represents the Lamb of Life when the Sun at the beginning of the Vernal Equinox crosses the Equator; in other words it is the "Passover" or "crossover" . . . In those far-distant ages the vernal equinox commenced in the Sign of Aries the Ram, the House of Mars. From the perfect equity of the Sun in its relation to the earth at this period of the year, giving as it does equal length of day and night to all the world, it became the symbol of equity, law, justice and judgment between men."— ("World Predictions," Cheiro.)

fruit, which she extends in the attitude of invitation to a minor constellation named Bootes, Jo-seppe or Joseph, who from its proximity to the Virgin of Summer, is sometimes impersonated as her betrothed, sometimes as the Father of men, Adam, yielding to the seductions of Eve, tempting him by the extended fruit she holds in her hand."

"The next and not least important figure in the legend is the impersonation of the evening star of spring, transformed from an angel of light into Lucifer, the leader of the rebel hosts and the morning star of Autumn. This evil star is followed by another important actor in the astral Drama, namely, the great Dragon, the antagonistic power of all systems, by whom the beneficent Sun-God is put to death on the Cross of the autumnal equinox; crucified between the two evil wintry constellations prevailing in November and December." . . .

"The discoveries of each succeeding age afforded to the astronomical priesthood a boundless field for the exercise of their favorite method of symbolical expression, thus, whilst we always find the main ideas of the scheme preserved intact, the divergent branches of ideality which spring forth from the parent root are countless." . . .

"In the paraphrase of the Christian history of the Sun-God, the writers represent one of the thieves crucified with the Savior of mankind as becoming penitent at the last dread hour of death—Jesus, in allusion to his approaching new birth, answers him, 'today shalt thou be with me in Paradise.' " [1]

"This is a highly ingenious and creditable mode of disposing of the difficulty which ancient astronomers experienced in representing the constellation of December at once antagonistic and favorable to the dying God. The Capricorn of Winter shares the Sun-God's evil fate, but becomes favorable to him in the hour of his new birth in 'Paradise.' "

"We have now brought the legend up to that point when it is to recommence with the renewal of the Zodiacal history. The *Sun of Righteousness* is now to be re-born in the *stable* of the goat, through the maternity of the *immaculate Virgin* and thus the light of the world, the *Lamb,* of Spring, the

[1]Luke 23:43.

275

Lion of the tribe of Judah, the good master of the twelve Zodiacal *apostles,* is ever sacrificed, that he may take away the sins of the world, and ever restored to life, that all may have hope of immortality in his resurrection, etc., etc., etc."

"Every symbol has a correspondential spiritual meaning and the esoteric philosophy veiled under this mass of symbolism is the real heart of its religious significance."

"So long as the famous astronomical religion was practiced and taught amongst those nations whom Christians contemptuously denominate 'the heathen,' it was denounced by them as the vilest of idolatries, but at the point where they attempt to build up a theology of their own, they first begin by stealing the astronomical myth, then transpose its origin to a far later date, rechristen its personages, locate them in fresh birth-places, declare them to be genuine personalities, invest them with the most sacred names and attributes, fall down and worship them, and then call upon the name of the Most High God as a witness to the credibility of their audacious fictions."

"India is the oldest nation that possesses scriptural as well as monumental records, dating back to the highest antiquity, even to prehistoric ages . . . The biographies of Chrishna and Buddha Sakia are closely accordant with the history of the Sun-God."

"Egypt taught the Sun-God's history; the stories of Osiris, Isis, Horus, and Typhon are direct transcripts of the astronomical scheme. The same basic idea prevailed in the sublime system of Zoroaster, The Chaldeans, Ethiopians, Phoenicians, and the most settled of the Arabian tribes, Babylon, the Scythian nations, China and Japan, Ceylon, Java, Philippines."

"The Druidical system of worship . . . recognized a Sun-God mediator with a complete Zodiacal history in the incarnated deity they called Hesus. Grecian and Roman mythology were a paraphrase of Egyptian solar worship. Hindus, Egyptians, Arabians, Parsees, Greeks, and Romans all drank at the same celestial fountain. The Jews . . . worshipped a Deity who was only one of the . . . astral tutelary spirits of the Egyptians."

"The truth that at least twenty different incarnate Gods

276

were celebrated in the East, and taught of in Greece, to each of whom was attributed a history similar in general details to that of the Christian Messiah, but the still more significant facts that these various incarnations were all supposed to have preceded Jesus in point of chronology, and that the miracles attributed to him had been sculptured in Temples gray with age before the date assigned for his birth, bring their own comment to every mind not closed against the light of reason by bigotry, or incapable of appreciating the truths of history from blind superstition."

The preface to "Solar Biology" (H. E. Butler) states: "Man is a world in miniature . . . an epitome and image of the universe itself. This being so, man necessarily holds a definite relation to all its parts, both near and remote . . . Man is not a citizen of the world merely, but of the solar system and the universe in all its parts, both visible and invisible; consequently there is not a star that shines or a sun that burns but what has expression in his being, either active or latent."

In "Astrology, Your Place in the Sun," by Evangeline Adams, we find astrology defined as "the science that describes the influence of heavenly bodies upon mundane affairs and upon human character and life. It is the oldest science in existence; it is not only prehistoric, but pretraditional; it is the science of the effects of the Solar Currents on the living things of our earth, especially on human life."

Astro-physics is scoffed at by many as superstition, largely owing to ignorance of the subject and also to observation of practices of novices who, limited in their understanding and interpretation, have brought the science into ill-repute. Thus it has become a fetish and a superstition causing many devotees to make daily examination of charts for observance of supposedly good days and unfortunate days, creating a condition of mental slavery.

The scientific aspect of astro-physics, on the other hand, has important value in that it points out the favorable and unfavorable characteristics of the individual. The individual having such knowledge may be able to fortify himself against the unfortunate tendencies and weaknesses indicated by the planetary aspects at his birth.

277

Astro-physics is not founded on belief but is demonstrable by anyone who will give careful study to the fundamental principles of planetary activities and their influence on mankind. Just as the sun and moon control the tides and as our very lives are dependent upon the sun's activities, it should be obvious that the sun, moon and planets have also a bearing on life.

This science should be taught in schools that the child may know his good and weak points and thus be aided in developing a balanced mentality and character. In other words, "Man, know thyself."

CHAPTER XV

The Golden Thread of Truth

CHRISTIANS send missionaries to "convert the heathen," yet countless centuries before the Christian era the sages of ancient "heathen" nations taught the great truths of life and soul development.

Through all true religions and in the various philosophies, precepts and teachings of the ages, although obscured at times by symbolism and allegory, runs the one Golden Thread of Truth.

Concerning the nature of God we find a consistent similarity in quotations from varied sources.

"Not in the sight abides his form, none beholds him by the eye. Those who know him dwelling in the heart, by the heart and mind become immortal." (Swetaswatara, Upanishad.)[1]

"But verily thou art not able to behold Me with these thine eyes; the divine eye I give unto thee." (The Bhagavad-Gita.)

"The Tao cannot be heard; what can be heard is not It. The Tao cannot be seen; what can be seen is not It. The Tao cannot be expressed in words; what can be expressed in words is not It. Do we know the Formless which gives form to form? In the same way the Tao does not admit of being named." (The Texts of Taoism.)

"Divine Unity is incomprehensible and known only through its manifestations. To recognize the manifestation of the cycle in which he lives is the supreme duty of man," is a Bahai principle. "The essential nature of God is entirely beyond human comprehension." (Bahá'u'lláh.)

"The Kabbalists regard God as ineffable and assert that He can only be known by his manifestations." ("Mystery of the Ages.")

---

[1] See "The Bible of Bibles," Dr. Frank L. Riley.

Confucius taught that the Supreme Being was a mentally immeasurable fact, and not one of comprehensive limits.

"The voice of the spiritual source of all light and knowledge is not heard directly by any embodied spirit in existence. It remains behind the impenetrable veil of eloquent silence, and speaks to the soul of man, through its own powers" (conscience), "by an eternal evolution." ("Illuminated Brahminism.")

"No man hath seen God at any time." (I John 4:12.)

"The King of kings and Lord of lords . . . dwelling in the light which no man can approach unto; whom no man hath seen, nor can see." (I Timothy 6:15, 16.)

"Great is the Lord, and greatly to be praised; and his greatness is unsearchable." (Psalms 145:3.)

"I acknowledge a universal God, being a Unity, and the primordial power of Good in the universe; self-existent, independent of forms, needing no locality for its existence, unmeasurable and not subject to the intellectual comprehension of any being." (Jacob Boehme.)

"Mind is Brahma; for from mind even are verily born these beings; by mind, when born, they live; mind they approach, (mind) they enter." (Taittariya Upanishad.)

"The Mind . . . is of God's very essence . . . and is not separated off from God's essentiality, but is united unto it, as light to sun." ("Thrice-Greatest Hermes.")

"For who hath known the mind of the Lord? or who hath been his counsellor?" (Romans 11:34.)

"Our God is a living God. His power fills the universe. He was before the world saw light. He will be when the world exists no more. He formed thee; with his Spirit thou breathest." (The Talmud.)

"But there is a spirit in man and the breath of the Almighty giveth them understanding." (Job 32:8.)

"In him we live, and move, and have our being." (Acts 17:28.)

"Ye are the temple of the living God." (II Corinthians 6:16.)

"Know ye not that ye are the temple of God, and that the Spirit of God dwelleth in you." (I Corinthians 3:16.)

"One God and Father of all, who is above all, and through all, and in you all. (Ephesians 4:6.)

"To us there is but one God, the Father, of whom are all things, and we in him." (I Corinthians 8:6.)

Vedantism maintains that all souls are divine sparks, derived from the Great soul.

"He is the living One. No God is there but He." (The Koran.)

"For with thee is the fountain of life; in thy light shall we see light." (Psalms 36:9.)

"Where the Spirit of the Lord is, there is liberty." (II Corinthians 3:17.)

"God is light, and in Him is no darkness at all." (I John 1:15.)

"God is the Light of the Heavens and of the Earth." (The Koran.)

"Everything that is made manifest is light." (Ephesians 5:13.)

Many parallel teachings have been given regarding the transitory nature of the mortal:

"Unhappy is he who mistakes the branch for the tree, the shadow for the substance." (The Talmud.)

"Ye love the transitory and ye neglect the life to come." (The Koran.)

"The things which are seen are temporal but the things which are not seen are eternal." (II Corinthians 4:18.)

"Vanity of vanities . . . all is vanity" (transient physical). (Ecclesiastes 12:8.)

"Flesh and blood cannot inherit the kingdom of God; neither doth corruption inherit incorruption." (I Corinthians 15:50.)

"All that is with you passeth away, but that which is with God abideth." (The Koran.)

"For we know that if our earthly house of this tabernacle were dissolved, we have a building of God, an house not made with hands, eternal in the heavens." (II Corinthians 5:1.)

"The Atma Bodha" states: "Similar to the image of a

dream the world is continually troubled by Love, by hate and other passions. As long as the dream lasts it appears to be real, but on awakening it passes into non-reality." (Likewise, upon awakening to a realization of a future life, the mortal things are recognized as evanescent and transient.)

Moral precepts of the different religions often convey the same truths.

"And why beholdest thou the mote that is in thy brother's eye, but considerest not the beam that is in thine own eye? ... First cast out the beam out of thine own eye; and then shalt thou see clearly to cast out the mote out of thy brother's eye." (Matthew 7:3, 5.)

"Man sees the mote in his neighbor's eye but knows not of the beam in his own." (The Talmud.)

"If the wise man of world who carefully picks holes in the character of others, expends the same skill on himself, what would prevent him from breaking through the bonds" (of ignorance)? (The Jivanmukti-Viveka.)

In "The Moral Aphorisms of Confucius," Marcenus R. K. Wright states that Confucius taught:

"Seek and cling to an upright purpose in life and love thy neighbor as thyself."

"A just and happy life may alone be realized as a result of obedience to true moral principles."

"It is the duty of every man to first perfect himself and then to aid in the work of perfecting others. Human nature is our inheritance, it came to us as a divine gift, yet it is only in the complete subjugation of its compromising qualities that we are enabled to find perfect peace of mind, social joy, and freedom."

"A good portion of our time should be allotted to the work of self-examination and self-correction. We should check our hasty impulses, desires and emotions, and hold them under the control of reason" (and will).

"It is not enough to know of virtue, it is necessary to possess it. It is not sufficient to admire it, it is necessary to practice it."

"Sincerity and constancy of purpose are redeeming mental qualities."

"It is a pleasure to know the truth and a sin not to love it, and yet those who love it are not equal to those who follow its light."

"Every person should try to cultivate to the fullest extent, the better qualities and characteristics of his own nature, and should employ them with a view to social acceptance and fraternal happiness. Those who do this are not very far from the true path of mental harmony, joy, contentment, and peace."

"Do unto another what you would that he should do unto you, and do not unto another what you would not should be done unto you. Thou needest but this law alone. It embraces the foundation and principle of all the rest."

The Bible is replete with axioms of a like nature as the foregoing.

"Whatsoever ye would that men should do to you, do ye even so to them." (Matthew 7:12.)

"Love worketh no ill to his neighbor: therefore love is the fulfilling of the law."[1] (Romans 13:10.)

"Love your enemies, bless them that curse you, do good to them that hate you, and pray for them which despitefully use you, and persecute you." (Matthew 5:44.)

"He that loveth his brother abideth in the light." (I John 2:10.)

"He that loveth not his brother whom he hath seen, cannot love God whom he hath not seen." (I John 4:20.)

"Let us not love in word, neither in tongue, but in deed and in truth." (I John 3:18.)

"Thou shalt love the Lord thy God with all thy heart, and with all thy soul and with all thy mind. This is the first and great commandment. And the second is like unto it. Thou shalt love thy neighbor as thyself. On these two commandments hang all the law and the prophets." (Matthew 22:37-40.)

"When thou doest alms, let not thy left hand know what thy right hand doeth." (Matthew 6:3.)

"Except ye . . . become as little children, ye shall not enter into the kingdom of heaven . . . Whosoever therefore

[1]See "Nine Ingredients of Love," Chapter X, "Christian Science," Page 191.

shall humble himself as this little child, the same is greatest in the kingdom of heaven." (Matthew 18:3, 4.)

"He that is slow to anger is better than the mighty; and he that ruleth his spirit than he that taketh a city." (Proverbs 16:32.)

"Though I speak with the tongues of men and angels, and have not charity, I am become as sounding brass, or a tinkling cymbal." (I Corinthians 13:1.)

"The path of the just is as the shining light, that shineth more and more unto the perfect day." (Proverbs 4:18.)

"Pure religion and undefiled before God and the Father is this, to visit the fatherless and widows in their affliction, and to keep himself unspotted from the world." (James 1:27.)

Knowledge of self, mastery over the physical and understanding of life's purpose, variously referred to as "deliverance," "salvation," "at-one-ment," "unification," "redemption," etc., have always been taught as an attainment necessary for the progress and evolution of the soul.

"The Atma Bodha," or book of soul knowledge, a free translation of an ancient Sanskrit manuscript written upon palm leaves, declares:

"One cannot arrive at final deliverance without knowledge . . . Knowledge dissipates ignorance as light dissipates the darkness of heavy clouds. When the previous ignorance has been dissipated by knowledge . . . then the spirit itself manifests itself in a manner shining like the sun. The soul . . . becomes manifest in intelligence as the reflection on the surface of a mirror."

"Of all means there is but one knowledge that is efficacious for the obtaining of deliverance, even as there is no cooking without fire can one not arrive at final deliverance without knowledge."

"Know then that all things possessing form and weight are not what they seem, but are only external representations of more interior correspondence."

"There is no Being within, without, above or beyond the One Being. All the interior, movable world is the Spirit of the One, and the external world is the same soul. Nothing exists apart from the One."

"All the varieties of being are comprised in the One Being, veritable and intelligent, who is bound up with all, eternal all, penetrating even as the gold is in all variety of ornaments."

"Renouncing all (undue) attachments to an external and fleeting happiness, satisfied with the happiness of a soul, the wise man is forever resplendent in the interior light and similar to a Lamp, does he himself protect."

"The soul whose condition of being is knowledge desires not the knowledge of another on the subject of its own knowledge, in the same wise as a lamp giving its own (light) has no need for another lamp to be seen."

"The soul illuminated by . . . knowledge . . . drives away darkness, penetrates all, shines and all is illuminated. This is the great completion of existence, it is the great and final deliverance from sin, from pain and also from death."

"He therefore who undertakes the pilgrimage of the soul that is within his own without considering the state of the heavens, or the country, or the time, dissipates the cold and the heat and attains unto a perpetual happiness free from all impurity. This one, freed completely of works becomes omniscient, all penetrating and Immortal."

Matthew 13:46: "The kingdom of heaven is like unto a merchantman, seeking goodly pearls; who, when he had found one pearl of great price, went and sold all that he had, and bought it."

"Know the Divinity that is within you, that you may know the Divine One of which your soul is but a ray." (Proclus.)

"To live in accordance with one's religion is to live interiorly, since one then looks to the Divine . . . Heaven is within man, and those that have heaven within them come into heaven . . . A man whose moral life is spiritual has heaven within him . . . Heaven within man is acknowledging and being led by the Divine. The first and chief thing of every religion is to acknowledge the Divine." (Swedenborg.)

Boehme taught salvation, not from a dead and historical person . . . but by the Christ within . . . by the mind becoming selfconscious in the light of the spiritual soul.

285

"My little children, of whom I travail in birth again until Christ" (the spirit of understanding) "be formed in you." (Galatians 4:19.)

"Ye shall know the truth, and the truth shall make you free." (John 8:32.)

"The Father . . . shall give you another Comforter, that he may abide with you forever, even the Spirit of Truth" (the desire to understand life's purpose). (John 14:16, 17.)

In "Mystery of the Ages," by the Countess of Caithness, a comparison of various religious and philosophical teachings is given.

"The truth, namely . . . the crucifixion of the earthly man" (replacing ignorance with understanding) "as necessary for the salvation" (freedom) "of the heavenly man . . . crucifixion of the lower nature (the Son of Man), in order that the higher should be lifted up . . . has been revealed to humanity at different epochs and in different parts of the world; it is the most ancient, and thereby will probably be the most enduring on earth . . . since it is the only means of uniting earth with heaven, or of preparing the Son of Man to become the Son of God; it is, therefore, substantially the religion of all past, as of all coming ages."

"The Gospels are the histories of an inward and regenerating Principle[1] . . . which is the Saviour of humanity, for it redeems man from the prison house of earth; and the development in him of this Principle transforms the Son of Man into the Son of God. Call it the Spirit of Truth, or call it Love, or Life; or call it Wisdom, the Logos, or the Sixth Principle in man, as do the Buddhists; or the Key-Stone of the Arch, as do the Royal-Arch Masons; or the Head-Stone of the Corner,[2] as do the Scriptures; it is always the highest state to which man can attain."

"The Egyptians, Hindus, Persians, Greeks, Druids, Semites, and others, had their mystic myths, wherein the life of an individual hero delineates the course of Divine Re-Birth."

[1] "The regenerating principle" does not demand bodily tortures, asceticism, etc., but implies recognition of the higher laws while man lives a natural life. "First . . . that which is natural, then that which is spiritual." (I Corinthians 15:46.)

[2] "The stone" (reason) "which the builders rejected, the same was made the head of the corner." (Luke 20:17.) "Thou art Peter, and upon this rock" (reason) "I will build my church." (Matthew 16:18.)

286

"Practical Buddhism may be thus summarized: To see, feel, speak, behave, live, act, think, and aspire RIGHTLY. It teaches Love and Justice for all; that the Path to Divine Union is by that Supreme Principle—Divine Love, which alone unites the human with the Divine."

"Both Buddhism and Brahminism have the same object in view; namely, to humanize the animal and divinize the human, by freeing the Soul from earthly passions and from the influence of the material world: Attainment of perfect liberation to the Soul-state is called by the Brahmin Miksha, and Absorption into the Infinite Being, while the Buddhist considers Nirvana as a total annihilation of the lower self."

"There is a difference not only in words but in views between the two systems, yet the *object* of their practice is essentially one. The ethics of both Systems are almost the same, only in external ceremonial lies the chief difference; but on most physical and psychical rules of life they are both agreed."

"The essential teachings of Taoism which have served China for centuries: Everything comes from one originally, the same entity. Man must cultivate indifference to the pains and pleasures of the world; live in harmony with Nature. Concord between the human will and the Universal Reason constitutes the highest form of virtue."

"These same points were taught by the Greek Philosophers, Pythagoras, Parimenides, Zeno, Plotinos. Theories common in China were taught by Anaxemenes, Anaxagoras, and Xenophanes."

"Jewish Kabbalists claim the Bible to be an occult Book wherein their Kabbalistic system is embodied in allegories and Symbols . . . having mystic truth as their foundation. The Kabbala transmits such knowledge as was chosen to commit to writing . . . Of the inner life of the Jews comparatively little is known, but it can be traced even in the Bible, that a traditional (occultism) was extant, which the Nazarites and the Schools of the Prophets, and later, the Essenes and Kabbalists, and possibly also the initiated Talmudists, perpetuated, but which all Kabbalistic schools that followed Akiba and Simon Jochai, consolidated into a scientific system in the books Jezira and Sohar . . . which reveal

287

the basis of (occult knowledge) of the Hebrews; however, these works are but little known to the orthodox Jews."

"The Talmud is the protective fence around the written Law, which in turn is the symbolical vehicle of the Divine Kabbala. (Precepts directing towards a Divine Life.) Thus there were two traditions, an Exoteric tradition perpetuated in the Talmud, and an Esoteric tradition wherein the Kabbala was transmitted. The Exoteric tradition is permeated with Kabbalism, although the mere Talmudists know it not."

"The mystic Tora or Kabbala is not the Pentateuch but the tradition of the Divine Word, the God in our own Being. The written Law is by the Kabbalists assumed to be a concealed path to the unwritten or occult Law which is a guide to the Divine Word . . . or Manifestation of the Absolute."

"Godfrey Higgins states in 'Anacalypsis': 'The Essenes were a fraternity of Hermetists . . . The doctrines of Zoroaster, Pythagoras, Plato are all contained in the Jewish Cabala.' "

"Dr. Oliver, accredited lecturer for Freemasonry, claims that Freemasonry has come down from the Essenes, a Jewish Sect . . . a secret brotherhood . . . devoted to piety and devotion to God, and that the Essenes were in possession of what they call the Temple Secrets in the days of Solomon."

"The systems of the Kabbala and Esoteric Masonry are identical, and for this reason the Masons call their temple the Temple of Solomon . . . Solomon built a visible *TEMPLE* to inculcate the grades and secrets of the Invisible Soul Life . . . It was Architectural Occultism."

"The story of Hiram Abiff: is that of the Divine Spirit, the Son of the Widow, or Spiritual Soul, which in undeveloped and material conditions is separated from her Divine Source, thus widowed; the three fellow-craft's-men who slay him are the three lower principles, viz., the Body, the Ego, and the animal or earthly Soul."

" 'Head-Stone of the corner' (like the Key-Stone of the Royal Arch Mason), symbolizes the Christ Spirit in Man."

Philosophers and thinkers of the Middle Ages could not come out openly regarding the facts of life here and hereafter for fear of their lives and of persecution by the church, therefore the Rosicrucians spoke only in symbols. But there is today no need of medieval secrecy concerning occult teachings.

Franz Hartmann, in "An Adventure Among the Rosicrucians," states: "The true Alchemist requires no ingredients for his processes, such as he could buy in a chemist's shop . . . all the description of . . . retorts, mortars, filters . . . distilling apparatus, etc., in books on alchemy was written to prevent the selfish from prying into mysteries which they were not fit to receive."

"The highest processes of alchemy require no mechanical labor; they consist in the purification of the soul, and in transforming animal man into a divine being."

"The invisible principles of which the constitution of man is made up are called his 'metals,' because they are more lasting and enduring than flesh and blood. The metals which are formed by his thoughts and desires will continue to exist after the perishing elements constituting his physical body have been dissolved."

"Man's animal principles are the base metals of which his animal organization consists; they must be changed into nobler metals by transforming his vices into virtue, until they pass through all colors and turn into gold of pure spirituality. To accomplish this it is necessary that the grossest elements in the form should die" (be subdued) . . . "so that the light of the spirit penetrate through the hard shell and call the inner man into life and activity."

"The microcosm of Man is a true counterpart, image, and representation of the great Macrocosm of nature. In the former are contained all the powers, principles, forces, essences, and substances which are contained within the latter from the Supreme and divine spiritual principle, called God, down to the grossest state of the universal one Life, in which it is called Matter."

"The Hermetic Philosophers of the Middle Ages, called the Brotherhood of the Golden and Rosy Cross, investigated the underlying principles of the Christian religion and gave forth their findings in certain Symbols which were called 'secret' because they can be understood only by those who possess the key to their understanding . . . the Key of Spirituality" (intuitive discernment of their meaning) "and Reason."

289

"Ever since the days of the great Reformation, when the Bible became the common property of the people who were unable to understand the secret meanings of its fables and allegories, which were known only to the initiated, the Cabalists, Alchemists, and Rosicrucians, the Christian religion has been studied more in its intellectual than in its spiritual aspect." (The biblical stories have been believed literally; their inner meaning has not been discerned.)

In "The Light of Egypt," by Sri. Ramatherio, the symbol of the Rosicrucians—a cross with a red rose upon its center—is thus explained: "The cross can be found on the walls of tombs and temples in Egypt. To the mystics of ancient Egypt or the Orient it means man's body in either a posture of salutation to the rising sun (with arms held out in horizontal position) or man's body being crucified by the labors, trials, tests, and sufferings of life."

"The Egyptian mystics added a red rose to the cross. The rose was made symbolical of the inner consciousness, the spirit, the SOUL of man. The fact that the rose gradually opened from a tightly closed bud into full bloom and expression, and then slowly faded, drooped, and passed out of sight, made itself suggestive of the soul of man which came into the youthful body imprisoned, slowly evolved to manifestation and beauty, and slowly weakened in its expression until it seemed to be no more. The evolution of the rose seemed to typify the evolution of man's soul."

"Years of observation convinced these sages that the tests and trials of life, the experiences, lessons learned and suffering endured, contributed to the evolution of the soul; to them it seemed that the soul of man was evolving through the experiences of the body. Since the cross has ever been to them the symbol of the body of man in its sufferings, they added the rose to the cross and created the symbol which has but one explanation: The Rose (soul) evolves and gains beauty while being crucified upon the Cross (the body.)"[1]

The Rosicrucian teachings are clearly presented in "Cosmology" by Franz Hartmann.

"If men desire to know that which is immensely superior to their personal selves, they must step out of these selves

_____
[1]See "Passion Cross," Chapter VII, "Dogma Spiritualized," Page 159.

and by the power of Love embrace the infinite All . . . they must realize practically . . . that the Universal Spirit is one, and that in him and by his power we live and have our being, and that we should love wisdom above all, and all humanity, as if they were a part of ourselves."

"How can man partake of the consciousness of the Universal Spirit so long as he clings to the consciousness of being merely a very limited personality?"

"Upon the recognition of this truth are based all the fundamental doctrines of the religions of the world; it is the rock (Petra) upon which the universal spiritual church of humanity is built; it is allegorically represented in the Bhagavad-Gita by the battle which Arjuna has to fight with his own personal Egos, to enable him to become united to Krishna; it is represented by the Christian Cross adorned with the figure of a dying man; for it is not the Christ-principle which dies upon a Cross, but the semi-animal self which must suffer and die so that the real man may rise into a glorious resurrection, and become united with the 'Christ.' It is not physical death which is represented in this beautiful allegory, but the mystic death, the death of personal desires, personal claims, and personal considerations."

"The Cross is a symbol of victory over self, of triumph, and the beginning of immortal life."

"Christ is a symbol of Spiritual consciousness, Life and Light, the divine element in humanity, which if it manifests itself in man, becomes the personal Christ in individual man. 'Christ' means, therefore, an internal spiritual living and conscious power or principle."

" 'Christ' originally signifies a universal spiritual principle, co-existent from all eternity with the 'Father,' i.e., the Divine Source from which it emanated in the beginning."

"Those who cannot rise up to the sublimity of this conception look upon 'Christ' as being merely a historical person, who in some incomprehensible manner took upon himself the sins of the world."

"Father: The incomprehensible Absolute, the cause of all existence, the Centre of Life, becoming comprehensible only when he manifests himself as the 'Son'—Light. In the same sense a geometrical point is merely an abstraction and incomprehensible, and must expand into a circle before it can become an object of our imagination."

"Cross: A symbol expressing various ideas. The creative power of Life is a spiritual aspect, acting within the Macrocosm of nature and within the Microcosm of Man. It also represents Spirit and matter ascending and descending. The perpendicular beam represents Spirit, the horizontal bar the animal or earthly principle, being penetrated by the divine Spirit."

"Universal as well as individual man may be symbolized by a Cross. Man's animal body is a Cross or instrument of torture for the Soul." (Passion Cross.) "By means of his battle with the lower elements of his constitution, his divine nature becomes developed. By means of his physical body man is 'nailed' to the plane of suffering appertaining to terrestrial existence. The animal elements are to die" (be subdued[1]) "upon that Cross, and the spiritual man is to be resurrected to become united with the Christ. 'Death upon the Cross' represents the giving up of one's own personality and the entering into eternal and universal life" (esoterically, Christ consciousness).

"God: The eternal, omnipresent, self-existent cause of all things; in its highest meaning this term is necessarily beyond the intellectual comprehension of imperfect man, because the imperfect cannot conceive the perfect, nor the finite the infinite."

"God is the only eternal Reality, unknowable to man; all we know of him are his manifestations" (as revealed in objective nature). "We cannot possibly form any conception of the unmanifested Absolute; but as soon as the latter becomes manifest it appears as a Trinity of Thought, Word and Revelation—i.e., as the 'Father,' the 'Son' and 'Holy Ghost.'"

"The God of the Universe . . . is an eternal power, unchangeable as the Law . . . the eternal power of love, the source of all being . . . whose rays are the Light of Intelligence and the principle of immortal Life . . . Universal religion is based upon the recognition of the truth that all humanity is one, and that we should always be guided in our

[1]See "A little Child shall lead them," Chapter VIII, "Pictorial Religion," Page 173.

actions by our consideration for the welfare of all, in pref-
erence to all personal considerations." (Selfishness is the
principal cause of "evil.")

"At-one-ment: Unification with the eternal one is the only
aim and object of all true religion" (obtained through reason and understanding, not sentimental dreaming). "All
things are originally one; they are all states of one universal
divine consciousness. They merely appear to be different
from each other on account of the illusion of Form. The
Centre is one . . . To become reunited with the Centre is to
enter the Real and to become divine and immortal. After a
man has become united with his own higher self, he may
become united with Christ."

"This process of regeneration and unification is taught
in all the religions of the East, but although the whole
Christian religion is based upon this truth it is nevertheless
universally misunderstood by modern Christians who expect
to obtain salvation rather through the merit of another
than by their own exertion. To understand the process of
regeneration and unification requires an understanding of
the real nature of man and of his relations to nature."

"The spiritual power which constitutes the real man . . .
is a universal principle which fills, surrounds, and penetrates
all things . . . The universal eternal power of the spiritual
sun of the Universe enters the heart of man . . . as a ray
of spiritual light and stimulates the higher elements of the
soul into activity and life . . . facilitating the development
of the spiritual faculties . . . and unfoldment of the soul."

"This Light, being the Life and the Truth shining into
the hearts of men, is the 'Christ,' or 'Redeemer of mankind' " (or "at-one-ment" which Christians misconstrue as
"atonement"). "It is universal, and there is no other
redeemer; it is known to the wise of all nations, although
they do not all call it by the same name; it existed in the
beginning of creation, and will exist at its end; it is the flesh
and blood, the substance and power, of the inner spiritual
man in his highest divine aspect."

"Only the higher self of man is immortal, and he who
desires to enter the eternal life must strive to grow out of
his lower animal self" (realize he is in the world but not of

the world), "and become able to unite his soul with his own spiritual ego, or Christ.' "[1]

"This fundamental truth forms the laws of all true religion, and all the principal religious systems upon this globe are founded upon this final unification with God. The wise men of all ages know of the birth of Christ, not of a man called 'Christ' but of the divine Saviour, who may be born in every human heart."

"The Christ is the 'Son of God,' a ray of Light from the eternal spiritual sun of the universe, shining into the hearts of men.[2] . . . Nature produces the Christ. She is an eternal mother, for all forms are evolved from Nature. . . . Yet she is an ever immaculate virgin, for she has no connection with any external God; the fructifying power of the 'Holy Ghost' lives and acts within her own centre."

"The duality of man in his material and spiritual aspect is universally recognized; it is a truth which forces itself continually upon the attention of every one who is able to think. The final union of the divine elements existing in the organization of men with the sum and substance of the divine elements existing in nature, is the truth upon which all reasonable religious teachings are based . . . the truth of . . . the one-ness of nature and the divine eternal Spirit within."

"Individual man is an image of Nature. His constitution is based upon the same laws upon which Nature as a whole is constructed . . . man's organism resembles universal nature in everything but the external form. . . . He contains within himself, either germinally, potentially, or actively all the powers and principles, substances and forces contained within the great organism of nature, and moreover the great and the little world continually act and react upon each other; the elementary forces of nature act upon man, and the forces emanating from man—even his thoughts—react again upon nature . . . the two are actually only one."

"These truths are as old as the world, and they had been known many thousands of years before the advent of mod-

---

[1] "For to this end we labour and strive, because we have our hope set on the living God, who is the Saviour of all men." (I Timothy 4:10.)

[2] "I am the light of the world; he that followeth me shall not walk in darkness, but shall have the light of life." (John 8:12.)

ern Christianity. They have often been impressed upon mankind by great reformers and sages, and have been again forgotten by man."

"The Christian teachings as well as the Brahminical books, whose origin dates from prehistoric times, all tell the same tale in various allegorical forms. 'In him was life, and the life was the light of men.'" (John 1:4.)

"As the images of the Gods of the Greeks and Romans were not intended to represent persons, but consisted merely of figurative personifications of powers of nature, likewise the persons spoken of in the Bible are personifications of the same powers or principles which still exist today as they existed before the Bible was written . . . They are mythological allegories and represent living truths. True natural science is the basis of all true religion."

The "Rosicrucian Prayer"[1] expresses clearly a conception of Universal Power and Wisdom symbolized by Nature:

"Eternal and Universal Fountain of Love, Wisdom and Happiness; Nature is the book in which thy character is written, and no one can read it unless he has been in thy school. Therefore our eyes are directed upon Thee, as the eyes of the servants are directed upon the hands of their masters and mistresses, from whom they receive their gifts. Oh thou Lord of Kings, who should not praise thee unceasingly and forever with his whole heart? For everything in the Universe comes from thee, out of thee, belongs to thee and must again return to thee." . . .

"Thou alone art the Lord, for thy Will is the fountain of all powers that exist in the Universe; none can escape thee. Thou art the helper of the poor, the modest and virtuous. Thou art the King of the world, thy residence is in Heaven and in the sanctuary of the heart of the virtuous."

"Universal God, One Life, One Light, One Power, thou All in All, beyond expression and beyond conception! O Nature! Thou something from nothing, thou symbol of Wisdom! In myself I am nothing, in thee I am I. I live in thy I, made of nothing, live thou in me, and bring me out of the region of self into the eternal light. Amen."

---

[1]"Cosmology," Hartmann.

Swedenborg wrote: "The Lord's church is universal, and is with all who acknowledge the divine and live in charity." The creed of Thomas Paine was: "The world is my country; to do good is my religion."

Oriental minds recognize the similarity of esoteric Christianity to their own ancient teachings but they repudiate the dogmatic teaching of Christian missionaries that belief in a vicarious atonement, namely, that Jesus died for our sins, is the chief requisite for a supposed future "salvation."

These doctrines may be accepted by the untutored oriental, at least partly, because of favors and benefits received thereby, but to the oriental scholar such doctrines are illogical and belittling to Universal Spiritual Principle, which the oriental mind recognizes and adores, and which makes no mistakes, as implied by the Christian dogma.

That the broader view of religion held by the oriental scholar has a liberalizing influence upon the missionaries themselves is evidenced by the recent disturbance of the Presbyterian Board of Foreign Missions, owing to the statements of Mrs. Pearl S. Buck, famous novelist, missionary and student of Chinese life and literature, who was accused of heresy because of references made to the Christian doctrine that the "heathen" races are damned unless they hear the gospel, as "a magic religion."

Mrs. Buck is quoted as declaring: "I agree with the Chinese, who feel that their people should be protected from such superstition. We have sent ignorant people as missionaries, we have sent mediocre people, we have sent arrogant people, we have sent superstitious people who have taught superstitious creeds and theories and have made the lives of hungry-hearted people wretched and sad."

"It does not matter whether Christ was magic in a supernatural sense or not," Mrs. Buck stated, as quoted by the press. Christ, to her, is "that force shaping out of the universe, still living, still tireless in truth. I see He is not often truly believed in, even by those who profess to be His followers; He who is most simple and unafraid, how can men who are not simple and who are full of little fears or of some great fear truly believe in Him? No magic is needed, no creeds, nothing except the pondering of ourselves into that greatest simplicity."

"And what if Christ never lived? If there existed mind or minds, dreams, hopes, imaginations, sensitive enough to the human soul and all its needs, perceptive enough to receive such heavenly imprint on the spirit as to be able to conceive a personality like Christ's and portray him for us with such matchless simplicity as He is portrayed, then Christ lived and lives, whether He was once one body and one soul, or whether He is the essence of men's highest dreams."

The dogmatic interpretation of religion is slowly giving way to a broader concept; this was indicated even in the attitude of the Presbyterian Board of Foreign Missions which, according to its duty to the Church, was obliged to accept Mrs. Buck's resignation, but did so "with regret."

As there are many highways leading to one city and each traveler follows without condemnation the one most convenient, so are there many roads of thought leading to the goal of understanding, and none may condemn the road another travels, for all lead eventually to Truth.

CHAPTER XVI

The Soul's Journey

THE various interpretations of religion have undoubtedly been the cause of more divergence of opinion, of strife and commotion in the mental world than have all other questions pertaining to existence, physical and mental. Yet, when bias and dogmatic creeds are eliminated, the meaning of religion becomes so simple that "wayfaring men, though fools, shall not err therein."

Benjamin Franklin, when eighty-four years old, wrote: "Here is my creed: I believe in one God, the Creator of the Universe; that He governs it by His Providence; that the most acceptable service we can render Him is doing good to His other children; that the soul of man is immortal and will be treated with justice in another life respecting its conduct in this. These I take to be the fundamental points in all sound religion."

Religion is defined as "a binding back," and implies a conscious realization that we are a part of a Source. "All are but parts of one stupendous whole, whose body Nature is, and God the soul." (Alexander Pope.)

"We are all God's children. I am the brother of the Jew and the Parsee and the Mohammedan and the Buddhist. We must have a religion that will take in all mankind," was the statement of Sir Arthur Conan Doyle, quoted in the recently published biography, "Arthur Conan Doyle, A Memoir," written by the Rev. John Lamond, D.D., and containing an epilogue, a beautiful tribute to her husband, by Lady Conan Doyle.

In religion too much emphasis has been placed upon blind devotion and too little upon the use of the reasoning faculties, for the latter lead directly to understanding. Reasoning and understanding illumine the soul and that illumination enhances a natural devotion.

Continued study of fine works of art develops a spirit of admiration and appreciation, for "A thing of beauty is a joy forever"; likewise in spiritual science, the more the soul comprehends of life's meaning and nature's marvelous revelations, the greater is the happiness attained, leading the soul from "glory to glory." "The soul of man is divine; contemplation of the divine essence is the noblest exercise of man," declared Philo, the Neoplatonist. "Science, Religion, Art, and Philosophy are indirect paths to the fountain of existence," wrote the Countess of Caithness.

Through failure of religionists to give to nature and life the intelligent and unbiased study which alone affords true interpretation of life's meaning, vast numbers misjudge the divine nature of God. Seeing only the seeming wrongs and upheavals in the world they reject a Supreme Being entirely; not perceiving the Divine Plan, they judge God by the externals, which are only the spiritual digestive processes necessary for bringing the soul to self-realization.

Truth reveals the mystery. Through practice of clear discernment of mind, and separation of the soul life from undue attraction to mortal illusions, not by evading life's duties but by patient endeavor to meet them, will the soul, day by day, gain fuller discernment of the Great Theme.

This is the perception of which Franz Hartmann writes in "Boehme": "Only when man's spiritual perceptions are unfolded and he attains divine knowledge of self then will he know the Christ and all the celestial powers whose aggregate goes to make up the kingdom of God existing within himself. . . . The religion of the living Christ is based upon the recognition of an eternal process going on in the macrocosm of nature and in the microcosm of man."

"The true Christ is neither an 'adept' nor a 'Mahatma,' nor a Reformer, a mortal person, nor anything whatsoever that differs from God, but is Divinity itself manifesting itself in Humanity, and thereby saving mankind as a whole, and each individual separately considered, from ignorance and suffering, to the extent as mankind or such an individual person receives Him (light) in him or her. The redemp-

299

tion from spiritual darkness depends on the presence of the redeeming power of the spiritual light within the darkness itself." . . .

"There is a divine element in humanity, by means of which humanity may be redeemed from materialism and ignorance and be brought to realize again its originally divine state. Moreover each human individual constitutes for itself a little world wherein are contained all the powers, principles, and essences that are said to exist in the great world, the solar system wherein we live. In each of these little worlds the great work of redemption, which is described in the Bible as having taken place in the great world, is continually going on."

"Forever the divine Spirit descends into the depths of matter within our corporeal being, and, by the power of light and love of Christ within the soul, overcomes the lurid fire of the wrathful will within for the purpose of re-establishing in man the divine image of God."

"Forever the Christ is born amidst the animal elements in the constitution of man, teaching the intellectual powers therein; crucified on the cross, in the center of the four elements, and resurrected in those who do not resist the process of their own regeneration whereby they may attain life in the Christ." . . .

"This work of evolution and redemption is going on continually and everywhere. . . . The light of the Spirit comes from the sun of divine wisdom, the sacred Trinity of Will and Intelligence and its manifestation; and from the depths of the human heart up-wells the light of love, over-ruling the arguments of the intellect that has been mis-guided by external appearances . . . The universal God, the Christ, begins to live in him. Then the illusions end, and the interior truth becomes revealed. . . . In the living Truth itself is the Light to be found."

"There is a spirit in man, and the breath of the Almighty giveth them understanding." (Job 32:8.)

In order to comprehend the invisible, intangible nature of the Unmanifest, objective illustrations and comparisons are required. Let us postulate God as a great Harp and Humanity its strings not yet in tune. Each string must ultimately become attuned to the nature of the Harp in order that harmony may be realized.

To illustrate further, a musician learning to play an instrument appreciates more fully, as he studies and practices, the revealed beauty and harmonies which cannot be perceived without an instrument. That the scope of harmony may be increased, instrument after instrument is added, each attuned according to its nature, culminating in one great symphonic orchestra.

Similarly, each soul is an integral part of Life's Harmony but, as a musician must practice to overcome difficulties, so must the soul endeavor to overcome ignorance, selfishness, jealousy and all obstructive conditions which would unduly hold the soul in the trammels of the illusory, objective attractions.

When self-seeking is replaced by love for Truth and a seeking after Truth, Love and Harmony prevail and the soul will discern that, as each instrument in the orchestra must recognize the other instruments, so must each soul harmonize with other souls, and through helping them to find their places in the great Orchestra of Life will find itself in tune with God, in one Harmony of Understanding, which constitutes "heaven."

Thus each soul, through the ascendency from the cruder mortal state gradually evolves to a realization of Life's purpose and ultimately becomes a conscious integral part of the Whole. The saying, "being lost in God," should not be understood to imply annihilation, but as each instrument in the orchestra still remains individual while being, in a sense, lost in the orchestra, so each soul still retains its identity although being a part of the grand, harmonious Orchestra of the Universe.

As another illustration, let us assume God to be like a river in which bubbles are floating here and there—individualized humanity. Each bubble, unaware of its source, perceives itself as an independent entity; failing to recognize that it is a part of the stream, it drifts along and finally becomes engulfed in the eddies along the shore, enmeshed in various creeds, cults and dogmas, there to remain, its progress checked.

After drifting from one creed or cult to another some individuals become discontented with the limitations in which they find themselves. Discontent evolves thinking and thereby knowledge is added to their faith. Thus they are liberated from limitations and consciously realize themselves as part of the stream in which they live and move and have their being.

Boehme wrote in "Three Principles": "The living soul, from the eternal will of the Father, was breathed into man, and this will has no other purpose than to give birth to His only Son" (understanding). This great philosopher has also said that God's activities are a Love-Play, or God revealing himself to himself. "God the One is becoming God the many."

By analysis it would seem that this explains much of the mystery or purpose of existence. Let us illustrate and say that the ocean is God and that this ocean is conscious of itself as a whole but that the individual drops of water in the ocean are not conscious of the whole. However, the Creator wishes every atom in his being to become conscious of its nature and its part in the whole.

Recognizing intelligence as invisible, we postulate that the spirit germs, or atoms, in the whole contain the element of becoming; these spirit atoms, being intangible, unconscious of themselves, yet containing the element of becoming, cannot evolve without being projected into objectivity, such as we find ourselves in, in the physical form.

God, being Spirit, in order to carry out his purpose of causing every atom in his being to become conscious of the whole, projected his invisible nature into objective form, revealing a universal or cosmic boundless ocean of eternity.

Floating about in this great ocean are bodies of planets and suns, a grand, enormous workshop. The globes are first gaseous bodies, which slowly transform themselves into liquid and solid substances, the conditions gradually evolving until they will sustain life, vegetable, animal and, lastly, human life.

As spirit atoms cannot develop self-consciousness without contact with objective forms, the Great Over-Soul, or God, recognized the necessity for an objective universe;

302

therein the infinitesimal spirit, in a microscopical cell, with its limitless possibility of becoming, takes on a form and evolves a transient, physical body with various organs and functions. Through this the indwelling spirit, by means of the special sense organs (sight, hearing, taste, smell and touch), is enabled to contact the objective. "Knowledge has its beginning from the mind; its introduction from the senses."

Liebnitz taught that the soul contains certain principles which external objects awaken. Lavater said, "The soul itself during its earth life, perfects the faculties of the spiritual body, by means of which it will apprehend, feel and act in its new existence."

Jung Stilling expressed the same thought: "The Soul does require the outward vigour of sense, in order to be able to see, hear, smell, taste and feel in a much more perfect state."

What is it all but an involved plan through which the sojourner must discover himself and ultimately realize his oneness with the All?

"The end of all things of creation is that there may be an external conjunction of the Creator with the created universe . . . the end is for man to be more and more nearly conjoined with Him, for thus man possesses heaven more interiorly . . . and by that conjunction becomes wiser . . . and happier, because it is from wisdom and according to it that man has heaven, and by means of it has happiness." (Swedenborg.)

Many ask, If God is Love and Wisdom, and if there is a realm which some call Heaven, why are we placed in this plane of obstacles, apparent contradictions and injustice? Would it not be reasonable to assume that the solution of the mystery lies in the fact that if we were born into a heavenly condition of perfection it would have little or no meaning for us since we would have had no contrasting experience?

There can be no consciousness manifest without something to be conscious of. "God introduces His will into nature for the purpose of revealing His power in light and in majesty, to constitute a kingdom of joy. If there were no

303

nature originating within the eternal unity, there would be nothing else but eternal tranquility." ("Grace," Boehme.)

"The whole of the divine Being is in a state of continual and eternal generation comparable to the mind of man, but immutable. There are continually thoughts born from the mind of man, and from them arises desire and will. From desire and will originates action, and the hands do their work, so as to render it substantial. Thus it is with eternal evolution." ("Three Principles," Boehme.)

Being born into the rough school of life with a small amount of free will we act according to our own devices and stumble about, causing pain to ourselves, mental as well as physical. To stub one's toe once is pardonable but to continue stubbing it over the same obstacle is foolish.

Pain causes thinking and thought is the solver which gradually unravels the mystery of life and shows us how important this life's school really is in that it compels us ultimately to comprehend an underlying purpose which was previously hidden from us, owing to our ignorance of the why of life.

The turmoil of life is a necessity. "Let us also rejoice in our tribulations; knowing that tribulation worketh patience." (Romans 5:3.) The so-called right and wrong in life are only factors, or re-agents, calculated to slowly reveal the plan of justice, or wisdom, which is above both good and evil.

As an illustration, suppose a spectator finds himself upon a plateau with a valley on one side where the people are born ideally good, and on the other side a valley where the people are born in a condition of evil.

The individuals of the first group have no knowledge, they have only their own condition to contemplate and of this they have no realization since they have seen nothing else. Having contacted no outer condition to cause thinking, no thinking has been developed. Nor do the individuals of the second group recognize any evil since they have not experienced anything else and are not aware of any other condition.

The spectator, representing wisdom, which is superior to good or evil, analyzes the two situations and perceives

304

the necessity and importance of intermingling these opposites. The consequent experiences will cause pain and anguish, grief and sorrow, but one definite result will be accomplished, the unfolding of thought and understanding, the good and evil acting as re-agents in arousing the slumbering higher consciousness.

Thus is carried out the implied purpose of the School of Life. Knowledge and wisdom are attained through discernment of Nature's Plan, which is gained by the experiences the soul has acquired during its journey in this primary grade of existence. "The ultimate goal of cosmic process is the perfection of human character." (John Fiske.)

The mind that can look beyond the transient, stern school of every day life realizes that there are many roads to ultimate understanding. The Man of Nazareth said: "The publicans and the harlots go into the kingdom of God before you" (Matthew 21:31), referring to the chief priests and elders. The latter had not experienced the pangs of sorrow nor had their souls suffered and endured, hence their hearts were lukewarm.

Whereas, when "publicans and harlots" realize their mistakes they boast of nothing, and, perceiving the higher ideals, they become enthusiastic and eager to broaden their comprehension of the spiritual meaning of life, which too often they have been denied the opportunity of ascertaining during their earthly career.

Born in squalor and raised in iniquity, they are subjected to the evils of ignorance and are shunned by those in better stations of life, those who, from lack of the Christ spirit of sympathy and love for the least of God's children, are only concerned about their own comfort and pleasures, unmindful of the dictum that no man can live to himself alone and that all are in a broader sense their brother's keepers.

"For none of us liveth to himself." (Romans 14:7.)

"Let no man seek his own, but every man another's wealth." (I Corinthians 10:24.)

"Look not every man on his own things, but every man also on the things of others." (Philippians 2:4.)

"With the same measure that ye mete withal, it shall be measured to you again." (Luke 6:38.)

"For all the law is fulfilled in one word, even in this: Thou shalt love thy neighbor as thyself." (Galatians 5:14.)

"Let us love one another; for love is of God." (I John 4:7.)

"The true Christian does not belong to any particular sect . . . He has only one science, which is Christ" (the Christ spirit) "within him; he has only one desire, namely, to do good," wrote Boehme.

We recently received from an inmate of a State Prison a letter which read in part:

"A few days ago I picked up your book, 'Thirty Years Among the Dead,' and started idly turning its pages in order to discover the nature of a book bearing such an odd name. I thought to myself, 'This should be worth a good laugh,' but the light attitude with which I had started reading soon became dead earnest. I took the book with me and did little else until I had read every word of it from cover to cover."

"I sincerely believe that the reading of this volume marks a turning point in my life. I have always felt that my greatest need was for a religion, the teachings of which I could believe in with my whole heart and soul. Although I have tried and tried, over and over again, to make myself believe a creed of some orthodox Christian church, I could never bring myself to accept such a religion. Such creeds always leave too much to the credulity of the individual to satisfy me."

"I have had a university education and have always tried to keep an open mind in the reading and discussion of any subject, especially one with which I was unfamiliar, and to accept truth where I find it. I was reared in a strict Christian home and cannot even remember when I started attending Sunday School. As I grew older and began to form ideas of my own, I ceased to accept all that my teachers told me and even formed a doubt, deep down in my mind, as to the existence of an all-powerful God who punished all who would not accept the teachings of his holy book, the Bible. Fight as I might against such sacrilegious thoughts, I could not dislodge them from my subconscious mind. My skepticism grew until the idea of a just God who would doom a mortal soul to everlasting punishment simply

306

because it could not believe in Him seemed absurd. I soon lost all my 'religion' and ceased attending church. I decided it is better to be an agnostic than a hypocrite."

"Your teachings and philosophy are most acceptable to me because of their frank logic and dismissal of any preconceived ideas on religion. One does not have to accept them in blind faith; he can reason them out for himself and not fail to see the truth in them. I especially like the idea of doing good to others and serving them because, since God is in everyone, you are then serving and helping not only the individual, but God Himself."

The ego, an invisible entity, springs from the Invisible and, through generation into physical form, enters the doorway of the mortal into this primary school of earthly experience, existing invisibly while in a material body, and in this school of necessity the unconscious soul is to unfold consciousness of its being.

"The qualities cannot know the Soul, but the Soul knows all qualities. . . . He who sees all things in the Soul, and the Soul in all things does not slight anything. It is more refined than an atom and cannot be approached by argumentation" (but by reasoning). ("The Atma Bodha.")

Having attained recognition that this journey from the Invisible through the transient objective is but for a season, and having developed the soul qualities through experience and discernment of the laws of life, the Ego again emerges from this objective material into the Invisible Real.

All are traveling along that road through the valley of this transient, external life, ultimately to enter the higher life. As the soul journeys along this path, through experience it slowly recognizes that the sign-posts of right and wrong along the wayside are the guides by which the soul will eventually attain wisdom and a consciousness of the importance of this earth experience, which finally liberates the soul from the illusion and attractions of the transitory mortal.

Liberation of the soul has been defined in many ways. In "Thrice-Greatest Hermes" we find: "This is . . . rebirth— no more to look on things from body's view-point."

"Spirit Life in Higher Realms" states: "The whole of

life's philosophy may be reduced to one aim—the subjugation of the animal in man."

"Hatred, revenge, envy, jealousy, anger, intemperance, lust and selfishness are all animalistic inheritances. They are not divine by any means. Vanity, conceit, arrogance, pride, fault-finding, self-righteousness, etc., are modifications of the first-named, or the virtues perverted by animalism, and are all effects of selfishness. . . . Only such impulses as charity, benevolence, sympathy, generosity, kindness, justice, truthfulness, etc., are of the soul."

"The practice of temperance, justice and charity frees the spirit from material attraction. If one has prejudice, he must develop an opposite tendency through the agency of charity to conquer it. Bigotry is neutralized by tolerance; frivolity by gravity; penuriousness by generosity; selfishness by benevolence; vanity by modesty; conceit by forgetfulness of self; hatred by sympathy; lust by abnegation, and so on. These are called virtues, but they are only agents to root out their antitheses. Every kind act adds to future happiness, whether in the physical body or out."

"The true divinity in man is composed of love, intelligence and will power. From these all good arises when exercised naturally."

Maitland-Kingsford in "The Perfect Way" wrote: "The result of the Soul's steadfast aspiration towards God—the Spirit within her—and of her consequent action upon the body, is that this also becomes so permeated and suffused by the spirit as, at last, to have no will of its own, but to be in all things one with its soul and spirit, and to constitute with these one perfectly harmonious system, of which every element is under full control of the central Will. It is this unification, occurring within the individual, which constitutes the atonement.[1] The process, however, is one which each individual must accomplish in and for himself. Being an interior process, consisting in self-purification, it cannot be performed from without. Perfection is attained by experience which implies suffering . . . This suffering must be borne by each man for himself. To deprive anyone of it by putting the consequences of his acts upon another,

---

[1] Acquiring consciousness of "at-one-ment" with the All, with Life.

so far from aiding that one, would be to deprive him of his means of redemption."

Our spirit co-worker, Dr. Root, in addressing the audience at one of our circles, said:

"There is a life after this and it is progressive. There is a life of happiness but you must try to find it. You must have understanding so that you can progress to a more beautiful life of happiness."

"Understand and learn that God is the life of everything and everyone. In each one is that spark of the Divine— God. Call it 'Life,' 'Electricity,' whatever you wish, but that is THE LIFE throughout all the universe."

"Try to find the God within you if you would be happy and contented. Do not only pray—act. You must work, and do your work to the best of your ability. You can overcome trouble because you have the power to overcome. When you worry you become exhausted; your thoughts go around until you are in a dark condition."

"Understand that you are a part of God and that you have it within your power to create conditions; find that power. Where there is the will, there is life and power within you to act; do your part."

"Make the best of your own life and open your hearts to your spirit friends who are anxious to help you. Why should you doubt them? When you doubt you make a wall around yourself; the more you doubt, the higher will the wall become."

"When a mother passes out could she be happy in the spirit world if she did not look after her children here? Would she not be selfish to do otherwise? Could she enjoy her happiness in the spirit world when she knew her children needed her guidance and protection?"

"A mother's love is strong and she will often be with her children to guide them and make their troubles easier. Yet the majority of persons are afraid of the spirits of their loved ones. Why should they be? They were not afraid of them in earth life; why should they be afraid of them when they have gone to a happier world? Why not make it pleasant for them by recognizing them and realizing their presence; then they can help so much more easily."

"How many know where they are going from here—where they will go after the sleep of death? They do not care; they merely 'believe,' that is all. You could not make a trip to Europe by belief; you would never reach there. You must know conditions and make preparations. It is necessary to do the same before starting on the journey to the spirit side of life. Obtain all the understanding you can while here."

"You cannot go from one country to another advantageously without learning the ways of the new country; then how could you step directly from this earth life into the Great Beyond without having understanding?"

"Learn all you can, before you pass out, regarding the other side; then you will not be an earthbound spirit causing trouble and suffering to yourself and others."

"Some who believe that after death they will sleep until the 'Last Day' hypnotize themselves into a sleep that may last for many years, as time is calculated on earth, although on the other side of life there is no time."

"The majority only believe, they do not want to understand. For years the Church has taught its followers to believe, but now people ask for knowledge, not belief. The truth is spreading more and more."

"Those who scoff are spiritually blind; they are of the physical, blinded by business, or money, or material interests, and they shut the door to spiritual truths. But the truth will be known; there will be understanding. Before long the world will understand."

"Learn all you can while here regarding the beauties of the other side; be happy and contented and learn to know the truth. Every one of you will some day step over the border to the spirit world; learn to understand the other side of life. You must learn to know yourselves and to develop the highest that is in you."

"You cannot pass on to the higher life except through understanding. Unless you have knowledge of the next life you have no light; all is darkness. Light is understanding, and, if you do not take that light with you, you are in darkness;[1] you must learn to find that light."

[1]See allegory of "The Ten Virgins," Chapter VII, "Dogma Spiritualized," Page 155.

"Doubt, dogma and creeds are like sandbags hung around the neck; they must be thrown off. You must be free and have understanding and you will find yourself much happier. You have the power to create your own conditions."

"Hatred, jealousy and envy all belong to the dark; when you develop these you live, in your own heart, in the fire of 'hell.' When you learn to overcome these and develop love, kindness and sympathy you are then in 'heaven.' 'Heaven' and 'hell' are conditions."

"You must have peace in your heart and an understanding of the real life, then you will find bliss and happiness when you reach your home in the spirit world."

"In the spirit world, where understanding exists, all is music and harmony; it is a beautiful condition. There each is a note in the wonderful harmony of life."

"In earth life there is more discord than harmony; but the lesson of life is to find yourselves and become one with the Harmony of Life. If you had the grandeur of music on earth as we have it in the spirit world, you could not develop your soul. You would not strive; you would only listen and enjoy the beautiful harmonies. Each is here to find himself and realize himself in a higher and better life."

"The first lesson which must be learned is to live for others and to find yourselves. God placed you here to learn to find yourselves through mistakes and suffering. When you have learned that lesson then you will better understand others and will know that you must live for others, not for self. To serve is the first lesson. Help each other."

"Forget all doubt. Let all sorrow pass out of your life. Learn to think wisely; do the very best you can and you will have success in life."

"Gloomy thoughts attract gloomy conditions; smile and be happy and you create happy conditions around yourself. Be cheerful; sing, trust in God. Understand his wonderful manifestations; look within yourself and live happily. You are a part of God; when you doubt yourself you doubt God. Live happily and you will be happy."

"Change your thoughts and you will have prosperity; life will be better. Learn all you can of the life after this; the more you learn the happier you will be. Your burdens will be lighter because you can overcome troubles and worry."

"Learn self-mastery over your physical body as well as over the conditions around you. You have strength and power; use them."

"Happiness is attained by understanding that life is everlasting and that the next world is only a counterpart of this, but one far more beautiful. Close the door to selfishness and ignorance and let only love, kindness and happiness remain."

"Plant the seeds of happiness in your heart; do the best you can to help others; be kind to others and let the seeds of happiness grow in your heart; think happiness. Live in that thought; overcome all gloom and downheartedness. Let these be in the past; do not think of them. Cast them aside. Lift up your heart in happiness, cheerfulness and joy, and try to give sunshine to everybody. When you live in the thought of sunshine and happiness you will overcome all gloom and sorrow."

"Try to conquer the earthly conditions of selfishness, jealousy and ignorance. Learn to know the truth of nature. Learn all you can; do not condemn others because then you only condemn yourself."

"No one has a right to condemn another; God alone is the Judge. Learn to understand God; God is Love, not hatred. Do not have undue desires; be free. Do not be a slave to anything. Life on this plane is only temporary; learn about the life after this; know where you are going. Be happy; live for others, not self."

"Do justice to yourself; you will then also do justice to others. Live in Truth and Love and help your fellowman. Learn about nature's forces; learn that you are God. Do not only believe in God; understand him, know that you yourself are a part of that which you call God. Search within and you will find God. Find yourself and try to understand Life."

Truth is arrived at by attaining knowledge of things as they are. Mystically, this attained truth is "the Son of Man" which, contemplating the transient nature of existence in this mundane sphere, realizes that while the soul is in the physical, yet it is not a part of the physical, and that the soul's advent into this formative plane is only the first stage of the soul's progressive journey.

Having attained the consciousness that "the things which are seen are temporal, but the things which are not seen are eternal" (II Corinthians 4:18), the soul understands the true meaning of the precept, "If a man keep my word, he shall never see death." (John 8:51.)

For such an one transition is but a brief sleep and a glorious awakening into a higher grade of mental life, a conscious and joyful entrance, through the Gateway of Understanding, into the World Immortal.

THE END

Thirty Years
Among the Dead

By
CARL A. WICKLAND, M.D.

$4⁰⁰

Published by
NATIONAL PSYCHOLOGICAL INSTITUTE
Incorporated
2206–2208 W. 11th ST.,
LOS ANGELES 6, CALIFORNIA

●

"The most striking of all . . . posthumous communications are to be found in 'Thirty Years Among the Dead,' by Dr. Carl A. Wickland of Los Angeles . . . Dr. Wickland and his heroic wife have done work which deserves the very closest attention from the alienists of the world. If he makes his point, and the case is a strong one, he not only revolutionizes our ideas about insanity, but he cuts deep also into our views of criminology, and may well show that we have been punishing as criminals people who were more deserving of commiseration than of censure . . . The discovery, when fully made out, will be one of the root facts of the psychology and jurisprudence of the future."

"THE LAND OF THE MIST," Sir Arthur Conan Doyle.